Individuation and Identity
in Early Modern Philosophy

Individuation and Identity
in Early Modern Philosophy

Descartes to Kant

Kenneth F. Barber
and
Jorge J. E. Gracia, *editors*

State University of New York Press

Published by
State University of New York Press, Albany

For information, address State University of New York Press,
State University Plaza, Albany, N.Y., 12246

Production by Marilyn Semerad
Marketing by Nancy Farrell

Library of Congress Cataloging-in-Publication Data

Individuation and identity in early modern philosophy : Descartes to
Kant / edited by Kenneth F. Barber and Jorge J. E. Gracia.
    p.   cm.
Includes index.
ISBN 0-7914-1967-3 (alk. paper). — ISBN 0-7914-1968-1 (pbk. :
alk. paper)
1. Individuation (Philosophy)—History.   2. Identity.
3. Philosophy, Modern.   I. Barber, Kenneth F., 1940- .
II. Gracia, Jorge J. E.
BD394.I52   1994
111'.82—dc20   93-38028
                                                              CIP

10 9 8 7 6 5 4 3 2 1

Contents

Acknowledgments

The editors are indebted to David R. Raynor and Richard A. Watson for their helpful comments on an earlier draft of this book. Special thanks are also due Jane Bristol, Michael Gorman, and Gordon Snow for their help in preparing the manuscript for publication.

Introduction

Kenneth Barber

Some philosophical problems, by virtue of their importance relative to a philosophical system, are widely discussed by those safely within the parameters of the system—solutions are contested, distinctions are generated, and the promise of eventual resolution is entertained by all. Once the system comes under attack, however, leading either to its piecemeal or even wholesale rejection, those problems formerly of consummate importance may reduce to minor irritants mainly of antiquarian interest. Examples of this phenomenon are easy to find even, or perhaps especially, in our own century: Witness, to take just one case, the disappearance in the literature of discussions as to whether two persons can experience the same sense datum, a worry of underwhelming significance once the theory of sense data has been discarded and one that for the most part is of concern only to the historian of early twentieth-century philosophy.

One issue constituting the theme of this volume apparently shares the same fate, namely, the problem of individuation (or, more accurately, the cluster of related problems discussed under that heading) whose contending solutions were debated with much vigor during the medieval era,[1] but to which only passing reference is made by philosophers in the early modern period.[2] Thus, while Francisco Suárez in 1597 devotes 150 pages to the problem of individuation in his *Disputationes metaphysicae*,[3] the seminal work in early modern philosophy appearing a mere forty-four years later, Descartes's *Meditations*, not only fails to advance Suárez's discussion but refuses to acknowledge the existence of the problem. Although this neglect is rectified to an extent elsewhere in Descartes and in the later Cartesians, the problem of individuation is never restored by the Cartesians to the place of prominence it formerly held in medieval philosophy.[4]

And when one turns to the empiricists the situation is, if anything, even more peculiar: the problem of individuation is duly noted and then resolved, usually within the confines of a single sentence.

"All Things, that exist, being Particulars . . ."[5]

"But it is an universally received maxim, that *every thing which exists, is particular.*"[6]

"'tis a principle generally receiv'd in philosophy, that every thing in nature is individual."[7]

What was once a matter of intense debate is now dismissed by appealing to a maxim or received principle not meriting discussion.

An abrupt change in philosophical fashion of this magnitude is perforce a matter of interest to the historian of philosophy on at least two counts. First, one concerned with intellectual history, an enterprise broader than the pursuit of answers to philosophical questions, may inquire into the reasons why a philosophical problem no longer attracts widespread interest. In the present case the reasons no doubt involve a combination of factors, ranging from a redirection of philosophical preoccupation induced by the emergence of the New Science to a simple belief that the problem of individuation need no longer be discussed at length since it had long ago been solved.[8] Second, since philosophers in the early modern period were for the most part systematic, presenting ontologies rivaling their medieval counterparts in comprehensiveness if not in detail, one can ask how within their systems the problem of individuation could or should have been resolved even where explicit discussion of the issue is minimal.

While both inquiries have a role to play in developing our understanding of early modern philosophy, the authors in the present volume for the most part focus on the second or strictly philosophical issue, with excursions into intellectual history taken only when necessary to make intelligible the strategies of the philosophers under study. Despite the official view, characterized and partially endorsed in the above paragraphs, that discussions of individuation in early modern philosophy lack the prominence accorded to the issue by medieval philosophers, the chapters in this volume demonstrate that lack of prominence is not to be confused with pathological neglect.

Even leaving aside Leibniz and Wolff, neither of whom can be accused of ignoring the problem of individuation, Descartes, Malebranche, and Spinoza certainly present, or are forced to adopt under the pressure of positions taken on other philosophical problems, intriguing if not entirely satisfactory solutions to the problem. Nor, as Lennon shows in his chapter, should the contributions of the minor Cartesians be ignored in writing the history of individuation in the early modern period.

Although Locke, Berkeley, and Hume are less than preoccupied with individuation, the second issue constituting the theme of this volume—identity through time—does receive their attention, beginning with Locke's rather lengthy discussion in the *Essay* and ending with Hume's notorious and anxiety-ridden struggle with the problem of personal identity in the *Treatise*. The shift in focus by the empiricists, of course, does not eliminate the problem of individuation, since an account of an object (or person) remaining the same object (or person) through time presupposes that the object (or person) in question at each moment in time be different from all other objects (or persons).

The structural linkage between the problems of identity and individuation is obvious, but what is perhaps less obvious and of greater interest is that common to both the Cartesian and empiricist approaches to individuation and identity is the increasingly altered role accorded to substance in early modern ontologies. Indeed, it is the various modifications and/or rejections of one traditional doctrine of substance that lead to what is novel in recasting the problems in this period. And it is this matter that I wish to address in this brief introduction.

A SKETCH OF THE PROBLEM(S)

Objects in a perceptual field, to take the simplest case, are complex: they have several qualities (at a minimum, shape and color). Examples of such objects are quite ordinary; persons, trees, and books all may appear in one's visual field. These ordinary objects have four very general features that, in turn, generate four corresponding philosophical problems. (1) Such objects are, as one would say, individuals possessing a variety of qualities and, hence, complex. (2) Yet despite the observed complexity each individual is *one* thing, a unity, since the qualities in question are all attributed to the same individual (e.g., Socrates is both short and bald). (3) Furthermore, an individual is different or distinct from all other individuals appearing with it in the visual field. (4) Some of these individuals may also appear to endure through time, to have a continued existence as the *same* individuals even though undergoing various kinds of change, including change of quality and change of relation with respect to the other objects.[9]

The task of an ontological analysis is to present a catalogue and classification of the constituents of these individuals; if the analysis is successful then the commonplace features of complexity, unity, difference, and continuity through time are preserved insofar as various

items in the ontological inventory are said to account for or to explain
those features. The explanation is secured by showing that items in the
catalogue, or inventory, have certain broad, categorial dimensions that
allow their classification into ontological kinds.[10] Of the features to be
accounted for only difference and continuity through time (identity)
are of direct concern in this volume. A successful account of difference
(the problem of individuation) would consist in locating at least one
constituent of an individual that is not present in any other individual;
a successful account of identity would consist in isolating at least one
constituent of an individual that endures unchanged throughout the
history of that individual. The tradition under attack in the early modern period solves both of these problems neatly with one entity: substance.

Before turning to the solution under attack, however, it is worth
noting that complementary to the ontological enterprise there is an
epistemological task: How do we know (perceive, apprehend) the complexity, unity, difference, and continuity through time of objects?[11]
Again, with respect to the present volume only epistemic issues affecting difference and identity are of direct relevance although, as should
be obvious, any simple demarcation into nonoverlapping issues is inac-
curate both philosophically and historically.

These two concerns, ontological and epistemological, are uneasily
linked in the history of philosophy. In an ideal world, philosopher's
heaven as it were, the marriage of ontology and epistemology would be
completely harmonious in that all the entities catalogued and classified
by the ontologist would meet with approval by the epistemologist and
in turn all items on the epistemologist's short list of knowable entities
would be sufficient for the ontologist's account of the world. In a less
than ideal world, however, the two concerns are often at odds; the epistemologist complains about the cavalier attitude of his ontologically
inclined brethren who generate entities and distinctions in an uncon-
scionable manner, while the ontologist in turn dismisses the epistemologist as one blinded to the richness of the universe through a neurotic
fixation on a few favorite sense organs.

Less dramatically, but more sharply focused, epistemology and
ontology can be related in two ways. On what I call the *Strong Model* of
their relation, epistemological considerations serve as criteria for the
adequacy of an ontological system: putative candidates for inclusion in
the catalogue of existents must first pass a test for knowability and,
once included, their classification in terms of categorial features must
again meet the same rigorous standard. Failure to pass these tests is, or
ought to be, sufficient reason for discarding all or parts of the ontology

in question, no matter how firmly entrenched the latter may have been in a philosophical tradition. On what I term the "weak model," epistemology and ontology are understood to be parallel methods of investigation having in common only the fact that their respective inquiries are directed toward the same classes of objects. While the ontologist asks what it is *in objects* that *individuates* those objects, the epistemologist searches for features *in experience* that allow us to *discern* the difference among objects. The results of the two investigations need not be the same. Aquinas, for example, employs designated matter to solve the ontological problem of individuation and appeals to place to account for our ability to discern the difference among objects. Since on the weak model epistemology does not function as a control for ontological claims, the disparity in accounts embarrasses neither enterprise.

Broadly speaking, the weak model is dominant in medieval philosophy. Epistemological concerns are subordinate or at best parallel to ontological concerns. The existents, beginning with God, are given as are the categories available for their analysis. The task of the epistemologist is to support not to challenge the schema, and any attempt to reverse the subordinate role assigned to epistemology (or to advocate the Strong Model) would have been regarded not as an indication of philosophical acumen but rather as a potential source of heresy.

By 1641, however, the strong model has replaced its weaker medieval counterpart. In the opening paragraphs of the *Meditations* Descartes announces that he will suspend belief in the existence of anything not known with certainty. Ontological claims concerning the existence of material objects, of God, and even of the self, must be subjected to a most rigorous epistemological scrutiny before one (or at least Descartes) is entitled to accept those claims.

The reasons for the ascendancy of the strong model are various. The theological chaos engendered by the Reformation is certainly a contributing factor; competing and conflicting religious claims require adjudication, that is, rival beliefs must be shown to be false while one's own views demand proof of their truth. Reliance on mere probabilities is insufficient when the question is one of salvation. It is not surprising, then, that epistemological questions, especially the search for certainty, are promoted to the first rank of issues demanding resolution.

Nor are matters helped by the advancement of scientific theories wherein the real constituents of the physical realm are atoms, invisible to perception and hence unknowable by ordinary or commonplace standards. Thus the physical realm and God share an uncomfortable feature: both are transcendent in the sense that neither can serve as objects of perception. Securing knowledge of God and physical objects, then, becomes an epistemological project requiring great skill, a project difficult in the best of times and one apparently doomed at its inception in early modern philosophy by the concomitant revival and promulgation of skeptical arguments designed to show the impossibility of the enterprise.[12]

However fascinating the details of the genesis of the shift from ontological to epistemological concerns may be (and a number of these details are indeed discussed in this volume), the importance of the shift, for our purposes, lies not in its genesis but in its impact on the problems of identity and individuation. Aside from the obvious textual point, already noted, that discussions of identity and individuation become more abbreviated in the early modern period, the epistemological turn is significant for its effect on the *content* of those discussions. What could plausibly count as solutions to those problems is restricted by the imposition of new criteria; solutions formerly held to be uncontroversial are rendered puzzling, incomprehensible, or in conflict with newly discovered "truths" about the world.

By way of illustration, consider the impact of the epistemological turn on a standard (though by no means universally held) treatment of individuation and identity prior to the early modern period. One entity, substance, allegedly solves both problems; this is possible because substance is a complex entity, one part of which (matter, for example) becomes the principle of individuation while another part (form, nature, or essence, for example) accounts for, among other things, identity through time in the sense of explaining why an individual remains the same kind of individual despite undergoing changes of various kinds.[13] These two aspects of substance, the individuating principle and the continuity principle, if I may so put it, are linked in such a way that neither could function in the required way without the other. First, insofar as the nature or essence is something shared by many individuals, the individuating principle is needed to make sense of the claim that there are or can be many individuals of the same kind. Second, the continuity principle, that is, that an individual may remain the same individual through time, requires that the individual in question at each moment of its existence be distinct from all other individuals. In other words, merely securing the possibility of there being more than one individual with the same essence does not by itself guarantee the identity through time of an individual having continued existence unless the individuating principle is operative *at each moment* of the continued existence. Third, the individuating principle must not only be present at each moment but must remain itself the *same* individuating principle throughout the individual's existence.[14] Fourth, the continued existence of the same individuating principle by itself would not be sufficient for the continued existence of the same individual; without the attachment of the same essence to the individuating principle Socrates could change into a rock, a case in which one would be reluctant to say that it is the same individual. While this solution presents problems of its own (What is the sense in which a substance is complex? What is the sense in which designated matter and form are parts of such a complex? What is the relation between these parts?), nevertheless the theory fulfills the formal requirements for a solution in that the analysis offered reveals constituents whose job is to account for the various features of ordinary experience.

The entity in question (substance), when examined under the newly ground epistemological lens employed in early modern philosophy, is found to contain discomforting flaws of a magnitude unsettling even to those wishing to countenance its existence. When Descartes in the "Second Meditation" engages the question (1) of *what* we can know about material substance (e.g., a piece of wax) and the question (2) of *how* we know what we know about substance, he discovers that the answer to (1) is a resounding *less than previously thought*, while the answer to (2) is *not by our usual sources*. The senses, it turns out, yield information only about properties and reveal nothing about substance itself. What can be known about substance is furnished solely by reason, or the understanding, and what can be known by reason is restricted to just one aspect of the formerly complex entity, namely, the essence or nature of substance (extension in the case of material substance). The other aspect, matter, which had been the principle of individuation for material objects, disappears, leaving Descartes with the twin difficulties of having no principle of individuation and of having to equate, untenably, substance with essence.[15] The novel if not entirely satisfactory solutions to the problem of individuation presented by Descartes and other Cartesians are the understandable result of attempting to retain an entity considerably reduced in stature by the new epistemological constraints.

While Descartes, by conspicuous omission, casts doubt on the knowability of the individuating principle in the case of material objects, the difficulty is by no means restricted to the latter but is also replicated in the realm of mental substance. Many minds allegedly share the same essence (thinking) and yet are distinct from one another even though here, too, substance is equated with essence. What, then, is the principle of individuation for these nonspatial entities? Although it may be to Descartes's credit that in his single-minded pursuit of grand epistemological truths he refused to be sidetracked in the *Meditations* by various enigmas generated by his line of argument, nevertheless the options left for a resolution to the problem of individuation are clear: (1) adopt some version of monism, wherein the problem of individuating substances disappears, a move consistent with the equation of substance and essence but not a move palatable to most; or (2) secure another principle of individuation, one that is both epistemologically respectable and sufficient to accomplish the task. Not surprisingly, the second option dominates discussion, however limited that discussion may be in some cases, during the early modern period.

When one turns to Locke, the epistemological suspicion cast on the utility of substance for solving the problems of individuation and identity is baldly stated and overwhelming. Locke retains, inconsistently with his epistemological principle that all ideas must originate in experience, a vestige of the individuating constitutent in substance. But this vestige, substratum, becomes an "I know not what" and is relegated to a limited ontological role, that of providing support for qualities.[16] For individuation, Locke casts about in search of less problematic, less ephemeral entities.

The other element in substance, form or essence, also undergoes a transformation due to epistemological considerations. Unable to secure an experiential foundation for the classical notion of essence— real essence—Locke abandons it. Its replacement, nominal essence, becomes a collection of experienced qualities, a collection subject to change through addition or subtraction as our knowledge (experience) increases. And since nominal essence lacks the stability of real essence, it cannot be relied on to provide an acount of identity through time.[17]

The epistemological focus in Descartes and Locke, or what I have called the "strong model" of the relation between ontology and epistemology, is incompatible with the substance solution to the problems of identity and individuation. Interestingly this is the case even though Descartes and Locke do not employ the same epistemological principles, the former relying on innate ideas and reason for securing knowledge while the latter, rejecting innate ideas, accords a significant role to sensory experience.

The responses of Descartes and Locke to traditional ontological problems are of course echoed by other philosophers in the period. The obvious examples are Berkeley, who rejects material substance, and Hume, who rejects both material and mental substances; in each case epistemological concerns are a major factor in the rejection and in each case other principles of individuation and identity are consequently required. And while the list could be extended, it has been my intention in this introduction to suggest but not exhaust the possibilities for understanding individuation and identity in this period. The impact of epistemological considerations on ontological themes outlined above is elaborated in several chapters in this volume even though they are not and were never intended to be restricted to the framework sketched in this introduction. The philosophical tradition in the early modern period is too rich and diverse to be understood solely as a reaction to one model of substance in recasting solutions to the problems of individuation and identity, just as the medieval period itself would be misrepresented were one to claim that philosophers and theologians then were uniformly committed to a resolution of those problems using the model of substance outlined above. And, finally, while the epistemological turn does affect the content of ontological discourse, not all early modern philosophers are equally preoccupied with epistemology, and even those most under its sway are to various degrees influenced by other philosophical problems as well as by theological, scientific, social, and political concerns.

NOTES

1. Although the views of Aquinas, Scotus, and Ockham on individuation have been prominently featured in the scholarly literature, the issue was certainly not invented by those philosophers. For a detailed treatment of individuation in the earlier medieval period, see Jorge J. E. Gracia, *Introduction to the Problem of Individuation in the Early Middle Ages*, 2d ed. (München and Wien: Philosophia Verlag, 1986).

2. Obviously such a sweeping claim requires equally sweeping qualifications. While Berkeley's references to individuation may be fleeting, the same is clearly not true of Leibniz nor for the most medieval of early modern philosophers, Wolff.

3. Francisco Suárez, *Disputio metaphysica V*, in *Opera Omnia*, vol. 25, ed. Carolo Berton (Paris: Vivès, 1861).

4. I do not want to suggest that there is no continuity between the medieval and early modern traditions. In the case of Descartes the connection has been quite thoroughly explored. The seminal work in this area is Etienne Gilson, *Etudes sur la rôle de la pensée médiévale dans la formation du systême cartésien* (Paris: J. Vrin, 1951).

5. John Locke, *An Essay Concerning Human Understanding*, ed. P. H. Nidditch (Oxford: Clarendon Press, 1975), III, 27.3, p. 409.

6. George Berkeley, *Three Dialogues Between Hylas and Philonous*, in A.

Luce and T. E. Jessop, *The Works of George Berkeley* (London: Thomas Nelson and Sons, 1948), 2:192.

7. David Hume, *A Treatise of Human Nature*, ed. L. A. Selby-Bigge (London: Oxford University Press, 1958), I.I.VII, p. 19.

8. Julius Weinberg, in discussing Hume, notes that the reasons for the principle that everything that exists is particular are found articulated in Ockham. Without accusing Hume of having read Ockham, he rather suggestively claims that this is a case in which a philosophical principle has been firmly entrenched long after the supporting arguments have been forgotten. See Julius Weinberg, *Abstraction, Relation, and Induction* (Madison and Milwaukee: The University of Wisconsin Press, 1965), pp. 52–53.

9. This is not the only formulation of the problems nor do I claim that the formulation given here is unproblematic. Twentieth-century discussions, beginning with Moore and Russell, are as varied as their historical counterparts, and are too numerous to mention here. For a comprehensive overview of the most important literature in this century, see Jorge J. E. Gracia, *Individuality: An Essay on the Foundations of Metaphysics* (Albany: State University of New York Press, 1988).

10. Extension or attribution of these commonplace features and their categorizations to nonperceptual objects (e.g., mathematical entities and God) creates additional puzzles, some of which are of course relevant to understanding the ontologies in both medieval and early modern periods. Furthermore, note that while I apeak of these issues as ontological, philosophers in this period of course would have classified them as metaphysical since the word 'ontology' was not then in vogue. I intend this terminological anachronism to be harmless.

11. It should be noted that for the early modern period a satisfactory understanding of epistemological theories would require a detailed examination of the roles played by abstraction, innate ideas, and perception, including the various causal models of perception employed by those philosophers.

12. See Richard H. Popkin, *The History of Scepticism from Erasmus to Descartes* (Assen, Netherlands: Van Gorcum & Comp. N. V., 1960).

13. It should not be thought that this resolution of the problem is the only or even the dominant one in medieval philosophy. For a discussion of the various gambits entertained by those philosophers, see Gracia, *Introduction to the Problem of Individuation in the Early Middle Ages*, especially Chapter 1.

14. Pierre Bayle notes that under the Cartesian doctrine of the continual creation of substance by God a different substance could be created at each moment having the same modifications as its predecessors without any mortal being the wiser. See Pierre Bayle, *Historical and Critical Dictionary* (selections), trans. Richard H. Popkin (Indianapolis: Bobbs-Merrill, 1965), p. 204.

15. For a thorough criticism of the epistemological and ontological conse-quences of the identification of substance with essence, see Richard A. Watson, *The Breakdown of Cartesian Metaphysics* (Atlantic Highlands, N.J.: Humanities Press International, 1987), especially Chapter 14, "Descartes Knows Nothing."

16. Locke, *An Essay Concerning Human Understanding*, II.XXIII.2, p. 295.

17. Ibid., II.XXVII.12, p. 337.

The Problem of Individuation
among the Cartesians

Thomas M. Lennon

Leibniz said that numerically different individuals always differ qualitatively; it would be a violation of his principle of sufficient reason if numerical difference were the only difference between things. Whether some further principle of individuation is entailed, we can at least say that for him qualitative difference is sufficient for numerical difference. Certainly no further principle is required for Berkeley—at least not for the individuation of physical things like books and bananas. Again without controversy, we may say that on his bundle analysis of such things, things with all the same qualities would ipso facto be numerically the same; set identity is a matter of membership identity. A perplexing question raised by such analyses concerns how qualities differ. An apple differs from a banana not only numerically, but also in shape and color, that is, qualitatively; but how do shapes and colors differ? Does red differ from yellow numerically or qualitatively? Although such questions may be perplexing, I want to argue that on the Cartesian line I shall develop, *not only physical objects but also minds differ in the way in which red and yellow differ*, however the Cartesians may understand that difference.[1]

Elsewhere[2] I have argued that for Descartes there is but a single material substance, *res extensa*, of which the individual material things of our experience are modes, and that in this sense their essence is extension. Their essence just is *res extensa*, which is the thing that God creates when he makes it true, for example, that the interior angles of a triangle are equal to a straight angle. An individual thing of our experience, such as a piece of wax—what Descartes calls *extensum*—is individuated in *res extensa* by our sensations. What this means is that if we ourselves had no body, that is, if we had no sensations, we would never perceive individuals; all our perceptions would be of the universal. But it also means that without sensations, there would not *be* any such individuals. For an apple is not just extension, which gives it determinable geometrical properties, but also redness, which determines it to just a

13

set of those properties. Consider *Meditations* II. We learn that the wax is *known* through the mind alone, by which I take it that its essence, that is, extension, is known by the mind alone. But after learning this, Descartes raises and answers an often overlooked question: "But what is this piece of wax which cannot be known excepting by the mind? It is certainly the same that I see, touch, imagine and finally it is the same which I have always believed it to be from the beginning."[3] What this means is that objects like apples consist in part of sensations; at least in part, they are mind-dependent.

This result raises the question as to the analysis and individuation of mind. If objects of experience are individuated by sensations, what individuates minds? Here I can only report that while Descartes may be read as taking physical objects to be modes of a single material substance, he seems nowhere to regard individual minds as anything less than so many thinking substances.[4] Descartes's views on individuation are discussed elsewhere in this volume. My aim here is not to defend any of the above as Descartes's, but to show how it is found in certain of his self-proclaimed disciples. Indeed, I show in the third and fourth sections of this chapter that Descartes's alleged analysis of material things is extended by them to thinking things as well. In a brief first section I provide a bit of background whose aim is, among other things, to mitigate the impact of the obviously many texts in which 'substance' is used by these Cartesians, as by Descartes himself, to refer to individual things, including individual minds. In a second section I show the various other ways in which the Cartesians sought to deal with individuation—all of them uninteresting or unsuccessful, in my view. Finally, in the third and fourth sections I turn to the heart of the chapter, the heretofore almost totally ignored work of Robert Desgabets and Pierre-Sylvain Régis.

SOME BACKGROUND

In the seventeenth century the explicit treatment of the problem of individuation is not nearly commensurate with its perennial importance. There are several reasons for this. One reason relates to the emergence of mechanism, which undid the Aristotelian models of explanation, and in particular the appeal to final causes. On previous models it is important to individuate in order to have discrete loci for discrete teleological organizations. The mantis and the fly upon which it preys have radically different ends, even if those ends are thought to contribute to an overreaching universal end. With mechanism, however, teleology is either proscribed entirely (Descartes) or else severely restricted (Locke).[5]

A second reason for the overt neglect of the problem of individuation also relates to the emergence of mechanism. For the correlative problem of natural kinds had also undergone a radical change. On previous accounts, including especially the Aristotelian, but also the various versions of Platonism, hermeticism, naturalism, and the like, there are many different natural kinds. The significance of the great chain of being requiring that there be no gaps in nature, that every possible kind be instantiated, and so on, would have been upset or certainly at least diminished if the world were not plentiful, indeed overwhelmingly so, in its sortal diversity. Driven by mechanism, however, the thrust of the seventeenth century is to reduce natural kinds, even to the point of eliminating all but one of them. This is most obviously true of Cartesianism, whose material world is of one kind only, namely, the extended. But the thrust is also to be found in empiricism, as represented by Locke for example. We do not know the Lockean real essences of things, but the difference among all such essences may turn out to be, at least on the corpuscularian hypothesis that Locke often accepts and nowhere rejects, a difference in the primary qualities of their microscopic parts. That is, for Locke all material things are ultimately of the same determinable kind (having, e.g., shape), differing only in their determinates (e.g., specific shape). For these two reasons, the problem of individuation although still important tended to be ignored.

The upshot is that both in the atomist ontologies that typified empiricism and in the plenist ontologies typical of Cartesianism, substance became a mass noun rather than a count noun. In Aristotelian terminology, primary substances, which previously had been individuals, were abolished in favor of secondary substances, which previously had been only their essences.[6] To use some homely metaphors, for atomism substance was like a paint to be spread by creation on some spatial figures and not on others.[7] For the Cartesians of interest here, substance became the bread, not only of life, but of all else—sliced, as I argue, by our sensations.

Given the Cartesian dualism of Desgabets and Régis, there are qualitatively, and I argue, numerically two substances: *res extensa* and *res cogitans*. Many statements by them, and by other Cartesians, are ambiguous, however, and can be read as asserting the existence either of one substance or of a multiplicity of substances, of the two kinds. Régis, for example, begins the physics of his *Système* as follows: "There is no one who does not know that there is a substance [*une substance*],

extended in length, breadth, and depth, called *body*."[8] As Régis continues, however, we can only translate him as saying *one* substance and not
a substance in the sense of some individual substance or other. The
idea of one substance "is so comprised in all those that the imagination
can form that we necessarily know it or else never imagine anything."
There seem to me only two ways to avoid this translation. One is to
read Régis as asserting in the fashion of Locke that the idea of substance as the place-marker for a support (an I-know-not-what) is a component in our ideas of individual things; but this is implausible because
contrary to Locke, substance *is* known, as either extension or thought,
for these Cartesians. The other way is to say that the idea of any material thing is sufficient for the knowledge of all material things; this is
true for Régis, but only because material things are not so many different substances. In knowing one thing I know all just because in knowing the essence of one I know the essence of all.[9]

PATHS NOT FOLLOWED

Among the followers of Descartes, there are four tendencies discernible with respect to the problem of individuation. (1) One tendency is simply to ignore the problem; this tendency was exemplified
by the most acute of the Cartesians, Arnauld, although certainly not as
a function of his acuteness. (2) A second tendency is to individuate by
means of substance while yet satisfying the exigencies of the Cartesian
version of substance ontology. In the most systematic of the Cartesians,
Malebranche, this is in fact more than a mere tendency; it was an
explicit effort he made throughout his career. (3) Another, no less clear
response is to be found in the most deviant of the Cartesians, Cordemoy. His application of the independence criterion for substance
directly responds to the problem of individuation, but in a way that
undid the metaphysical core of Cartesianism and with it, perhaps, his
claim to being a Cartesian at all. (4) Finally, those who were most rigorous in working out the implications of Descartes's views for individuation, and who in this sense were the most faithful of the Cartesians, are
nowadays least known. Desgabets and Régis held that the difference
between individuals is the difference between modes, either of the
same or of different substances.

(1) Arnauld seems not to have had a view on individuation. At
least none readily emerges from his long debate with Malebranche, in
which the only related issue concerns how we perceive things as distinguished. Both he and Malebranche agree that perceptions are particu-

larized by our sensations—paradigmatically, a shape is distinguished within the visual field by a difference in color. They agree further that the sensation, of color, for example, is a modification of the mind. Their disagreement, which is the central issue of their debate, concerned the status of the perceived shape. For Malebranche, like all other perceived properties of extension it was independent both of the mind and of the shaped, but uncolored, thing in the material world that it represented to the mind. For him it was an Idea in the mind of God after which the material thing was created. For Arnauld, on the other hand, the perceived shape was in the mind as a modification of it. But their discussion, in both agreement and disagreement, was restricted to the individuation of our perception of material things and did not extend to the individuation of the material things themselves.[10] Still less did they address the individuation of minds, despite the theological concerns (such as conditions of salvation for individual souls) that drove their discussion of perception. To put it another way, although their disagreement revealed deep ontological differences, the issue between them was the discernibility of individuals, not individuation as such.[11]

(2) I do not give here an extended treatment of Malebranche's views on individuation, which are dealt with elsewhere in this volume. Rather, I treat them, briefly, only as an indication of the dialectical pressures of Cartesianism that drove others to take a more consistent position than did Malebranche on the problem of individuation.[12]

It seems clear that throughout his career Malebranche regarded individual material things as so many substances, meaning by substance what Descartes laid down in the *Principles*: that which, because conceivable apart, can exist apart from all else (but God).[13] But their individuation *qua* substances posed a problem for him. For example, when space or extension was identified by Descartes with homogeneous matter, the task of accounting for the differences among cohesion, contiguity, and union became problematic for obvious reasons. In the *Search after Truth*, Malebranche criticized Gassendi's non-Cartesian account of cohesion in terms of interlocking, branched, and crooked particles on the grounds that in failing to explain the cohesion of the particles themselves, the account only puts off the difficulty. Nor will it do, he says, to regard the binding particles as essentially indivisible, for their parts are conceivable apart from each other; hence, as substances, they can exist apart from each other. This means that on Malebranche's view every extended substance contains an infinite number of substances because every part of extension is at least conceptually divisible to infinity. The independence criterion of conceivability also means that every extended substance is contained by an infinite number of substances.[14] Furthermore, he seems committed to introducing an infinite number of modifications for each substance but one, for a modification is that which is inconceivable apart from that of which it is the modification, and the whole of which any substance is a part is inconceivable apart from its parts. That is, every substance but one has an infinite number of modifications, for every substance is a member of an infinite number of wholes except for the substance that is all of extension, which has no modifications. With such a dialectic, Malebranche's ontology, in which everything is either a substance or a mode, is not of much use with respect to the problem of individuation. To put it another way: if a substance is what can be conceived apart, ordinary material individuals cannot be so many substances.

Nonetheless, when confronted with the charge of Spinozism, Malebranche insisted that individual material things were so many substances. Against Mairan, who took material things to be modifications of extension, he replied that he could "conceive, imagine, sense by itself a cubic foot of extension, without thinking of anything else. Therefore, this extension [that is, presumably, the cubic foot of extension] is the substance and its cubic shape is its modification. This cubic foot is indeed a part of the larger extension, but it is not the modification of it."[15] At this point the concept of conceivability itself becomes problematic. In the end, individuation seems inscrutable on Malebranchean grounds, which is perhaps as it should be since for him the individual is as such unintelligible. That there are individuals, as opposed to the essences they instantiate, depends on the indifferent will of God. This is likely what Malebranch means in pointing to existence itself as what distinguishes otherwise identical things.[16] More than this, what his struggle shows is the pressure inherent in Cartesianism toward positions that were in fact developed by others.

(3) The conclusions at which Cordemoy arrived may obviously have been heterodox in Cartesian terms, but the premises from which he departed were at least arguably orthodox.[17] Without ever stating it in such terms, Cordemoy relies on the Cartesian independence criterion for substance. But he uses it to argue that each individual body is a simple and indivisible extended substance whose shape cannot change. That is, for Cordemoy, the text of conceivability apart leads directly to atomism. "Bodies are extended substances. . . . As each body is but a self-same substance [une même substance], it cannot be divided; its shape cannot change."[18] Matter, on the other hand is a collection [assemblage] of bodies, which compose it as its parts. "As each body cannot be divided, it cannot have parts; but as matter is a collection of

bodies, it can be divided into as many parts as there are bodies."[19] Furthermore, although each body is extended and perforce possesses extremities and a middle, it cannot be altered. "If . . . a self-same substance cannot in itself be divided [*une même substance ne se peut diviser en elle-même*] and if its nature is to be able to be extended, then, as soon as the substance is conceived to exist, we must allow that since it is the same in all its parts, none of its extremities can be separated from it."[20]

To answer the problem of individuation, Cordemoy thus appeals to substance as an individual; indeed, his tendency is to regard the individual as bare, that is, unnatured. To this Cartesian heresy, Cordemoy added the atomist conception of space as a nonmaterial container independent of the matter it might contain. If the matter in a vase or a room were annihilated, its sides would not ipso facto touch, for the bodies of which the sides are composed are independent of each other.[21] The void is thus possible, with the result that matter and extension or space cannot be identical as Descartes thought.

(4) Such anti-Cartesian views did not go unnoticed. Cordemoy's book was sent by Clerselier to Desgabets, who replied in no uncertain terms.[22] Aside from personal invective, Desgabets's rebuttal of the independence argument allows that parts of matter taken in relation to a common end are "formally and essentially" indivisible, but insists that the parts composing it are nonetheless separable.[23] The spring in the object before me is separable from it insofar as both are composed of bodies; but it is inseparable insofar as both compose a watch. Régis made the same kind of distinction, and answered the voided-room argument as follows. The walls of the room have an independent existence, but only "considered in themselves." "The disposition they have to compose a room is dependent on the space between them and consequently on some quantity and some matter."[24] Elaborating these Cartesian responses to Cordemoy's atomism involves many difficulties and anyhow is less important than Desgabets's and Régis's own answers to the problem of individuation. Each of them deserves an extended treatment.

DESGABETS

Desgabets's longest and most important work is the *Supplément à la philosophie de Monsieur Descartes*.[25] Although finally published in 1983, it nonetheless shows the ways in which it was possible in the period to develop Cartesian principles and it indicates the thinking that may have influenced others, especially Régis. The title of the work is indicative of

Desgabets's program. For Desgabets, as for other Cartesians such as Malebranche, Descartes's fundamental principles were correct but the use he made of them was sometimes defective.[26] Yet if Descartes "sometimes ceased to be a good Cartesian," we need turn only to Descartes's principles in order to find the remedy.[27] In this sense it was thought possible, as Malebranche put it, to base views opposed to Descartes's (and the boldness to defend them) on Descartes himself (and his way of doing philosophy).[28] Desgabets thus supplements Descartes's philosophy by supplying its defects, and he attempts to do so with respect to two topics that emerge from the *Meditations*: (1) the real distinction between soul and body, and (2) the existence of God.

The first, which is by far the longer of the two treatments, culminates in an argument of great importance to the issue of individuation. According to Desgabets, Descartes erred greatly when in his *Replies to Objections* II he allowed that only by faith do we come to accept that God does not afterward do what he, Desgabets, has just demonstrated separation of body and soul does not do, namely, annihilate the soul. That is, according to Desgabets, once it is demonstrated that the soul's separation from the body does not annihilate the soul, the soul's immortality can then be demonstrated and no appeal to faith is necessary. The reason for this is that substance, like eternal truth, is indefectible. Desgabets was among the minority of Cartesians who accepted Descartes's argument based on divine omnipotence that God is the "total and efficient" cause, not only of the existence of things but of their essence as well.[29] What this means is that the eternal truths depend on God's will, that is, he could have made it false that the three angles of a triangle equal two right angles or more generally that contradictories should simultaneously both be true.[30] While this strips geometrical truths of their necessity (they could have been otherwise if God had willed otherwise), they are nonetheless eternal (there is no time at which God in fact wills them otherwise). God makes geometry true by creating *res extensa* as its object.[31]

While God's will is perfectly free with a "freedom of indifference," it is eternal and immutable and therefore what he wills is eternal and immutable.[32] The upshot is that although substance is created, it is nonetheless eternal and immutable, that is, it is indefectible. However problematic this line of argument may be for Descartes's exegesis, it is abundantly clear in Desgabets, as I now indicate.

Desgabets explicitly links the creation of the eternal truths with the creation of other *things* (*choses*) such as the soul and matter, which are their "object and subject" (*objet et sujet*).[33] God is the author of both sorts of creation with a sovereign indifference, which is to say, absolute omnipotence. The problem this raises is that God could, however inconveniently to us, "annihilate" a truth such as the whole is greater than its parts. That he does not, however, seems to be derived from the same attribute that generates the problem, namely, divine omnipotence. "Everyone believes it justified to regard [such a truth] as fixed for all eternity, the reason for which is, according to Descartes, that God wills that it be what it is and that it would be absurd and even impious to place in Him contrary volitions, of which one would destroy what the other had done."[34] That is, just because he always and immediately has his way, God never has to change his mind, as it were, and try something else. Though absolutely indifferent, his will is fixed for all eternity.[35]

If the eternal fixedness of geometry follows from divine omnipotence, however, the eternal fixedness of everything else dependent on God's will also seems to follow. And indeed, this is just the conclusion that Desgabets draws in arguing for the immortality of the soul. "For if this so noble substance does not depend on God in a way other than the truths which do not withal cease to be immutable, notwithstanding their dependence, we must say that its existence is no less firm than theirs . . . which in no way prejudices God's prerogatives. Nonetheless, this is more than sufficient for my purpose, for it follows that a soul can no more be annihilated than a truth can cease to be a truth."[36] Desgabets apparently ignores an important disanalogy between the creation of the eternal truths and the creation of the soul, namely, that *ex vi terminorum*, there is no time at which the eternal truths are not, whereas for individual minds, if they are so many thinking substances, there is presumably a time at which they begin to be and before which they are not. My own view is that either Desgabets did not think through his position on this question fully or that, if he did, he drew back from expressing the consequences of it. What those consequences were, and why the expression of them should be problematic will become more obvious below. Meanwhile, Desgabets has no hesitation in arguing that matter is indefectible and indeed that if it were not, the foundation of the whole of Descartes's physics would be upset.[37] The obvious question this whole line of argument raises concerns the possibility of change. If everything happens according to God's will, indeed utterly as a result of it, and if that will is eternally fixed, then nothing would ever change. Yet the river flows, or at least appears to do so, *in omne volubilis aevum*, as Horace says.[38] What we have is Aristotle's problem with Parmenides: the experience, and presumed fact, of change in the face of a dialectic that says change is impossible.

I have indicated above the context for Desgabets's account of change. There is an analogous question about the necessity and contingency of truths. To be sure, all truth is contingent in the radical sense that all truth could have been otherwise with a different divine volition, which itself could have been otherwise. But presumably we still want to distinguish between the propositions of geometry, which are eternally true, and propositions about the weather, which are true only for a time. The difference for Desgabets is the difference between statements about substance and statements about modes. Consonant with his view that essences are created, he holds that there is no absolute possibility and that possibilities are defined only when substance is created. When God creates a substance he gives it a nature that defines the modes of which it is capable. "Only modes or things particularly as such [*les chose particulièrement en tant que telles*] have an actual coexistence in time, but matter *qua* corporeal substance . . . prior to its determinations through forms is not in time at all . . . it exists simply in itself, without any difference of present past and future time."[39] The variable individual things of our experience are modes, and only they are in time and change; their essence, the single corporeal substance of which they are modes, does not change. The important point that emerges for our story is not the account of modality but the view of individuals as modes that determine substance/essence to exist in a certain way. As Desgabets puts it in an earlier work devoted entirely to the topic of the indefectibility of substance: "matter considered in itself will be the essence of corporeal things, which matter will receive its existence when it takes on [*quand elle sera revetue*] its modes, which give it a particular and determinate mode of being [*qui lui donnent une manière d'être particulière et determinée*]."[40]

The problematic consequences of Desgabets's position for the individuation of minds now becomes clearer. For if minds are transitory modes of a single thinking substance as physical things are transitory modes of a single extended substance, then the indefectibility of substance cannot be appealed to in order to secure the personal immortality required by religious (and political) dogma. When I die my substance may be immortal, but I myself will not be around to receive the rewards of a good life or the punishments for a bad one. Desgabets avoided this problem, as far as I can tell, only by ignoring it. His follower Régis did not ignore it; *au contraire*, he acknowledged this consequence. The difficulty for this position can be made even worse, for even before either of us dies any difference between us seems not to be real. It is, to use a technical term, an 'appearance' or a 'phenomenon', as I now show.

A number of Cartesians were explicit in recognizing the importance of what might be called the principle of intentionality.[41] Desgabets's version of it goes as follows: "the simplest, best known and most necessary of all principles is that every simple conception always has outside the understanding a real and existent object that is in itself such as it is represented by thought."[42] Without this principle, he thinks, all certitude of our own existence, of the world, of God and of religion is upset; even the *cogito* is undermined without it.[43] Desgabets is thus at great pains to establish the principle against the obvious objections that can be made against it—for example, that we can think of such items as a golden mountain that are not real and existent, outside our thought, but purely possible, within our thought. (His long account of logical modality, which is only touched upon above, is in fact designed to meet just this sort of objection.) One of his arguments for the principle invokes a premise already limned above, namely, that real possibilities conceivable by us are created only when substance is created. The "pure" possibility of God creating different substances and thus a different range of possibilities conceivable by us is itself inconceivable. We can think as possible only what God has created.[44]

Desgabets at one point extends the argument as follows. "In addition to the fact that when we think of something, and when we think that it is already conceivable intrinsically and in itself, we have the power to give it an actual and real existence, in virtue of which it can also be shown that our thoughts always have a real object."[45] That is, just by thinking of anything we think of something possible, which shows that God has created some substance; but beyond that, we can *through our thought* determine that substance to exist in a certain way, which is to say that we determine its actual modes. This "production of things by thought" is likened by Desgabets to God's own creation, which brings into existence what he knows even as he knows it. What we do is to draw out of substance modes that consequently have a real and temporal existence; without this operation of the mind, modes have only a possible existence in substance.[46] It is in this additional sense that "our thoughts always have a real object," even when we think about such items as golden mountains. While Desgabets's main concern is to defend his principle of intentionality against objections based on such items as golden mountains, he extends his account to cover thoughts about, and the "production of," such items as the Alps. If I am correct, the account to which Desgabets commits himself is that: (1) only substances are individuated by themselves; (2) there are but two substances, thought and extension; (3) things, that is, individual minds and physical objects, are modes respectively of these two substances;[47] (4) the individuation of modes depends on our thought. All of these points are contentious as explications, certainly of

Descartes's position, but even of Desgabets's. I conclude by concentrating on just the final point, whose plausibility entails that of the previous three. I then turn to Régis, who carries out essentially the same program.

In Desgabets's terminology, substance exists intrinsically, mode extrinsically. "When an architect designs a house, it is very certain that he gives to matter, i.e. to the stone and wood, a form of a house which belongs to them extrinsically, although it is commonly imagined and said that this sort of being is only in thought and does not exist outside of the understanding, for an object which is known effectively possesses an extrinsic form of being known."[48] It is extrinsically that the predestined are chosen by God, he explains, and then continues: "All of geometry, architecture, etc. do nothing else but give that sort of being [i.e. extrinsic] to their objects: a pole divided into ten feet by mental designation [*par désignation mentale*], a cask divided into a hundred points, etc., are actually divided, and we believe that they have this determinate quality outside of the understanding. Men divided into regiments, companies, etc. really form these bodies. 20, 30, 40 pistoles are indeed such a number, and we cannot say that this has existence only in thought, because regiment, foot, 20 pistoles are real and corporeal things, and not thoughts, although their being as such comes to them through thought, which gives them that form and that extrinsic denomination."[49] I see no other reasonable interpretation of what Desgabets says here than to say that numerical distinctions in the physical world, that is, the individuation of it, depends on our thought. This is not a surprising result of the view that the things of the world are modes of a single substance and that modal distinctions depend on us. The rub comes when the same analysis is given to the world of minds and when both are read in the Parmenidean tradition of construing what is not real, that is, mind independent, as only apparent or phenomenal.

RÉGIS

Régis produced the most important systematic Cartesian treatise of philosophy as traditionally divided into logic, metaphysics, physics, and ethics. (But for Antoine Legrand's *Entire Body of Philosophy* of 1694, it was the only such systematic account.) In the *Système de philosophie*[50] Régis claims, like Desgabets, to be offering a purer version of Cartesianism than is to be found in the works of the eponymous author. While admitting to new explanations and definitions of, inter alia, mind, soul, understanding, motion, rest, quantity, and prime matter, he also says that they should be attributed to Descartes, "whose method and principles I have followed even in explanations that are different from his."[51] Régis's reading of Descartes seems to have been influenced by Desgabets on a great number of issues, but especially on those of most concern to us here.[52] He understands the connection between individual minds and material things on the one hand and thought and extension on the other in essentially the same terms as Desgabets, and thus is committed to the same account of individuation.

In a text cited in full and discussed below, Régis actually calls "body and mind considered in themselves *substantial beings* or simply *substances*, . . . and . . . all particular minds and bodies *modal beings.*"[53] Sometimes Régis does refer to himself as a substance; if I am right these instances must be disambiguated as references to his essence alone. But unless I am mistaken, he nowhere refers to his body, or any other particular body, as a substance. On the contrary, in discussing how we can know the existence, number, and duration of modal beings, he argues as follows. We have different sensations at different times that do not depend on us. Because they change they do not depend on God. For the same reason, they do not depend on body, at least not "considered in itself." Therefore, "when I sense in a given fashion, this depends immediately on body being divided into several bodies and its having received through this division modes that enable it to produce all the variety in my sensations, from which I conclude that several bodies exist."[54] This sounds as though different motions *cause* different sensations in us, as in Régis's Cartesian physiology they certainly do. But his point in *ontological* terms is that modes *result* from individuation through our sensations. On the basis of sensations like green and yellow, according to Régis, one picks out, that is, constitutes such objects as the earth and the sun that make up the sensible world as opposed to the so-called imaginary spaces that are termed such, not because they are void, but because the senses perceive nothing in them.[55] Individual things *result from* our projection of sensations on otherwise homogeneous and undifferentiated extension. On this view individual things *are* what Malebranche and Arnauld took to be the *representations* of things.[56]

Later in the *Système*, Régis distinguishes between *body* (that substance whose essence is extension) and *quantity*. Because of its essence, "size in itself" is an essential property of body; but quantity, which is a given size, is not an essential property—presumably for the reason that individual bodies can be of different sizes and perhaps change size. What is the distinction between body and quantity? "Quantity is nothing else but body itself considered according to size."[57] This distinction is sufficient to allow them to have different properties, as the distinction of reason between numbers and things numbered allows them to have different properties (e.g., oddness versus color). The difference in property crucial for the issue of individuation is divisibility. Infinite divisibility is an essential property of quantity, but not of body. If body were divisible, then "since all division brings a change to the thing divided," its essence would be changed, which is contrary to reason.[58] In fact, however, after division each part still has the whole essence of body. So there is no question here of matter being really divided by motion into individual bodies. The single material substance is the essence of all individual material things (bodies) which are so many quantities of it; but one still wants to know how those quantities are constituted. We still need an account of individuation.

The answer is that the mind in its perception individuates bodies. "From [his] doctrine it follows," Régis says, "first, that having some quantity or other[59] is of the essence of particular bodies . . . and second, that quantity is not an interior mode of body, but an exterior mode consisting in a certain manner in which body is conceived in relation to a given size."[60] Régis's exterior mode is the same notion as Descartes's extrinsic denomination or Desgabets's extrinsic mode. There are complications here, but the point clearly emerges that individual material things are modes of a single material substance and that their individuation depends on the conception of them.[61]

Régis's treatment of the individuation of material things is largely that of Desgabets. His advance beyond Desgabets lies in developing what is at best implicit in Desgabets concerning the individuation of minds. Régis is remarkably explicit in treating individual minds as modes of a single thinking substance. "Because body and mind considered in themselves do not contain in their idea any actually existing mode and considered as such or such they do, to mark this difference I shall call body and mind considered in themselves *substantial beings* or simply *substances*, because I conceive nothing in them that does not subsist in itself, and I shall call all particular minds and bodies *modal beings*, because in their idea they contain modes, which form part of their essence; thus by the word *modal being* in general I shall mean a being which contains modes in its essence."[62] The argument seems to be the following. From thought as an essence it no more follows that I am having a specific thought than it follows from extension as the essence of the object before me that it should have one shape rather than another. Furthermore, both essences are independent of the things of which they are the essences, while the converse does not hold—an asymmetry that Régis tries to capture with the Cartesian version of the substance-mode connection: modes depend on substances, but substances do not depend on modes, for a substance can be conceived without its modes, but a mode cannot be conceived without the substance of which it is the mode. Finally, Régis suggests that individual minds consist of their thoughts and bodies of their modes of extension, that is, shapes; for I can see no other way than in terms of class-inclusion to interpret the containment whereby, as he says, their idea contains modes that form their essence.[63] An individual mind, then, looks proleptically very much like a Humean bundle of perceptions.

The above is not the only point at which Régis anticipates Hume's analysis of the mind. In discussing duration, he argues that one often has the same idea at different times, which leads one to believe that it is produced by the same object. From this identity one gets the idea of duration—the perseverance of a body in being. Not only do modal bodies endure, but they also change—our ideas succeed one another, which also gives us the idea of duration. "Through this perpetual change of ideas I notice in my mind that I have an idea not only of my own duration but also of that of all the other modal beings that are the objects of my ideas."[64] To be sure, there is an important difference here between Régis and Hume. For Régis, the kinds of things bundled into minds and into bodies are essentially different, while for Hume they are essentially the same and are in fact bundled according to the same principles of association. Régis subscribes to dualism of kinds, Hume to neutral monism.[65] But for Régis, as for Hume, the idea of duration is not derived from either bodies or the mind, but rather from the *manner* in which the ideas ('perceptions' in Hume's terminology) composing bodies and the mind are presented.[66] If the idea of duration were derived from bodies or minds themselves, then for both Régis and Hume bodies or minds would be substances, that is, things remaining identical through change.[67] The point here, however, is less Régis's anticipation of Hume, than Régis's acceptance of the opening move in the Humean dialectic when he construes minds as bundles of modes, that is, as modal beings: "I have an idea not only of my own duration but of that of all other modal beings."

There is additional evidence for the set-theoretic analysis of individuation whereby individual things, minds and physical objects, differ insofar as the qualities constituting them differ. Régis at one point begins with a fair representation of the Cartesian notion of real distinction: "the true mark of the real distinction found between two things of the same nature is that these two things can be known without each other."[68] That they can exist apart, which is presumably what Régis means by their being really distinct, is known because they are known apart. He then produces three kinds of real distinction: (1) the generic, between things of different genera (e.g., a man and a stone); (2) the specific, between things having a common attribute (e.g., a man and a horse, which are both animals); (3) the numerical, "between things that have a same genus and a same difference, but do not have the same common accidents, which is how one drop of water differs from another."[69] All these kinds of real distinction rely on qualities for individuation, or at least on substances *qua* essences rather than substances *qua* individuators. This reliance is obvious in the first case, where a man *qua* thinking thing and a stone *qua* extended thing cannot be the same because they have different essences.[70]

It is even more obvious in the third case, where it would seem that two drops of water can differ only because of differences in qualities.[71] The second case is ambiguous because a man involves two essences; *qua* thinking thing his difference from a horse is generic, while *qua* extended thing it is numerical. For my argument concerning Régis's analysis of mind, the numerical is the crucial case, for Régis later argues, in connection with the problem of knowledge of other minds, that his soul is *really* distinct from the souls of other men because he senses and imagines through his body and they do not: "I also say that other souls are distinct among themselves because the use of language [*la parole*] clearly shows me that these different souls have different thoughts, from which I conclude that they are really distinct according to that kind of distinction that I have called *numerical*."[72]

Régis does sometimes refer to himself, presumably his mind, as a substance,[73] which for theologico-political reasons it would be in his interest to do, but he really cannot sustain this position. For one thing, on his account substances do not begin or cease to be, whereas surely minds must at least *begin* to be. The theologico-political problem of the immortality of the soul is thus raised for Régis in terms that he cannot ignore, and he tries to argue for the soul's immortality on the basis of the indefectibility of substance. But the substantial soul turns out to be, as it must for him, a universal soul: "as extension, which is the essential attribute of body is never corrupted, and it is only the modes making it this or that body that perish, we are forced also to recognize that thought, which is the essential attribute of mind cannot be corrupted. And it is only the modes determining it to be this or that soul, for example to be the soul of Peter, Paul, John, etc., which are destroyed."[74]

Régis is prepared, then, to maintain the merely modal status of minds even at the cost of supporting the theological and political heresy of denying individual immortality,[75] which he attempts to mitigate with a fideist skepticism. He begins the chapter entitled "that the soul is immortal" with the observation that apart from faith we can have no certainty on this question because the state of the soul after death depends on the will of God, which can be known only through experience (of which we have, and can have, none in this case) or revelation. So we are to believe that we are immortal because we are told on the best authority, revelation, that we are immortal. But what we are told to believe, it would seem, either is incomprehensible in the way the doctrine of the Trinity is, for example, or else results in the universal soul as explicated above. For in the next two chapters he argues that with death the soul loses its properties (such as sensation) that depend on the body and retains those that are independent (such as knowing itself). He concludes this line of argument by saying that death destroys everything but "what is substantial in man."[76]

The upshot is that the difference between individual minds is a difference between modes. This conclusion is not some suggestion at the periphery of Régis's system; it is found at the very core of his account of Cartesianism. Régis begins his metaphysics with an assertion of his own existence based on consciousness [*conscience*] of its truth. Simple, inner awareness [*connaissance simple et intérieur*] rather than reasoning produces this assurance, although he also says that the natural light teaches him that quite apart from their truth or falsity, he could not have perceptions if he did not exist.[77] From this he draws a conclusion about his nature, namely, that he is a thought [*une Pensee*], by which he means "a fixed and permanent thought . . . that exists in itself and is the subject of different modes of thought," which are in flux and change from one moment to the next as we think of different things.[78] This sounds as if each mind were an individual substance. But not so, for his concern is with his *nature*. "Since the thought that constitutes my nature exists in itself, and since all my modes of thought exist only in this thought, I shall say, in order to mark this difference, that the thought constituting my nature is a *substance*, and that all my different modes of thought [*manières de penser*] are only *modes* [*modes*], *modifications, modes of being* [*façons d'estre*] or in general *properties* of that substance. Extending it to every other subject, I shall mean by the word *substance* a thing that exists in itself; and by the latter words, what can exist only in a subject."[79] This is to say that if Peter and Paul have the same nature they have the same substance. The difference between them cannot be a difference of substance; the difference can be only of mode.[80]

That the difference between Peter and Paul can be only modal is all the more clear since Régis goes on to argue the Cartesian position on the basis that *his* substance cannot change. "The essences of things are indivisible and nothing can be added to or taken away from them without destroying them."[81] This is the position that Descartes takes in response to Gassendi's objection that the idea of God is not complete and innate, but is arrived at by a process of construction from experience: "[Gassendi appears] not to have attended to that common saying among Philosophers—that the essences of things are indivisible. For the idea represents the essence of the thing, and if something is added to it or subtracted from it, it is forthwith the idea of something else . . . after the idea of the true God is once conceived, although new perfections can be detected in it which had not previously been noticed, this does not cause any increase in that idea, but merely renders it more distinct and explicit, because they must have been contained in the very same idea, since it is assumed to have been true."[82] Régis says that essences are indivisible in this sense else *his* substance would change. The substance that does not change is his, but also Paul's, essence. The difference between them can be, like the difference between Paul's own thoughts, only a modal difference.

What, then, of my thesis, stated at the outset, that on the Cartesian line developed above, not only physical objects, but also minds differ in the way in which red and yellow differ? Whether minds and physical objects are individually *single* modes, or whether, as Régis seems more plausibly to construe them, they are individually *bundles* of modes, the difference between one mind and another, and between one physical object and another, will be purely conceptual—it depends on our thought. This difference will thus have, on one standard use of the term, the status of being *unreal*. Minds are modes of one substance, from which *we* distinguish them; physical objects are modes of another substance, from which *we* distinguish them. The difference between the two substances, however, will be—as the definition of 'substance' indicates—*real*, for they can exist apart from each other.[83] As a result, the original statement of my thesis is ambiguous. I meant the original statement to be an initial indication that numerical difference would be a function of the difference between qualities. We now see that there are two kinds of such qualitative difference: that between two essences, which is real, and that between their instances, which is unreal. The difference between red and yellow can be taken, as it is commonsensically perhaps, to be real; or it may be taken, as it was by these Cartesians, to be unreal. In any event, however, these are the two sorts of Cartesian numerical difference or individuation.

NOTES

1. What this means is that in the end my account of Cartesian individuation depends on the Cartesian answer to Porphyry's question about universals. Except for some elliptical comments along the way, however, I ignore this question here.

2. "Descartes's Idealism," in *Philosophy and Culture*, Proceedings of the XVII World Congress of Philosophy (Montreal: Editions Montmorency, 1988), 4:53–6.

3. *Oeuvres de Descartes*, ed. C. Adam and P. Tannery (Paris: J. Vrin, 1973) (hereafter *AT*), 7:31; *The Philosophical Works of Descartes*, trans. E. S. Haldane and G. R. T. Ross (Cambridge: Cambridge University Press, 1931) (hereafter *HR*), 1:155.

4. Consider the Synopsis of the *Meditations*: "all substances generally—that is to say all things which cannot exist without being created by God—are in their nature incorruptible, . . . and can never cease to exist unless God, in denying to them His concurrence, reduce them to nought; . . . body, regarded generally, is a substance, which is the reason why it also cannot perish, but . . . the human body, inasmuch as it differs from other bodies, is composed only of a certain configuration of members and of other similar accidents, while the human mind is not similarly composed of any accidents, but is a pure substance. For although all the accidents of mind be changed, . . . it does not emerge from these changes another mind: the human body on the other hand becomes a different thing from the sole fact that the figure or form of [certain—*quarundam*] of its portions is found to have changed" (*AT* 7:14; *HR* 1:141). More needs to be said about his text, but I take it to be sufficient for the *prima facie* plausibility of the above.

5. See especially Malebranche, who connects the issues of mechanism, causal explanations and the integrity of living things. See *Nicolas Malebranche: The Search after Truth*, trans. T. M. Lennon and P. J. Olscamp, *Elucidations of The Search after Truth*, trans. T. M. Lennon, *Philosophical Commentary*, T. M. Lennon (Columbus: Ohio State University Press, 1980), *Elucidations* 15; pp. 661ff. The mechanistic undoing of teleology was complicated by a theological constraint on the analysis of humans. At a remarkably early date (1311–12) the Council of Vienne condemned (*reprobamus*) as "erroneous and inimical to the Catholic faith [the view that] the substance of the rational or intellectual soul is not truly and of itself [per se] the form of the human body . . . anyone asserting, defending, or assuming that it is not should be regarded as a heretic" (H. Denzinger, *Enchiridion symbolorum*, 32d ed. [Barcelona: Herder, 1963], p. 284). Thus, although rejecting hylomorphism in all other contexts, Descartes (e.g., *AT* 3:503), Malebranche (*Elucidations* 8:582), and other Cartesians claimed that the soul is the substantial form of the body. Since for them the natural state of the soul was separate from the body, the individuation of souls posed a problem

not faced by Aquinas, for whom the soul's natural state is to be individuated by matter. I ignore this complication here.

6. *Categories* 5; 2all. For the problems generated by the failure of Descartes's Latin to disambiguate substance as qualified by definite and indefinite articles, and for much else of interest on these topics, see G. Rodis-Lewis, *L'individualité selon Descartes* (Paris: J. Vrin, 1950), Chapter 2.

7. See Newton's *De gravitatione et aequipondio fluidorum*, in *The Unpublished... Papers*, ed. A. R. and M. B. Hall (Cambridge: Cambridge University Press, 1962), pp. 132–33.

8. *Système de philosophie* (Lyon: 1690), p. 279. This work is discussed *in extenso* below. Except where indicated otherwise, all translations are my own.

9. 'Being' is another term that, like 'substance', 'mind', and 'body', deserves careful attention in this context. Régis and Jacques Rohault both define it as "that which exists, in whatever manner it exists" (Régis, *Système* [here and below: vol. 1], p. 69; Rohault, *Traité de physique* [Paris, 1671], part 4, chap. 4, par. 2). For the term 'body', see Régis, *Système*, p. 76: "by this word *body* I mean only an extension in length, breadth, and depth that exists in itself."

10. For Malebranche, an 'idea' that was a modification of the mind could represent to the mind nothing beyond the mind itself. Thus *Oeuvres complètes de Malebranche*, ed. A. Robinet, 20 vols. (Paris: J. Vrin, 1958–70) (hereafter *OC*), 6:55–56: "To perceive [*voir*] a sensible object—the sun, a tree, a house, etc.—two things are necessary: the modality of color, for Arnauld agrees that color is a modification of the soul; and a pure idea, viz., the idea of extension, or intelligible extension. For when we have a lively sensation of light attached or related to an intelligible circle removed from a certain intelligible space made perceptible by different colors, we see the sun, not as it is, but as we see it . . . all our perceptions are representative modalities. I agree that no ideas are necessary to represent perceptions. . . . But I deny that, without my *idea*, there can be any *perception* that represents to the mind a being distant from it. It is that alone which is in question." Thus, for Arnauld the representation resulted from one modification of the mind (color) individuating another (extension); for Malebranche it resulted from a modification of the mind color individuating intelligible extension in God's mind.

11. See Jorge J. E. Gracia, *Individuality: An Essay on the Foundations of Metaphysics* (Albany: State University of New York Press, 1988), p. 21.

12. I have given a more extended account of Malebranche's effort to solve this problem elsewhere in the context of his idealism in my *Battle of the Gods and Giants: The Legacies of Descartes and Gassendi: 1655–1715* (Princeton: Princeton University Press, 1993), chapter 4, section 14.

13. I sketch here Malebranche's views on the individuation only of material things. Nonetheless, it is worth drawing attention to Bouillier, who cites a text from Malebranche's *Meditations:* "I feel led to believe that my substance is

external, that I am a part of the Divine Being, and that all my various thoughts are only particular modifications of universal Reason" (*OC* 10:102). Bouillier points out that Malebranche rejects the view in no uncertain terms, but remarks, "one senses that it obsesses him, and seduces him as it were despite himself" (*Histoire de la philosophie cartésienne*, 3d ed. [Paris, 1868], 2:61). This is the slide toward Spinozism, which Malebranche also struggled with in accounting for the individuation of material things, as I show briefly below.

14. One way to conceptualize this dual relation of containment had by every extended substance is that if it did not obtain, there would be holes in space, which is effectively the conclusion that Cordemoy *accepted* in arguing an ontology of atoms and the void. See below.

15. To Dourtous de Mairan, 5 December 1713; *OC* 19:865. Thus, any Spinozist interpretation such as the above dialectic must be taken as rational reconstruction and not simply attributed to Malebranche, as perhaps the following is. "Every object that cannot be conceived as standing alone depends upon another and is therefore 'a manner of being, or a modification of substance'. Only two created substances fulfill this definition of a substance: mind, and matter . . . particular bodies are not substances, but 'modifications' or 'manners of being' of extension, body in general. Likewise, . . . thought alone is substantial. . . . Thus, although retaining much of the traditional definition of substance as being that subsists in itself, Malebranche abandoned the concept of particular substances that stand alone as ontological subjects" (Michael E. Hobart, *Science and Religion in the Thought of Nicholas Malebranche* [Chapel Hill: University of North Carolina Press, 1982], pp. 96–97).

16. To Mairan, 12 June 1714; *OC* 19:886. Cf. Rodis-Lewis, *L'individualité*, p. 51.

17. Gérauld de Cordemoy (1626–84) was a practicing lawyer who also frequented the leading *salons*, *conférences*, and *académies* of the period. He was known as a Cartesian and Baillet places him among those attending the Descartes funeral jamboree of 29 June 1667. The fine modern edition of his works at last makes his thought accessible; see it also for further bibliobiographical data (*Oeuvres philosophiques*, ed. P. Clair and F. Girbal [Paris: Presses Universitaires de France, 1968]).

18. *Oeuvres*, p. 95.

19. Ibid., p. 96. The failure to distinguish between bodies and matter, according to Cordemoy, leads to the mistaken view that all extension is divisible, indeed infinitely so. No individual body is capable of affecting our sense organs; hence it cannot be perceived; since no individual body is perceptible, the conjunction that results in matter cannot be perceived, only the resultant matter. "Because all the extension we perceive is thus divisible, we so join the notion of what is extended to the notion of what is divisible that we believe all that is extended is divisible" (ibid., p. 97).

20. Ibid., p. 98. For more on the historical significance of the modal quali-
fication 'to be able to be extended,' see the editor's note 7, pp. 306–7. That
Cordemoy says that individual substances are able to be extended, rather than
that they are extended, underlines the metaphysical atomism he was espousing
as opposed to the primarily physical atomism advocated by Gassendi, for example. For more on this topic, see my "Physical and Metaphysical Atomism:
1666–1682," in An Intimate Relation, ed. J. R. Brown and J. Mittelstrass (Dordrecht: Kluwer, 1989).

21. Oeuvres, pp. 103–4. Cf. Descartes, Principles 2:18.

22. "Lettre écrite à M. Clerselier touchant les nouveaux raisonnements
pour les atomes et le vide contenus dans le livre du Discernement du corps et
de l'âme." This letter exists only in ms.: Bibliothèque d'Epinal, ms. 143, 59. It is
discussed by Joseph Prost, Essai sur l'atomisme et l'occasionalism dans la philosophie cartésienne (Paris: H. Paulin, 1907), pp. 156ff.

23. "Lettre," cited by editors, Oeuvres note 12, p. 309 after Prost, in ibid.,
p. 168.

24. Système, p. 286.

25. Robert Desgabets (1610–78) was a Benedictine priest in contact with
various Cartesians. Aside from two opuscules on transubstantiation and blood
transfusion, he published only the Critique de la critique de la recherche de la vérité.
Until recently, his most important work has been in manuscript only, known
through two secondary sources. Now we have his Oeuvres philosophiques inédites,
in Analecta Cartesiana 2 (1983).

26. As, for example, on the crucial doctrine of the created eternal truths.
On this point Desgabets and Malebranche agreed that Descartes had erred, but
had contradictory assessments of his error. See Desgabets, Supplément p. 209
and passim; Malebranche, Eclaircissements 10, OC 3:127ff.

27. C'est "Descartes mesme qui se redresse luy mesme." Desgabets to N.-J.
Poisson, 9 March 1677, in Malebranche, OC 18:127. For a great deal more on
this aspect of Desgabet's thought, see J. Beaude, "Cartésianisme et anti-
cartésianisme de Desgabets," Studia Cartesiana 1 (1979): 1–24.

28. Recherche, OC 2:449. See F. Alquié's extensive treatment of this topic in
Le cartésianisme de Malebranche (Paris: J. Vrin, 1974).

29. To Mersenne, 27 May 1630, AT 1:151ff.

30. To Mesland, 2 May 1644, AT 4:118.

31. See my "Descartes's Idealism."

32. To Mersenne, 15 April 1630, AT 1:145–46.

33. Supplément, part 1, sec. 4.

34. *Oeuvres*, pp. 209–10.

35. Whether, and in what sense, God is capable of annihilating anything is an issue with several interesting contexts for the Cartesians. One is Malebranche's analysis of motion and rest, and his changes in Descartes's rules for the communication of motion. See his *Search after Truth*, 6, 2, 9; *OC* 2:429ff.

36. *Oeuvres*, p. 210.

37. *Supplément* part 1, sec. 5 and *passim*.

38. *Epistles* 1. 2. 43.

39. *Oeuvres*, p. 237.

40. Ibid., p. 27. I say an earlier work, but the chronology of Desgabets's works is problematic. The *Traité de l'indefectibilité des créatures* was begun at least as early as 1654 and the *Supplément à la philosophie de M. Descartes* was completed in 1675; but this is not to say that the latter could not have been begun before the former, or the former completed after the latter. See Introduction to *Oeuvres*, xvi, xx.

41. Consider Malebranche, for example: "It is certain that nothingness or the false is not perceptible or intelligible. To see nothing is not to see; to think of nothing is not to think . . . nothingness is not perceptible. Properly speaking, this is the first principle of all our knowledge" (*Search*, 4:11:3; *OC* 2:98).

42. *Supplément*, part 2, chap. 5, sec. 3.

43. Ibid., secs. 5–6.

44. The upshot is an ontological argument for everything that exists, at least for every substantial thing. What is conceivable exists and what exists is inconceivable except as existing: "all matter that is conceivable and possible being the same as that which actually exists according to Descartes, no matter can be thought of that does not actually possess outside the understanding everything perceived in it, it being ridiculous to say, on this view, that purely possible matter can be thought of" (*Oeuvres*, p. 233). For more on the connections among omnipotence, the eternal truths, possibility-actuality-necessity, intentionality, and the like, see my "The Cartesian Dialectic of Creation," in *The Cambridge History of Seventeenth-century Philosophy*, ed. M. Ayers and D. Garber (Cambridge: Cambridge University Press, to appear).

45. *Supplément*, *Oeuvres*, p. 243.

46. *Supplément*, part 2, sec. 7; *Oeuvres*, p. 243. This is not an especially eccentric reading of the Cartesian notion of modal existence. In *Principles* 1, 60–62, Descartes tried to establish a kind of distinction that was neither a real distinction (capability of existence apart based on conceivability apart) nor merely a distinction of reason, which depends entirely on us. This *via media* is

the modal distinction, which Descartes seems to have modeled on Scotus's *distinctio formalis a parte rei*: we distinguish between items that cannot exist separately, but unlike the distinction between a thing and its definition (Scotus) or between substance and its duration (Descartes), there is some basis for the distinction in the thing itself. The tendency of later Cartesians, however, was to regard all distinctions that are not real as distinctions of reason. Regis provides an example of this (see below).

47. In the presumably earlier work, *Indefectibilité des créatures*, Desgabets resists this parallel between minds and things: "matter and spiritual substances [*sic*], that is, all the things in the world considered according to their substantial and created being, which is the foundation of their accidents and states, cannot be annihilated" (*Oeuvres*, p. 21).

48. *Oeuvres*, p. 244. See *Replies to Objections* I, *AT* 7:102; *HR* 2:10.

49. *Oeuvres*, p. 244.

50. Published in 1690, it was, according to Pierre Bayle, written some eighteen years earlier but had its publication delayed by political problems. Régis himself said: "I am not one of those falsely modest types who say that their works have been torn from their hands. I admit that in good faith that I have produced this work with the aim of publishing it and that I would have done so ten years ago had fortune or envy not been opposed to my intention" Système, preface).

51. Ibid.

52. Bouillier cites Régis (1632–1707) as calling Desgabets one of the greatest metaphysicians of the century and supposes that Desgabets influenced Régis in his empiricist tendencies (*Histoire*, 1:531). With the Desgabets *Oeuvres* now available, many more of his views seem similarly traceable. For the account of their common doctrine of the creation of eternal truths, see my "Cartesian Dialectic of Creation," sec. 4.

53. *Système*, p. 101.

54. Ibid., p. 105.

55. Gassendi had resurrected the earlier notion of imaginary spaces and argues that they comprised a real being *suo modo* that is void of material extension (*Opera omnia* [Lyons, 1658] 1:183). Here Régis admits the notion, but characterizes it as the Cartesian *res extensa*.

56. Thus the criticism of Malebranche's disciple Lelevel, who claimed that Régis had confused ideas with the things of which they are ideas. Since, according to Lelevel, Régis incorrectly took matter to be the mind's immediate object, and since he also correctly saw that ideas are eternal, he was incorrectly led to regard matter as eternal. Given the confusion of matter with the idea of it, "one cannot avoid the excesses of Spinoza, who pretended that the substance

of the universe was not different from that of God and that all the changes occurring in bodies and minds were only different modifications of matter; or at least one says like Régis that substances have always been produced because one sees that it has always been and always will be" (*La vraye et la fausse metaphysique, ou l'on refute les sentimens de M. Régis sur cette affaire* [Rotterdam, 1694] p. 87). For an elaboration of the charge of Spinozism, and Régis's attempt to answer it, see my "Cartesian Dialectic of Creation," sec. 5. Except for an oblique reference through Hume below, I here ignore the difficult question of the individuation of God from creation.

57. *Système*, p. 280.

58. Ibid., p. 282.

59. *La quantité indeterminée*. By this Régis means not *in*determinate quantity, but quantity that is determined in some way or other, although not necessarily in a given way.

60. *Système*, p. 283.

61. One complication results from Régis's terminology. "Quantity is not distinct from body by a formal or modal distinction"—which suggests that individual bodies are not modes—"but by a distinction of reason," which is the distinction, however, "found between substance and exterior modes"—so individual bodies are modes after all. See ibid.

62. Ibid., p. 101. Occasionally Régis seems to use 'substance' as a count noun with respect to himself. Thus, in giving the synthetic account of his position he argues that "substance is what exists in itself and is the subject of several modes. . . . I exist in myself and am the subject of doubt and certainty: therefore I am a substance" (ibid., p. 96). But even this does not mean that Peter and Paul are not the same substance, and in the same synthetic account Régis goes on to say in arguing the existence of God that he has the idea only of two substances: the substance that thinks and the extended substance.

63. Régis says, "which form *part of* their essence," but I do not see what any other part could be.

64. Ibid., p. 106.

65. This is a crucial difference. For Hume would think that it enables him to avoid Spinoza's "hideous hypothesis." While minds and bodies may for Régis be bundles, the constituents of each are, *qua* essentially of the same kind, modes of a substance. Since there is no conceivable "specific difference" between object and impression, we are led to Spinozism according to Hume (*Treatise*, ed. Selby-Bigge, pp. 240ff.). I am grateful to W. Abbott for reminding me of this text.

66. Ibid., pp. 36–37.

67. Ibid., p. 204.

68. *Système*, p. 116.

69. Ibid. Régis's modal distinction and distinction of reason, also discussed in this text, nominally do not differ from Descartes's distinctions.

70. This is the case Descartes discusses as follows: "As for the distinction whereby the mode of one substance is different from another substance, or from the mode of another substance, . . . it appears to me that we should call it real rather than modal; because we cannot clearly conceive these modes apart from the substances of which they are the modes and which are really distinct" (*Principles* 1, 61, in *HR* 1:244–45). Alas, one of the examples given by Descartes is contrary to the interpretation of Régis that I am proposing: "as the movement of one body is different from another body [*sic*] or from mind." If my reading of Régis is both correct and Cartesian, the movement of one body should be only modally distinct from another body. See note 71.

71. This is Descartes's second kind of *modal* distinction: "As to [this] kind of distinction, its characteristic is that we are able to recognize the one mode without the other and *vice versa*, but we can conceive neither the one nor the other without recognizing that both subsist in one common substance. If, for example, a stone is moved and along with that is square" (*Principles* 1, 61, in *HR* 1:244).

72. *Système*, p. 135.

73. Ibid., p. 96.

74. Ibid., pp. 266–67.

75. The heresy, of course, is the moral heresy—ascribed to Hobbes and Spinoza in particular—which was thought to remove the ultimate sanction for all orderly existence. This was the main obstacle to the revival of Epicureanism by Gassendi and others in the period. See M. Osler, "Baptizing Epicurean atomism: Pierre Gassendi on the Immortality of the Soul," in *Religion, Science and Worldview*, ed. M. Osler and P. L. Farber (Cambridge: Cambridge University Press, 1985), pp. 163–83.

76. Louis de La Forge is another Cartesian who, in his *Traité de l'esprit de l'homme* (1666), took this line that led to a denial of personal immortality. For a discussion of the text in these terms, see R. A. Watson, *The Breakdown of Cartesian Metaphysics* (Atlantic Highlands, N.J.: Humanities Press International, 1987), pp. 175ff.

77. *Système*, p. 68.

78. Ibid., pp. 70–71.

79. Ibid., p. 72.

80. "Everything that exists is either a substance or a mode" (ibid., p. 73).

81. Ibid., p. 74.

82. *Replies to Objections* V, in *HR* 2:220–21.

83. It follows from this that a mind and a physical object will, as modes of really different substances, differ really. This is the problematic case discussed in note 70. Perhaps the best way to construe this case is in terms of the Scotist *distinctio formalis a parte rei*. Without our thought there would be no distinction, but the distinction is not without a real basis.

Descartes and the Individuation
of Physical Objects

Emily Grosholz

escartes's physics in the *Principles of Philosophy* and his theorationalist metaphysics in the *Meditations* offer philosophically suggestive accounts of individuation. In the *Principles* he explores a geometric and kinematic basis for the individuation of material bodies, in which he attempts to avoid the usual deficiencies of such accounts by referring to spatial features. In the *Meditations* he acknowledges the transcendent presence of individuals, which surpasses any apprehension in terms of determinate concepts. Given Descartes's dualism, individuation for material things is naturally different from individuation for spiritual things. Nevertheless, the two accounts are linked in interesting ways.

DESCARTES'S GEOMETRIC ACCOUNT
OF INDIVIDUATION IN THE *PRINCIPLES*

In the *Principles*, Descartes at first appears to make the spatial features of a thing the ground of its individuation. The individuals that figure in his physics are introduced in the first twenty-two sections of Part II as shaped volumes of material extension. This way of accounting for individuals does not seem promising, for a number of reasons. First, spatial (and temporal) relations are extrinsic to a thing, but a thing's individuality ought to be intrinsic to it.[1] Second, a thing's spatial (and temporal) features seem accidental rather than essential, and therefore, unlike individuality, posterior to its constitution.[2]

Descartes is aware of these difficulties, for he is very careful how he defines spatial features at the beginning of Part II. In section 10, he describes solid objects in terms of "internal place," a nonrelational, intrinsic version of spatiality: "Nor in fact does space, or internal place, differ from the corporeal substance contained in it, except in the way in which we are accustomed to conceive of them. For in fact the extension in length, breadth, and depth which constitutes the space occupied by a body, is exactly the same as that which constitutes the body."[3] This is not an implausible strategy, since a volume like a sphere or a torus or a cube has its own intrinsic shape and unity, independent of its extrinsic spatial relations.

What of the fact that if over time the object moves away, air, for example, might come to fill the place where it formerly was? Then, Descartes explains, although the object carries its internal place with it, the place that it formerly occupied remains where it was, and is defined externally. "External place" remains one and the same "as long as it remains of the same size and shape and maintains the same situation among certain external bodies by means of which we specify that space."[4] Thus, a body at any given moment of time has a place that can be defined intrinsically, its internal place, and a place that can be defined extrinsically, its external place. Descartes characterizes the difference between the two in this way: "The difference consists in the fact that, in the body, we consider its extension as if it were an individual thing, and think that it is always changed whenever the body changes. However, we attribute a generic unity to the extension of the space."[5] In other words, as Descartes explains in section 11, "the same extension which constitutes the nature of body also constitutes the nature of space, and . . . these two things differ only in the way that the nature of the genus or species differs from that of the individual."[6]

Thus, a shaped volume in a moment of time can be considered to be an intrinsically defined individual (when the extension is regarded as unique and inseparable from the relevant body), or as an extrinsically defined generic unity (when the extension is regarded as able to be occupied by different bodies). Every shaped volume, Descartes holds, exhibits this duality. So there is no extrinsically defined volume that cannot also be regarded as intrinsically defined and hence as occupied by an individuated body; this is the argument, in section 16, for the impossibility of the void.[7] So, too, internal place is a plausible, because intrinsic, way to ground individuation.

Descartes also claims that the spatial features of a body are essential, not accidental properties of the body. The mistake of distinguishing corporeal substance from extension, Descartes argues, has led others to suppose that the properties a thing has in virtue of being extended are accidental. "For when they distinguish substance from extension, or quantity: either they understand nothing by the word 'substance', or they have a confused idea of some sort of incorporeal substance, whose nature they falsely attribute to corporeal. And they call the true idea of corporeal substance 'extension', which they however, call an accident;

and thus they proclaim in words something quite different from what they themselves comprehend in their minds."[8] On the contrary, the essence of matter for Descartes is extension in the strongest possible sense, for all the properties of a material thing are to be explained in terms of that essence. Properties such color and texture thus turn out to be not mere accidents, but what the Scholastics would have called *accidentia propria*, understandable through the essence of the body.[9]

Indeed, extension is so intimately related to material substance that Descartes calls it the "principal attribute" and claims that there is only a distinction of reason between them. This means that, as Descartes argues in the Second and Sixth Meditations, a clear idea of material substance cannot fail to include extension. It also means that a clear idea of extension cannot fail to include that of material substance. This claim seems less obvious, and Descartes offers a separate argument for it in the *Principles*,[10] as well as in the *First Replies* to the *Meditations* and letters written during the same period. Sometimes, Descartes observes, we render an idea incomplete and inadequate by abstraction, as when we consider a shape apart from the substance whose shape it is.[11] In the *First Replies*, Descartes writes: "Thus, for example, there is a formal distinction between the motion and the figure of the same body, and I can quite well think of the motion without the figure and of the figure apart from the motion and of either apart from the body; but nevertheless I cannot think of the motion in a complete manner apart from the thing in which the motion exists nor of the figure in isolation from the object which has the figure."[12] What completes the incomplete, generic notion of extension is the concept of an extended thing; only in terms of the latter can the former be completely understood. Descartes uses this argument as well to deny the possibility of the void.

Descartes appears to have made the spatial features of an object so intrinsic and essential that they can account for the object's individuality. In the first set of arguments, Descartes compares the relation of external place and internal place to the relation of genus or species and the individual; in the second set, he compares the relation of extension and a material body to the relation of an incomplete and a complete concept.[13] Combining these arguments, we may suppose that in the case at hand Descartes assimilates the relation between species and individual to the relation between genus and species, as if they could both be treated as relations of abstraction between concepts. Thus, as the concept of polyhedron abstracts from the concept of a cube, for example, the latter abstracts from the concept of a material, actually existing cube. But is this a philosophically satisfactory account of individuality?

A charitable interpretation can be given to Descartes's strategy. Descartes claims that the process by which we move from knowledge of concepts to knowledge of individuals is the reverse of abstraction. It takes us along a series, from an instantiable to an instance, itself perhaps an instantiable, to a further instance of the latter, and so forth, until the process terminates in knowledge of an item that has no instances of its own. Concepts of instantiables are incomplete (and therefore capable of further instantiation), whereas concepts of individuals are complete. This account then has something in common with Gracia's, for whom the necessary and sufficient condition of being an individual is noninstantiability.[14] Moreover, Descartes also appears to claim that knowledge depends on the possibility of the termination of such series, that is, on knowledge of individuals.

This observation sheds new light on the *Meditations*, for now it seems that the objects of knowledge that Descartes puts first in the order of reasons are all individuals. The knower knows himself first, as a separate and indeed isolated thinking thing; then God, whose infinity and transcendence prove that he is 'alterior' to the knower; and finally, extended things. For Descartes, the intuitionist, ideas are not primarily ideas of universals, but are rather confrontations with the presence of existing individuals.[15] If this is the case, then Malebranche significantly distorts Descartes's doctrine by taking ideas, the "seeing all things in God," as knowledge of universals, and by relegating to the senses acquaintance with particulars.[16] However, as I argue below, Malebranche does not merely distort Descartes, but elaborates on Descartes's account of the role of the faculties in knowledge, an account that sits uneasily with some of his other philosophical commitments.

Despite the interest of Descartes's way of characterizing physical individuals in terms of their spatial features, important difficulties remain. Descartes himself cannot rest content with it, and in the later sections of Part II of the *Principles* he adds kinematic and dynamic considerations to the definition of the objects of physics. I treat this development below, but first examine other limitations in the account just described.

DIFFICULTIES WITH DESCARTES'S
GEOMETRIC ACCOUNT OF INDIVIDUATION

There are two sorts of difficulties. The first has to do with the process of abstraction and its inverse; the second, with the extrapolation of Descartes's arguments about regions of space to space as a whole. To address the first, we must ask what exactly reversing the process of abstraction in order to arrive at knowledge of individuals looks like, in the particular case of Cartesian extension. When we abstract to the concept of polyhedron from the concept of cube, for example, we render indeterminate what is determinate in the cube. That is, we eliminate the determinate condition that the figure has six congruent, square faces; for a polyhedron may have *n* faces, which need not be square or even of the same shape. Thus the reverse process that takes us from the polyhedron to the cube makes determinate certain features that characterize polyhedra as a class in an indeterminate way.

But when we abstract to the concept of a cube from the concept of a material, actually existing cube, what do we leave out? Initially, we might say that we eliminate the determinate condition that the material, existent cube has faces of area *r* and so a certain size; and a location at (*a, b, c*) in the real world. Does then the reverse process that takes us from the concept of cube to that of a material, existing cube render determinate features that characterize cubes as a class in an indeterminate way? This is a hard question to answer. Does a cube per se have a size and location at all? For whereas shape seems to be intrinsic, size and location seem to be extrinsic and relative to the ambient space in which the cube is taken to be. Indeed, to speak in an anachronistically modern way, only in a metric space, with an origin and axes, does a cube have a size and location. And a cube in a metric space has these features not because of its 'cubeness', but because of the metrizability of the space. In an ambient space defined only by the equivalence relation of similarity, for example, a cube *per se* can be defined in terms of its shape, but it will not have size or location.

Thus, unless the concept of cube is taken to be the concept of cube-in-a-metric-space, the item simply does not *have* the requisite indeterminate features to be rendered determinate by the process alleged to be the reverse of abstraction. And there seems to be no good reason why, in defining a cube, we should be forced to specify one sort of ambient space rather than another. Moreover, even if we identify the concept of cube with cube-in-a-metric-space so that position and size can be said to belong to the concept of cube *per se* in an indeterminate way, the question of how position and size in a metric space are related to position and size in physical reality remains. For unless that question can be settled, the process that is the reverse of abstraction will not make sense.

Descartes, of course, has something like an answer to the question, for the point of his pronouncements about extension is that the space of his geometry can be identified with the space of the real world. And

he assumes, although never explicitly in the modern sense, that the former space has metric properties. Thus for him the process that is the
reverse of abstraction, the rendering determinate of certain features
indeterminate in, for example, the cube, goes through without a hitch.
For a modern reader, however, the embedding of the cube in a metric
space and the relation of a given metric space to reality may seem more
problematic than Descartes realized.

This difficulty is intensified if we notice that the process of abstraction to the concept of cube from that of a real, material cube also elim-
inates the conditions of materiality and actual existence. This 'abstraction' and its reverse process are puzzling. For materiality and existence
also are not determinations of some indeterminate features of a cube; a
cube per se does not have these features at all. To put it another way,
materiality and existence are not generalizable, as number of faces and
shape of face are. We do not say that a cube can be instantiated by
cubes of n degree of materiality, or by cubes that exhibit an ordered
variety of alternatives to materiality. Nor do we make similar claims
about degrees of existence or ordered alternatives to existence. Number and shape are generalizable, and the abstractions and instantia-
tions such generalizability makes possible remain unproblematically at
the level of the conceptual. But the concepts of materiality and existence do not function in the same way; they are not generalizable, and
both point beyond the realm of the merely conceptual.

Thus, there are important disanalogies between the move from
genus to species, and the move from species to physical instance, in the
cases Descartes is considering. Yet he avoids reckoning with these disanalogies. I think the reasons for this are that, first, Descartes sometimes needs mathematical entities that look ontologically robust
enough to be individuals, as in the Fifth Meditation in which knowledge of mathematicals must precede acquaintance with the material
world. And second, in certain cases he does not want to admit that the
objects of his physics, defined geometrically, are not ontologically
robust enough to function as individuals.[17] Descartes's assimilation of
the objects of mathematics to the objects of physics cuts both ways.

Mathematical entities, however, are never individuals, with the
possible exception of certain sets.[18] Numbers and geometrical figures
are structures that always admit further instantiation.[19] But geometrical figures have the appearance of being individuals, because they are
spatial configurations with an intrinsic unity. The shape of a geometrical figure like a cube belongs to it independent of its external relations,
and constitutes it as a whole greater than the sum of its parts. Thus
shape seems to allow a geometrical entity to be one thing in itself, as

real individuals usually are. Descartes often profits from this semblance.

In the next section I examine the claim that the objects of Descartes's physics, defined geometrically, do not function properly as individuals because they are too closely assimilated to mathematical objects. But are the objects of physics really individuals? On the one hand, physics deals with schematic exempla that illustrate universal laws; such schemas admit instantiation and so cannot themselves be individuals. On the other hand, when universal laws are supplemented by appropriate boundary conditions, physics is also supposed to describe correctly certain kinds of actually occurring events, such as an eclipse of the moon or the eruption of a geyser, in which real individuals presumably take part.

If such boundary conditions can be used to pick out and exhaustively describe an individual (or set of individuals), then it seems that that individual and its individuality can be captured by determinate concepts. Yet the collection of determinate concepts that picks out the individual is instantiable, and must be distinguished from the individual itself. The presence of the individual, that which does not admit instantiation, cannot be captured by instantiables, and can only be pointed to by peculiar predicates like 'existent' and 'material'. These predicates do not add any further content to a concept in physics (at least not in seventeenth-century physics), but indicate that what is referred to lies outside the realm of determinate concepts.

Even if we grant Descartes that matter must be added to the concept of a cube in order to yield the complete concept of an individual cube, another difficulty arises, for then it seems that matter, not shape or spatial location or some other spatial feature, is the principle of individuation. But, as Gracia points out, severe difficulties accompany this choice of principle. Matter as such does not seem to be individual. Indeed, matter *qua* matter is shared by all material things and thus seems to be instantiable.[20] Historically, in order for matter to serve as a principle of instantiation, it has been combined with a particular set of spatial dimensions: "this" matter is, for example, this cube of matter in this place. But then the real principle of individuation is once again to be shape and spatial location; so it is not at all clear why extension needs to be enmattered to be individual.

A second difficulty with Descartes's attempt in the *Principles* to make spatial features the intrinsic and essential basis of individuation is that his arguments cannot be extrapolated in any obvious way from bounded regions of space to space itself. The distinction between internal and external place, for example, makes no sense when applied to space as a whole. For space as a whole has no shape, since it has no boundaries; and it has no position relative to other bodies considered at rest with respect to it, for there are no other bodies. This distinction and its subsequent reintegration as species and individual instance of the same spatial volume therefore support arguments against the void only in the case of a finite, bounded void; they do not weigh against the existence of the infinite void that empty physical space would be.

Likewise, the completion of the incomplete concept of mathematical space as a whole does not seem to lead to a clearer or more adequate concept, or indeed to anything comprehensible. For if the instantiation of a sphere would be a spherical volume of matter, the instantiation of space as a whole would be what Descartes in a letter to Henry More calls "quiescent matter," the indefinitely infinite, utterly inert, undifferentiated entity of matter that God injects motion into, in order to separate it into parts.[21] This entity has no internal articulation and so is without cognizable structure; it is a surd. One hesitates to call it an "individual," for though it does not seem to be instantiable, it also does not instantiate anything else. It has no characteristics. Once again, the argument against the void that hinges on the argument from complete concepts does not work with respect to the infinite void that empty physical space would be.

Descartes's arguments generate these difficulties because of the following considerations. Mathematical space and the bounded regions that articulate it are instantiated by physical space and the possibilities of location it offers physical objects. So understood, the appropriately chosen mathematical space and physical space are isomorphic; in the abstracting move from the latter to the former, no aspect of the structure is rendered indeterminate, for the mathematical space just is the structure of physical space.[22] But the former still needs to be distinguished from the latter. Physical space along with its possible locations is not instantiated by anything further; it is occupied by physical objects, but 'being occupied by' is a very different relation from 'being instantiated by'. Physical space is therefore apparently an individual, insofar as it is existent and noninstantiable. And the physical objects that occupy it are not its parts. Indeed, physical space does not have parts any more than mathematical space does; it has an articulation of possible places that is the condition for its being the partless, holeless, connected, unbounded, homogeneous, isotropic whole that it is.

So far I might seem to be merely agreeing with Descartes about the identity of mathematical and physical extension. But Descartes's account of geometrically determined individuals given in the beginning of Part II of the *Principles* leaves out physical space, the infinite void, altogether. For Descartes, there is just mathematical space (clearly itself not an individual, but an instantiable structure) and matter, at first quiescent and then broken up by God's injection of motion into it. The difficulty is that the isomorphism I suggest holds between mathematical and physical space cannot hold between mathematical space and matter so conceived, either quiescent or broken up into moving bits. It cannot hold in the first case because quiescent matter is a surd and has no structure. And it cannot hold in the second case because the parts of matter do not behave like geometrical unities: they cannot be superimposed.

Another way to make my point is to say that Descartes needs to let quiescent material extension correspond to mathematical space as a whole, while material extension broken up into bits after God's injection of motion corresponds to the articulation of mathematical space into bounded unities. But this correspondence cannot hold. For mathematical space is a partless, boundless, holeless, connected, isotropic, homogeneous whole at the same time that it is articulated; its articulations are not its parts, but the condition for its kind of wholeness. Descartes's material extension, however, would need to correspond to mathematical space as a whole before God's injection, and to its articulation into bounded regions only afterwards; and those moving bits would also be parts of matter, pulverized now but considered as a totality. In sum, material objects do not instantiate bounded volumes in mathematical space, as Descartes claims; they occupy possible locations in physical space, and physical space instantiates mathematical space.

KINEMATIC AND DYNAMIC ASPECTS
OF INDIVIDUATION IN THE *PRINCIPLES*

Descartes is aware that geometric shape alone cannot account for the individuation of the objects of physics. He is able to generalize the feature of spatial location to give a kinematic rather than static account of physical objects in sections 23 through 53 of Part II of the *Principles*. In section 13, he defines external place as a body's situation among other bodies, and observes that it can be used to define a body's motion, if the body changes its situation with respect to other bodies designated as at rest.[23] In section 25, he defines "one body" as "everything which is simultaneously transported; even though this may be composed of many parts which have other movements among themselves."[24] A body can be considered one individual if all its parts share a common motion (or a common rest) with respect to the surrounding context of bodies. Descartes makes the connection between the definitions clear in section 28, where he underlines the 'one body/one motion' doctrine: "I have also added that the transference is effected from the vicinity of those bodies contiguous to it into the vicinity of others, and not from one place to another; because, as has been explained above, 'place' can be understood in several ways, depending on our conception. However, when we take movement to be the transference of a body from the vicinity of those contiguous to it, we cannot attribute to that moving body more than one movement at any given time; because at any given time, only a certain number of bodies can be contiguous to it."[25]

Thus, the conception of a physical individual must include not only geometric shape and a determinate location, but the further feature that, over time, its parts share a common motion. Apparently the complete concept of an extended thing also includes that it has parts, and that those parts move together. Why does Descartes allow such equivocation about the basis for individuality in his physics? This question is best answered by examining his laws of impact, for in one sense they require objects that are assimilated to geometric unities, and in another sense, they function properly only when the objects that figure in them are kinematically or even dynamically defined.

Descartes uses his laws of impact in two incompatible ways. He uses them to organize and conserve the furniture of the world; in the seven rules given in sections 46 to 52 of Part II of the *Principles*, the same bodies that enter into collisions also emerge from them, and their interaction conserves the product of bulk and speed, something like the modern notion of momentum.[26] Since sometimes the interacting bodies emerge from the collision contiguous and sharing the same motion, Descartes must assume that they nonetheless retain their separate identities in virtue of their original geometric shapes. If not, the drift of the universe will inexorably be to larger, slower objects, and ultimately the extreme case of quiescent material extension.

But impact, as the only form of interaction among material bits, is also the sole physical means for breaking up physical individuals, for changing the shape, size, and number of existing objects. Descartes of course never tries to quantify this process of shattering, but he does suggest that an impacting object can always break off a bit from another object, as long as that bit is smaller than the impacting object.[27] This means that the collision is considered to take place between the impacting object and the bit to be broken off, before it is actually broken off. In this case, the latter is being considered as one thing not in virtue of common motion of its parts (different from all the bodies that surround it), but of geometric shape. Yet once again, unless Descartes can account for shattering, the end result of his laws of impact will be quiescent material extension.

Conversely, while a geometric definition of unity for material things is needed to keep matter from lumping together too strongly, unity in virtue of common motion does not seem strong enough to keep matter from being pulverized into the dust of subtle matter, if shattering is allowed as a possible outcome of impact. As Descartes explains in section 55 of Part II of the *Principles*, individuation based on common motion of parts entails "that the parts of solid bodies are not joined by any other bond than their own rest (relative to each other)."[28] So if one part of a material thing happens to be set in motion relative to the other parts, that event will have no consequences for any other part; the rest will simply persist in the same state. According to Descartes's laws of motion then, every collision can result in shattering, for either body could carry away with it a part of the other body, so long as that part were sufficiently small. Otherwise put, the unity of physical bodies so conceived cannot maintain itself against the disruptive effects of the sole form of physical interaction; and indeed, in Descartes's plenum every body is in the midst of a collision at every instant of its existence.

The kinds of unity that Descartes postulates for his physical objects are deficient for one reason or another. In any case, the formal unity proposed for these objects would be a necessary condition only for their existence as individuals for physics; and that existence must transcend their employment as mere exempla in the three laws and seven rules that Descartes gives in Part II of the *Principles*. Descartes is aware of this limitation, for in the *First Replies* he observes that his conception of body as an extended and mobile thing, while complete in one sense, is still incomplete in another. It does not carry with it the evidence of its existence as the idea of God does. "For I can well enough recognize that that idea [of a perfect body] has been put together by my mind uniting together all corporeal perfections, and that existence does not arise out of its other corporeal perfections, because it can equally well be affirmed and denied of them. Nay, because when I examine this idea of body I see in it no force by means of which it may produce or preserve itself, I rightly conclude that necessary existence, which alone is here in question, does not belong to the nature of a body."[29] The objects of Descartes's physics require a dynamic dimension to achieve even the formal unity required for their existence as individuals; Descartes tries to furnish this dimension through his doctrine of continuous creation.[30] Yet the dynamism rests with God, the true and sole seat of activity in the natural world.[31] Descartes's physics, as is commonly argued, lacks a convincing dynamics. And because of the way he locates activity, force, and order in the realm of spirit, his physics as a whole also lacks, as it were, ontological conviction.

KNOWLEDGE OF INDIVIDUALS IN THE *MEDITATIONS*

If one compares Descartes's claim that knowledge in physics requires complete concepts (that is, knowledge not only of geometrical, and perhaps kinematic and dynamic, features but also of the individual things that have those features) with some of his pronouncements in the Sixth Meditation, a puzzling inconsistency arises. The two entities that Descartes claims to know first in the order of reasons are individuals: the self and God. But these two individuals are known as spirits; the self is known as a thinking thing and the Cartesian God is a Christian God insofar as he must be distinguished from his material creation. And the faculty employed in such knowing Descartes claims is the understanding alone. The self's confrontation with the objects of physics, however, is more problematic.

When one knows the objects of physics as mathematical, as the knowing self does at the beginning of the Sixth Meditation in virtue of Descartes's arguments in the Fifth, one knows them only as "generally regarded," not as particulars.[32] The realm of pure mathematical concepts, like that of the chiliogram, is grasped by the intellect alone. To do physics in a way that allows talk about the sun and the moon, and other individual material bodies with which the experimenting scientist concerns himself, the knower must resort to the imagination and the senses. Not only must the objects of physics be enmattered to be individual, but the knower must be enmattered as well, for the operation of the imagination and especially the senses depends on the body. The intellect can operate without the body, according to Descartes, but to use the senses, the spirit must turn to the brain, using and 'reading' it.[33]

Thus, the progression from knowledge of universals to knowledge of individuals in physical science is not merely from incomplete to complete concepts, a transition the intellect alone could make. It also requires the testimony of the senses, through which we encounter an external, material individual. In spite of himself, Descartes must admit that there is something beyond the addition of determinate concepts that characterizes our coming to know an individual.

Indeed, the way in which the thinker knows himself and God, two
spiritual individuals, in the opening Meditations, also confirms this
transcendence of determinate concepts. The self's awareness of itself
in the Second Meditation has no content that could not be belied by
the evil demon, and yet that awareness constitutes unimpeachable
knowledge of an existent. And the self's knowledge of God is in terms
of an idea that is infinite; that idea's transcendence of the determinate
contents of all the other ideas over which the self presides proves that
its original is God.[34]

In these two cases, then, the intellect for Descartes has a peculiar
function. It does not just know things through abstract, universal,
determinate concepts, but confronts its own existence and that of the
divine Other. This metaphysical possibility stems from Descartes's intuitionism: an idea for Descartes is not merely a concept, but a contem-
plation as well. It is a spiritual 'seeing', usually what the spirit is able to
construct. In cases that transcend such construction, the spirit contem-
plates its own existence in the idea 'I think', and the Other in the idea
'God'.[35]

If the ideas of the intellect so construed can be the vehicle for
acquaintance with spiritual individuals, why can they not also allow
Descartes to know the physical individuals he needs for his physics?
The confrontations with the self and God in the Second and Third
Meditations require transcendence in the object of knowledge, taking
it beyond the construction of concepts. Descartes locates no such transcendence in the objects of physics. What is knowable in physics, as in
mathematics, is what is constructible. For Descartes, that which lies in
the objects of physics beyond their constructibility is not a transcendence upwards, but simply their material existence. Materiality in
Descartes' system cannot be known per se, but can be only encountered
causally, as it were, when the particles of the object collide with the
material constitution of the human body. Existence in the self and God
can be "seen" with the eyes of the soul, the intellect, but existence in
nature is degraded, to be met with only as impact, the blind bumping
of one body on another that is sensation.

Thus, Descartes vacillates between the claim that knowledge of
physical individuals is just the completion of incomplete concepts, and
that it is an encounter requiring sensation and imagination, as well as
the intellectual deployment of concepts. In the first case he emphasizes
the constructibility of physical objects; in the second, their materiality.
The puzzle of quiescent material extension reasserts itself here; the
conflicting demands of Descartes's metaphysics give him good reasons
both to refuse and to bestow upon it cognitive structure.

Descartes's bits of matter are mere associations of instantiable features, geometric shape, matter, motion, perhaps force, and so seem not to achieve the status of noninstantiables, true individuals. So his rational reconstruction of the genesis of the universe, in which the sun, moon, and planets, as well as all other naturally occurring individuals, arise out of swirling nexuses of such bits, is unconvincing. For Descartes, the whole of nonhuman nature consists of intricate machines. Perhaps then his metaphysics does not require true individuals in nature, which confront the self with the kind of imperious, transcendent existence that characterizes God and other souls. This difficulty in altered form continues to pose unsolved problems for the metaphysics underlying modern science.

Ironically, the epistemological issues just raised, in conjunction with Descartes' allegiance to the order of reasons, also pose serious problems for the coherence of his account of spiritual individuals in the *Meditations*. In the Third Meditation, the alterity of God is introduced before the externality of material nature: Is true alterity really possible without spatial externality? Perhaps it could be, given the right set of metaphysical assumptions (although I doubt it), but it seems not to be possible in Descartes's system. Indeed, Descartes's attempt to introduce spatial externality via the purely spiritual route of the mathematicals in Meditation Five is just the point where God's presence threatens to engulf the knowing self, and his alleged alterity wavers. Even after Descartes has saved the internality of the self from the threat of the evil demon, it is not clear that he can keep God from violating the separateness of the self.

Descartes's account of our knowledge of material nature raises these questions most pointedly. In the purely intellectual revelation of the Second Meditation, the "I think, I am," the self knows itself as essentially a thinking thing. The faculty of intellect constitutes the self as the imagination and senses do not; if he lacked the latter, Descartes claims, he would still be the same person, but the power of intellect is the essence of his mind.[36] And Descartes can recognize himself as an individual and God as an infinite, perfect individual distinct from his own finite, imperfect self without invoking the corporeal faculties that depend on the 'substantial union' of body and soul. No other spirit can disrupt the internality of the soul's certainty of its own existence. And the idea of perfection cannot fail to reveal the Existent that gives rise to it.

Many commentators have observed that Descartes needs a bridge from the realm of spirit encountered in the first four Meditations to the realm of external, material nature that is to be the subject of his science. The realm of physical individuals can be apprehended only through the senses and imagination along with the intellect, and thus with the aid of the body. So part of Descartes's bridging is effected through the 'substantial union' of body and soul. All the same, the very existence of the body is still at issue in Meditation Five. There, the central portion of Descartes's bridge from spirit to matter is, of course, the mathematicals.

Martial Guéroult argues in a Kantian vein that the mathematical ideas Descartes claims to know with certainty in the Fifth Meditation, before the introduction of the substantial union, are necessary conditions for any possible knowledge of an external world.[37] They are the conditions to which any such knowledge must conform in order to be objective, whether or not the external world should prove to exist. They guarantee objective knowledge, because they provide invariant structures in the flux of sense experience. On Guéroult's account, then, the introduction of the mathematicals at this juncture does not violate the order of reasons, and ushers in the material realm in an appropriate way.

If this is the case, then mathematicals and in particular geometricals, while not themselves individuals, provide objects of knowledge for the disembodied intellect. But how shall these complex unities, these invariant structures, be located in Descartes's metaphysical scheme? They cannot be located in the self, for the self is pure spirit at this stage and thus unextended; extension cannot be discovered in the self as a thinking thing. Nor can Descartes explain how an unextended thinking thing could have an idea that represents extension.[38] They cannot be instantiated in nature, for nature is so far only a possibility that might be overturned. The only other location for them is God. Extension is an unlikely divine attribute, so it is presumably a divine thought, an eternal essence in the mind of God.

But then Descartes's acquaintance with the mathematicals in the Fifth Meditation is a confrontation with, not God, but ideas in the mind of God. His intellectual knowledge of mathematics is his knowing God's knowing. And in this case, his mind is as it were fused with the mind of God, and the integrity of his internality, the self-certainty that kept him immune from the evil demon, is violated. Metaphysical systems that try to do without spatial externality often generate this kind of problem. God without the otherness of a material universe, souls without the expressive otherness of bodies, tend to collapse back into an undifferentiated spiritual oneness. Philosophers such as the late Leibniz, or Malebranche and Berkeley, who try to abolish the category of matter altogether, find that they are left with the difficult task of opposing this unifying tendency of spirit.

Spirit, as consciousness, is always one; thinking that thinks thinking is just more thinking. But undifferentiated spirit is no more an individual than undifferentiated matter. The impasse that Descartes is brought to here suggests that a metaphysics that can sustain the existence of individuals requires not only self and other, but also a material realm where the other can be encountered as an object of knowledge and as spatially external.

CONCLUSION

Descartes the scientist wants to unify mathematics and physics, and his treatment of material individuals is the result of this effort. But because Descartes understands the unification in too emphatic a way, identifying the subject matter of geometry with material extension, the integrity and individuality of his physical objects are finally unconvincing. Descartes the philosopher tries to develop human knowledge according to the order of reasons, and so to elicit scientific knowledge from the self's intuition of its own existence and of God. But the consequent spiritualizing of extension vitiates the self's autonomy, and threatens the individual human spirit with dissolution in God. In general, the tendency of Descartes's metaphysics is toward overunification, despite his reputation as a dualist, and this tendency interferes with his attempts to solve the problem of individuation.

NOTES

1. See the discussion in Jorge J. E. Gracia, *Individuality: An Essay on the Foundations of Metaphysics* (Albany: State University of New York Press, 1988), pp. 33–36 and 184–91.

2. Ibid., pp. 150–55.

3. *Principles of Philosophy*, ed. V. R. Miller and R. P. Miller (Dordrecht: D. Reidel, 1983), pp. 43–44.

4. Ibid.

5. Ibid.

6. Ibid., p. 44.

7. Ibid., pp. 46–47.

8. Ibid., sec. 9, p. 43.

9. D. Garber connects Descartes's doctrine with this term in Chapter 3, pp. 66–69 and Chapter 5, p. 151 in his *Descartes's Metaphysical Physics* (Chicago: University of Chicago Press, 1992).

10. *Principles*, Part II, sec. 18.

11. Letter to Gibieuf, 19 January 1642, in *Oeuvres de Descartes*, ed. Charles Adam and Paul Tannery (Paris: J. Vrin, 1964), 3:474–75.

12. Replies to Objections I (response to Caterus), in *The Philosophical Works of Descartes*, ed. E. S. Haldane and G. R. T. Ross (Cambridge: Cambridge University Press, 1912), 2:22.

13. In his essay in this volume, "Christian Wolff on Individuation," Jorge Gracia points out that philosophers of the seventeenth century characteristically conflate the ontological and epistemological aspects of the problem of individuation. Descartes's move here is a good case in point.

14. Gracia, *Individuality*, pp. 43–56. Of course, Descartes conflates the noninstantiability of the individual with the completeness of its concept, a confusion that Gracia is careful to avoid.

15. For an interesting discussion of Descartes as an intuitionist, see J. Vuillemin, *Necessité ou contingence: L'aporie de Diodore et les systèmes philosophiques* (Paris: Les Editions de Minuit, 1984), pp. 208–29.

16. See, for example, the arguments in Dialogues 2 and 3 of Malebranche's *Dialogues on Metaphysics*, ed. W. Doney (New York: Abaris Books, 1980).

17. See arguments in my *Cartesian Method and the Problem of Reduction* (Oxford: Oxford University Press, 1990), Chapter 3.

18. Penelope Maddy argues for this point in the second section of Chapter 3 in her *Realism in Mathematics* (Oxford: Oxford University Press, 1990).

19. This kind of position is developed in M. Resnik's "Mathematics as a Science of Patterns," *Nous* 15 (1981): 529–50; 16 (1982): 95–105.

20. Gracia, *Individuality*, pp. 156–58.

21. Letter to Henry More, August 1649, in *Descartes: Philosophical Letters*, trans. A. Kenny (Oxford: Clarendon Press, 1970), pp. 256–59.

22. Here I feel I am treading the fine line of anachronism. I avoid the issue of nonstandard models, since it seems inappropriate to a discussion of a seventeenth-century theory.

23. *Principles*, p. 45.

24. Ibid., p. 51.

25. Ibid., pp. 52–53.

26. Ibid., pp. 64–69.

27. Ibid., Part II, sec. 63, pp. 75–76.

28. Ibid., p. 70.

29. In Haldane and Ross, *Philosophical Works*, 2:21.

30. Ibid., 1:158–59.

31. D. Garber argues this point in his *Descartes's Metaphysical Physics*, Chapter 9, and takes issue with A. Gabbey's position in "Force and Inertia in the Seventeenth Century: Descartes and Newton," in *Descartes: Philosophy, Mathematics and Physics* (Sussex: Harvester Press, 1980), pp. 230–320, esp. pp. 230–40.

32. See passages from Meditations five and six in Haldane and Ross, *Philosophical Works*, 1:179–80, 185–86. M. Wilson also makes this point in her *Descartes* (London: Routledge and Kegan Paul, 1978), pp. 202–4.

33. The case of the imagination is a bit ambiguous; see Wilson, *Descartes*, pp. 200–201.

34. M. Guéroult gives this interpretation in *Descartes' Philosophy Interpreted According to the Order of Reasons*, trans. R. Ariew (Minneapolis: University of Minneapolis Press, 1984), Chapter 5. And E. Levinas treats the idea of infinity in the *Meditations* in similar terms in *Totality and Infinity*, trans. A. Lingis (Pittsburgh: Duquesne University Press, 1969), sec. 1, A, 5, pp. 48–52.

35. See Levinas, ibid.; and J. Vuillemin's remarks apropos the idea of God in relation to Descartes's intuitionism in *What Are Philosophical Systems?* (Cambridge: Cambridge University Press, 1986), pp. 125–26.

36. See passages from Meditations two and six in Haldane and Ross, *Philosophical Works*, pp. 153, 186.

37. Guéroult, *Descartes' Philosophy*, 1:27–9, 148–52, 239–40.

38. This is J. Laporte's contention in *Le Rationalisme de Descartes* (Paris: Presses Universitaires de France, 1950), Chapter 4; Guéroult disagrees with it (*Descartes' Philosophy*, 1:93–98), but I find Laporte's arguments more convincing in this case.

Malebranche and the
Individuation of Perceptual Objects

Daisie Radner

$\mathcal{M}$alebranche's doctrine of seeing all things in God is meant to explain how the human mind can have the sort of knowledge it has of the material world, given what the mind is and what matter is. How can the mind have general ideas of extension and its properties when the mind can have only particular modifications? How can the mind have sense experience of particular bodies when bodies are the sort of things that cannot be perceived by themselves? The vision in God is designed to answer both questions. Not only do we conceive all things in God, but we also sense all things in him. This dual application of the doctrine gives rise to a uniquely Malebranchian problem of individuation. Briefly stated, the problem is this: How can we have sensible perceptions of particular things if the immediate object of these perceptions is something general? In the first section, I show how the problem arises for Malebranche. In the second section, I explore its solution within the framework of his philosophy.

THE PROBLEM

According to Malebranche, things not in the mind are perceived by the mind in one of two ways: either directly (by being present to the mind) or indirectly (by being represented to it). Presence to the mind consists in the capacity for self-revelation: an object is present to the mind if and only if it is capable of producing a perception of itself in the mind. Physical objects are not present to the mind in this sense, for they cannot act upon the mind. Thus physical objects are not perceived directly; they can be perceived only indirectly. Some other thing, which is perceived directly, must represent them or make them known to the mind.

In Malebranche's system, when one sees the sun, the ontology of the situation is as follows. There is a *perception* or act of perceiving. Every perception has an object; to perceive is to perceive something.

The immediate and direct object of the act of perceiving is an *idea*. The existence of the idea is a necessary condition for the existence of the act of perceiving it; one cannot perceive a nonexistent idea. The idea in turn represents or makes known the sun. The existence of the sun is not a necessary condition for the existence of the idea; an idea can represent a nonexistent object. Each of the three entities involved in the perceiving situation—the act of peceiving, the idea, and the object represented by the idea—is in a different substantial realm. The sun is in the physical world as part of extended substance. The act of perceiving is in the mind as a mode or modification of it. The idea is in God.

In *The Search after Truth* (3.2.6), Malebranche gives several reasons, some theological, for the doctrine of seeing all things in God. His main argument is from the generality of ideas.[1] This argument is of special interest here because of what it reveals about the relation between the general and the particular.

Every creature, Malebranche says, is a particular being. A particular being, insofar as it has a given determinate property, is precluded from having innumerable others. A triangular object cannot at the same time be circular or square. A circular object with a diameter of five inches cannot also have a diameter of two or ten or fifty inches. Ideas, by contrast, are not subject to this sort of limitation. The idea of a circle represents circles of all possible diameters. To think of a circle in general is not merely to think of what is common to all circles, nor is it to let a particular circle stand for all circles. Rather, it is "to perceive an infinite number of circles as a single circle," as Malebranche says in the *Dialogues on Metaphysics and on Religion* (*OC* 12:53; cf. 9:954). The idea of a circle in general is itself a general entity, in that it includes all particular ideas of circles in a unity. It, in turn, is included, along with the general ideas of a triangle, a square, and so on, in the more general idea of figure. All ideas are included in the idea of being in general; they are, in Malebranche's words, "participations in the general idea of the infinite" (*OC* 1:441; *S* 232). Since all created things are particular and the idea of the infinite is general, this idea is not created. Moreover, since all ideas are included in it, none of them is created either. Anything in the human mind would have to be, like the mind itself, created and particular. Hence ideas are not in human minds. God is the only being that can contain all ideas included in one. Hence all ideas are in God. The divine efficacy ensures their presence to the mind. "All our ideas, therefore, must be located in the efficacious substance of the Divinity, which alone is intelligible or capable of enlightening us, because it alone can affect intelligences" (*OC* 1:442; *S* 232). God reveals his ideas to us by producing in our minds perceptions having his ideas as immediate and direct objects.

In the Tenth Elucidation of *The Search after Truth,* Malebranche cautions against a misunderstanding of his view:

It should not be imagined that the intelligible world is related to the sensible, material world in such a way that there is an intelligible sun, for example, or an intelligible horse or tree intended to represent to us the sun or a horse or a tree, or that everyone who sees the sun necessarily sees this hypothetical intelligible sun.

Thus, when I said that we see different bodies through the knowledge we have of God's perfections that represent them, I did not exactly mean that there are in God certain particular ideas that represent each body individually, and that we see such an idea when we see the body (*OC* 3:153-54; *S* 627).

The vision in God, by which we have knowledge of corporeal things, is really a vision of intelligible extension: "But I do say that we see all things in God through the efficacy of His substance, and particularly sensible things, through God's applying intelligible extension to our mind in a thousand different ways" (*OC* 3:154; *S* 628).

In his correspondence with Arnauld, Malebranche emphasizes that intelligible extension is not matter itself but God's idea of matter. It is "*the Archetype* of bodies, or that in God which represents bodies" (*OC* 6:232); "that which represents matter to God" (*OC* 6:243); "the idea that God has of bodies both created and possible" (*OC* 6:204); "the model of created extension of which all bodies are formed" (*OC* 9:926); "the *archetype* or the *idea* by which God knows all material objects and on which he has formed them" (*OC* 6:99); "the object of the geometers, the idea by which all bodies are known and on which they are all created," as Augustine says (*OC* 6:68; 9:1058). As a general idea, intelligible extension includes all particular ideas of bodies and their properties. "The general idea of created extension, which contains the ideas of all particular bodies, or from which the particular ideas of all bodies can be drawn, just as one can form or fashion all particular bodies from created extension—the idea, I say, of local extension, or intelligible extension, is only God's substance, not taken or understood absolutely, but considered insofar as it is relative to created extension, or insofar as it is imperfectly imitable or participable by it, as Saint Thomas says" (*OC* 9:1068-69; cf. 6:201; 9:942, 959).

The analogy between drawing ideas out of intelligible extension and forming bodies from created extension suggests that particular ideas are in intelligible extension only as bodies are in an undifferentiated mass of matter—that is to say, potentially. Malebranche seems to endorse this view when he compares intelligible extension to a block of marble:

> It is not, however, that there are properly *intelligible* figures in the intelligible spaces that we know, no more than there are *material* figures in material spaces, which would be entirely immovable. It is rather that, as all possible figures are in a block of marble potentially, and can be drawn from it by the movement or action of the chisel; likewise all intelligible figures are potentially in *intelligible* extension, and are discovered there, according as this extension is diversely represented to the mind according to the general laws that God has established, and according to which he acts in us without ceasing. (*OC* 6:208–9)

The analogy underscores the problem that Malebranche has created for himself. Intelligible extension and material extension differ in an important respect. A block of marble is in itself particular, just as the statues formed from it are particular. It can, in principle, be fashioned into a statue of anyone; but once it has been made to represent Julius Caesar, it is precluded from representing innumerable other individuals. Intelligible extension, by contrast, is "general and always the same" (*OC* 6:61). It is no less representative of all bodies for having one particular idea drawn out of it. Intelligible figures are *potentially* in intelligible extension only in the sense that they are potentially *perceived* in it. When they are actually perceived, it is not that something exists in intelligible extension that did not exist before. It is rather that the mind is modified in such a way that it can apprehend what was in intelligible extension all along.

Intelligible extension reveals itself to the mind by affecting the mind with a perception having itself as object. The perception can be either pure or sensible. Malebranche explains in the *Conversations chrétiennes*:

> When the idea of extension affects or modifies the mind with a pure perception, then the mind simply conceives this extension. But when the idea of extension touches the mind more vividly and affects it with a sensible perception, then the mind sees or senses extension. The mind sees it, when this perception is a sentiment of color; and it feels it or perceives it even more vividly, when the perception with which intelligible

extension modifies it is a pain. For color, pain and all other sentiments are only sensible perceptions, produced in intelligences by intelligible ideas. (*OC* 4:75-76)

As sensible perceptions, color and pain have a different ontological status from ideas. Color and pain are modes of the mind, whereas ideas are not. Ideas are the immediate objects of acts of perceiving; color and pain are species of mental acts having ideas as their objects. Thus Malebranche writes to Arnauld (19 March 1699): "For, in short, the soul's perception in one who sees or feels an arm is only the perception, which is called either color or pain, of the extension which composes the arm; I mean the immediate and direct perception of the ideal extension of the arm, without which one can neither see nor feel it, as experience teaches us" (*OC* 9:961-62). Similarly, he writes to Dortous de Mairan (12 June 1714): "For it is certain that sensible perceptions are only modifications of the soul different from the idea or the object immediately perceived. Thus if I look at my hand, I will have the perception of it, color; if I regard it in water, I will have the perception of it, coldness; and if I have gout at the same time I regard it in cold water, I will have the modification or perception of it, pain" (*OC* 19:884; cf. 15:9).

Sensible qualities serve to differentiate objects in the sensible world. Malebranche writes in the *Conversations chrétiennes*: "It is color alone which makes objects visible: it is solely by the variety of colors that we see and distinguish the diversity of objects" (*OC* 4:76; cf. 12:19). In the *Écrit contre la prévention* of 1704, he compares the perception of individual objects in intelligible extension to the perception of objects in a painting: "In order to see different bodies, it suffices that the idea of extension or intelligible extension affects or touches the soul with diverse colors. For indeed, painters need only an extended canvas and diverse material colors in order to represent all visible bodies, by distributing diverse material colors on their canvas in accordance with their art" (*OC* 9:1066; cf. 6:78).

The analogy with an artist's canvas suggests that intelligible extension has parts that function like material parts. The Tenth Elucidation reinforces this suggestion. In reply to the question of how the sun can appear larger when it is on the horizon, even though God's idea of it does not change, Malebranche describes intelligible extension as having greater and smaller parts: "All that is needed for this is that we sometimes see a greater part of intelligible extension and sometimes a smaller. Since the parts of intelligible extension are all of the same nature, they may all represent any body whatsoever" (*OC* 3:153; *S* 627).

Moreover, the parts of intelligible extension seem to stand in relations of contiguity and distance to one another. In response to the question of how we perceive bodies as moving, even though the parts of intelligible extension "always maintain the same relation of intelligible distance between them," he explains that the appearance of motion is "due to the sensation of color, or the confused image remaining after the sensation that we successively attach to different parts of the intelligible extension" (*OC* 3:153; *S* 627). Here intelligible extension seems to function like a moving picture screen, which depicts moving objects by successive illumination of spatially contiguous parts.

In the controversy with Arnauld, however, Malebranche soundly rejects the notion that intelligible extension is extended like a canvas or a screen. "I have never believed nor said that intelligible extension was of the same nature as matter. I have never confused the idea or Archetype of bodies with the bodies themselves, the divine substance as representative of creatures with the creatures. I have never thought that *intelligible* extension was *locally* extended, like bodies. I have never imagined that it was greater in a greater space, and smaller in a smaller. I am not, thank God, stupid and impious enough to have opinions so bizarre and so contrary to faith" (*OC* 6:210). "The idea of extension or intelligible extension is not, in itself or according to its absolute reality, locally extended. . . . It is only intelligibly extended, that is to say, only representative of a formal extension. It has only intelligible parts, greater and smaller intelligibly, not locally" (*OC* 9:954–55). "What the word *extension* signifies, when joined with *intelligible*, has no greater or smaller parts, unless one means by *intelligible* parts, those which, be they infinitely great intelligibly, occupy no place and have no relation to place" (*OC* 6:203).

Since an artist's painting is locally extended, like the real world it portrays, the analogy is ill suited to show how intelligible extension represents material extension. That is not its function. The relevant aspect of artistic representation is not the relation between the canvas, or the figures painted on it, and the bodies represented; rather, it is the relation between the canvas and the painted images. The analogy is simply intended to illustrate how colors make a variety of objects visible. On this level, the analogy ought to work; for the artist tries to capture how things appear to an observer, not what they are in themselves. A cow in the foreground looks larger than a barn far away, so that is how the artist paints it. The cow shape occupies a larger area of the canvas than the barn shape, just as it occupies a larger area of one's visual field in viewing the real scene. The figures are positioned in the painting at the same relative distance to one another as they occupy in the visual field.

Just where the analogy is strongest, it loses its usefulness as an aid to understanding how objects are seen in intelligible extension. Visual objects have expanse. They occupy greater or smaller areas of the visual field, and they are locatable with respect to one another. In short, they seem to have the very features that Malebranche is so careful to deny of intelligible extension itself. An artist's canvas has locally extended parts, whether it has colors spread over it or not. Intelligible extension, by contrast, has only intelligible parts, which nevertheless function like spatial parts when color is 'attached' to them.

An adequate account of intelligible extension must encompass both the generality of the idea and its role as object of sensible perception. Malebranche claims that the general idea of extension is "rendered particular" by color and other sentiments (*OC* 3:149; *S* 625; *OC* 6:61; 17–1:282). An adequate solution to the problem of the individuation of perceptual objects requires putting flesh on this phrase. How does sense perception make particular what in itself is general?

THE SOLUTION

Some commentators have proposed that intelligible extension and particular ideas constitute an axiomatic system. On this interpretation, particular ideas are 'contained' in the general idea of extension in the sense that they are derivable from it as theorems from a set of axioms.[2]

This proposal has one advantage for the problem at hand: it makes sense of Malebranche's denial that the intelligible world contains discrete intelligible objects, each destined to represent a different body. The theorems of an axiomatic system are interrelated. Derivations of different theorems can have some steps in common. One theorem can be used to derive others. According to Malebranche, the ideas by which we see bodies are not the ideas of bodies per se but the ideas of figures. "I have said so often, that in order to see the sun as actually existing, it suffices that I see an intelligible circle which is rendered sensible to me by a brilliant light" (*OC* 6:241). "For when one has a vivid sentiment of light, attached or related to an intelligible circle, distant by a certain intelligible space, rendered sensible by different colors, one sees the sun, not such as it is, but such as one sees it" (*OC* 6:55). We do not see all there is to the sun, or rather all there is to God's idea of the sun. We only see a small circular object. The idea that is present to us, the idea made sensible by light, is the same idea that is also present to us when we view any other round object. This point can be expressed in terms of axiomatization as follows. We do not apprehend the theorem that is

God's idea of the sun. We only perceive one step in its derivation, namely, what such an object will look like to an observer in certain circumstances—a step that is common to the derivation of other theorems.

Attractive as it seems at first, the axiomatic view of intelligible extension has two deficiencies. The first has to do with the linguistic nature of axiomatic systems. Axioms and theorems are statements. According to Malebranche, the immediate objects of sense experience are particular ideas. If particular ideas are theorems, then when we look out over a meadow, what we see directly are statements. Malebranche would never accept this consequence.

The second deficiency arises if the axiom system of intelligible extension is taken to be an uninterpreted system.[3] On this version, the created world becomes a model of the axiomatic theory. A model is a system of objects and relationships that provides an interpretation of the terms that makes the axioms true. Any system that provides such an interpretation is a possible model of the axiomatic theory. In creating the material world, God wills that one possible model should exist. But if he knows the model only by the uninterpreted axiom system, he has no way of knowing which model he has brought into being, or even whether it is a material world at all—a situation hardly befitting an omniscient deity.

Malebranche uses the word 'model' to describe the relation between intelligible extension and the created world (*OC* 9:926, 956, 959, 968). The word has a different meaning for him than it has on the axiomatic interpretation, however. On the latter interpretation, the created world is a model of the axiom system of intelligible extension. Malebranche's modeling relation goes the other way: intelligible extension is the model of created extension. The difference in meaning is reflected in the phrases 'a model' and 'the model'. On the axiomatic view, the created world is one of many possible models of a given axiom system. For Malebranche, intelligible extension is the model of an infinite number of possible material worlds (*OC* 9:910; 10:99). It is *the model* in the sense of being the pattern or set of specifications for constructing any one of these worlds.

What is needed is an interpretation of intelligible extension that keeps the advantage of the axiomatic view while avoiding its pitfalls. An interpretation is adequate only if it captures the following three features of Malebranche's doctrine: that the ideas in intelligible extension are systematically interrelated; that these ideas serve as objects of sensible as well as pure perceptions; and that intelligible extension is the model or archetype on which the world was created. The third feature has some interesting ramifications.

God must have knowledge of the material world, since he created it and he knows what he has made. Not even God can know matter directly. "God derives His light only from Himself; He sees the material world only in the intelligible world He contains and in the knowledge He has of His volitions, which actually give existence and motion to all things" (*OC* 3:61; *S* 573; cf. *OC* 6:62, 118; 9:959; 10:97). It is tempting to dismiss this sort of statement as just another affirmation of God's independence. But there is more to it than that. Intelligible extension must be explicated so as to allow it to play the role that Malebranche demands of it in this passage: it must provide God with enough knowledge to create matter and to know what he has made.

Malebranche's God may be compared to a blind geometer. Armed with the definitions, axioms, and postulates of Euclidean geometry, the blind geometer knows what a circle is and how to construct one. Suppose that the blind geometer's constructive activity is perfectly in accord with his will, so that whatever he wills takes place exactly as he wills it—something that is not true of a human blind geometer, but that would be true of an all-powerful divine one. The blind geometer could then be said to know what he wants to make, to know how to make it, and to know that he has made it—all without ever having direct acquaintance with the finished product.

Malebranche asserts several times during the controversy with Arnauld that intelligible extension is the object of study of geometry (*OC* 6:68–69, 201; 9:930, 942, 1058). In fact, he says, intelligible extension is the subject of Arnauld's own book on geometry, "in which he measures spaces which are *only intelligible*" (*OC* 6:203). In geometry, space is treated not merely as a system of axioms, but as that in which figures may be constructed. For Malebranche, as for Kant, spatial objects do not merely supply an interpretation of the terms that make the axioms of geometry true. Geometry is *about* constructing spatial objects.[4] Cartesian geometry is primarily concerned with construction problems. Algebra is a tool for solving these problems, but it by no means dispenses with the need for doing the constructions. Once a problem has been formulated and solved algebraically, one still needs to know whether something can be constructed that will satisfy the equation. One proves that the solution exists by constructing it.[5]

The divine geometer has his own form of construction problem. It involves creating locally extended objects on the basis of ideas in the divine reason. The activity of God as blind geometer precludes the reduction of geometry, the science of intelligible extension, to algebra.[6] When God wills to create a curve characterized by a certain equation, he needs to know not only the equation but also what constitutes generating it in a coordinate system. The latter sort of knowledge is not reducible to algebra in seventeenth-century mathematics.

Malebranche's God needs something akin to a Kantian pure representation of space as object.[7] Like a Kantian intuition, Malebranchian intelligible extension is singular. There is one unique idea of extension that is shared by everyone, including God. Diverse ideas are parts of it. These intelligible parts are not constituents out of which it is composed, nor are they related to it as species under a genus. They can only be thought of as *in* intelligible extension.

The intelligible parts of intelligible extension are ideas of parts of material extension. One has the idea of a figure when one thinks of extension as being limited in a certain way. "Thus, since the mind can perceive a part of this intelligible extension that God contains, it surely can perceive in God all figures; for all finite intelligible extension is necessarily an intelligible figure, since figure is nothing but the boundary of extension" (*OC* 3:152; *S* 626). The idea of extension continues to represent extension as capable of being bounded in an infinite number of ways, even when one conceives of extension as bounded in a certain way, for instance, by a closed curve all points of which are equidistant from a given point. Intelligible figures are thus *in* intelligible extension in a different sense than created figures are in material space. For if a material surface is actually bounded by a particular curve, it is thereby precluded from being bounded in an infinity of other ways. To construct an actual circle is to impose a limitation on matter itself. Ideas are in God "without any limitation or multiplicity," whereas finite creatures are such that their "particular nature excludes all the others, or includes infinite nonbeings, so to speak, the nonbeing of all the others" (*OC* 9:954).

Ideas are related to one another in ways that the objects represented by them can never be related. For this reason, the intelligible world cannot be considered isomorphic with the material world. God can create a number of circles with different diameters, in accordance with his ideas of particular circles; but he cannot include these created circles in a unity, as the ideas of them are included in the general idea of a circle.

Ideas are revealed to us in their aspect of generality only when we have pure perceptions of them. "One conceives a circle in general, or an infinity of circles, because having the idea of space or of greater and greater lines to infinity, one takes no one of them for the diameter of the circle that one conceives" (*OC* 6:209). The circle that one conceives is the sort of thing that has no counterpart in the created world, where each circle has a given diameter as opposed to every other possible diameter. That which I see when I think of a circle in general, Malebranche says in the *Réponse à Régis*, "actually is general. . . . Certainly the idea of a circle in general represents to me nothing but itself. For it is evident that there is no circle in general in the world, and that God himself cannot create one, even if he could create an infinite extension" (*OC* 17-1:302).

The aspect of generality is totally absent when ideas affect us with sensible perceptions. Although still in themselves general and included in a unity, the ideas are perceived as particular and discrete. When a portion of intelligible extension is made sensible by color, we see a determinate figure, for example, a circle with a diameter of two feet. Intelligible extension is not really limited when color is 'attached' to it, as material extension is actually limited by boundaries; for color is not in the intelligible world but in the mind. Nevertheless, insofar as color makes the ideal circle sensible, it limits the representative function of the idea for that perceiver. It becomes the idea of a certain circle to the exclusion of every other.

Bodies have determinate figures. We see bodies by ideas of determinate figures, but not necessarily the same determinate figures that the bodies actually have. For instance, we see the sun by the idea of a circle made sensible by light. The circle is sometimes greater and sometimes smaller, but never more than two or three feet in diameter. The sun itself, however, is a million times larger than the earth and does not change size (*OC* 4:62). The idea by which we see the sun is not the same as the idea according to which it was created. This is what Malebranche means when he says that there is not an intelligible sun destined to represent to us the real sun, so that all who see the sun see this supposed intelligible sun. God has an idea of the sun, an idea that served as the model for creating the sun; but he does not reveal this idea to us, at least not in sensation. God's idea of the sun is the idea of an astronomical body of a certain size and shape, with a certain configuration and arrangement of parts, capable of having certain properties in certain conditions, and entering into certain lawful relations with other bodies. Among these lawful relations are those pertaining to optics: it is part of God's idea of the sun that it should appear to human observers on earth as a bright circular object, larger or smaller depending on its position with respect to the horizon, but never more than two or three feet in diameter. The idea by which we see the sun represents the sun only as it relates to our own visual system.

Besides intelligible extension, there is also intelligible mind in God. Unlike intelligible extension, intelligible mind is not revealed to us. We know our own soul and its states only by consciousness or inner feeling (*OC* 3:451–53; *S* 237–39; *OC* 6:245; 17–1:298–99). Just as God does not have direct acquaintance with the material world, likewise he has no direct experience of the mental world he has created. The blind geometer is also an unfeeling psychologist. "God clearly knows the nature of my perceptions without having them; because, having in himself the idea or the archetype of my soul, he sees in this intelligible and luminous idea how the soul has to be modified in order to have such and such a perception, whiteness, pain, or any other which he does not feel" (*OC* 17–1:289; cf. 6:162). As the model or archetype on which the mind is created, intelligible mind or the idea of mind provides God with the knowledge of how to modify the mind in order to produce in it various types of sensations. The mind, deprived of access to the idea of itself, lacks this sort of knowledge. There is no human counterpart of the divine psychology. "Having no clear idea of my mind, and knowing it only by consciousness or inner feeling, . . . I do not know distinctly what pain is, for example; I do not know clearly how my mind must be modified in order to feel it. God knows plainly what pain is in the clear idea he has of minds in their archetype, but he does not feel it. I, on the contrary, often *feel* this disagreeable perception or modification, but I by no means *know* it" (*OC* 9:917; cf. *OC* 2:97; *S* 319).

In sensation, God as unfeeling psychologist mimics his constructions as blind geometer. He creates minds, and, when the occasion warrants, he creates in them particular perceptions of ideas of bodies and their properties. When the perceptions are sensible, the ideas are perceived as though they, too, were particular. Although the ideas we see are God's ideas, we do not see them the way God sees them, certainly not in sensation. "God, who sees in himself things such as they are, does not see this paper such as I see it; but he sees plainly that I see it white, because he knows that I have to see it thus according to the laws of the union of soul and body" (*OC* 6:221). God's idea of the paper's shape and size is included in his idea of figure in general. He knows how to limit material extension in order to form a determinate figure, but he has no direct apprehension of the actual determination in space. Likewise, he knows, by his idea of mind, that sensible perceptions of portions of intelligible extension make those portions appear discrete and limited to the perceiver. He knows how to give a mind a sentiment of color so as to make it see a determinate representation of a figure, but he has no direct acquaintance with how this ideal figure looks to the human observer.

The constructions of the blind geometer are material; those of the unfeeling psychologist, mental. Yet the two sets of constructions have a resemblance to each other that neither shares with the idea that is its archetype. Sensible perceptions are particular, as material figures are particular. A sentiment of white is not a sentiment of green nor of warmth, just as a three-foot circle is not a thirty-foot circle nor a square. The particularity of sensible ideas is a function of the particularity of the perceptions of them. As representations of the actual properties of material objects, sensible ideas fall woefully short. But as representations of the particularity of material objects, they serve us better than if we had access to the very models on which these objects were created.

My account leaves two questions not fully answered. First, exactly how are particular ideas included in the general idea of extension? Second, exactly how do sensible perceptions make ideas appear discrete and limited? My failure to answer these questions satisfactorily is, I maintain, not a deficiency of my account but a point in its favor. In interpreting a philosopher, one should leave room for the philosopher's own acknowledged unknowns. In order to answer each of these two questions, one needs some item of knowledge that Malebranche denies we have. The second question is about how the mind must be modified in order to perceive an idea as a determinate representation. In order to answer it, one must have access to the idea of mind, which is not given to us. The first question has to do with the manner in which ideas are in God. Here, too, one runs up against a Malebranchian unknown. "If I am asked to explain clearly how the Divine Word contains bodies in an intelligible manner, or how it can be that the divine substance, though perfectly simple, is representative of creatures, or participable by creatures, without having the imperfections or the limitations of creatures, I shall reply that it is a property of the infinite which seems incomprehensible to me, and I shall stop there; for it has been a long time since I have troubled myself with meditating on matters which are beyond my comprehension and which pertain to the infinite" (*OC* 6:204).

NOTES

1. *Oeuvres complètes de Malebranche*, ed. André Robinet, 20 vols. (Paris: J. Vrin, 1958–70, 1:440–42; *The Search after Truth*, trans. Thomas M. Lennon and Paul J. Olscamp (Columbus: Ohio State University Press, 1980), p. 232. Hereafter these editions are cited in the text as *OC* and *S* respectively. For a full reconstruction of the argument, see my *Malebranche* (Assen: Van Gorcum, 1978), pp. 53–55.

2. See, for example, Gustav Bergmann, "Some Remarks on the Philosophy of Malebranche," *Review of Metaphysics* 10 (1956): 207–26; Paul Schrecker, "Le parallélisme théologico-mathématique chez Malebranche," *Revue philosophique de la France et de l'Etranger* 125 (1938): 215–52; Richard A. Watson, "Foucher's Mistake and Malebranche's Break: Ideas, Intelligible Extension, and the End of Ontology," in *Nicolas Malebranche: His Philosophical Critics and Successors*, ed. Stuart Brown (Assen: Van Gorcum, 1991), pp. 23–34.

3. Schrecker admits that this Hilbertian conception of axiomatization is inappropriate. "Le parallélisme théologico-mathématique chez Malebranche," p. 223.

4. For discussion of Kant and the role of construction, see Michael Friedman, "Kant's Theory of Geometry," *Philosophical Review* 94 (1985): 455–506.

5. For discussion of the role of algebra in Descartes's geometry, see Morris Kline, *Mathematical Thought from Ancient to Modern Times* (New York: Oxford University Press, 1972), pp. 304–17.

6. Léon Brunschvicg claims that Malebranche reduces geometry to algebra (*Les étapes de la philosophie mathématique* [Paris: Félix Alcan, 1929], p. 132). The lack of textual evidence for this claim is noted by Jean Laporte, "L'étendue intelligible selon Malebranche," *Revue internationale de philosophie* 1 (1938): 26–27.

7. "I term all representations *pure* (in the transcendental sense) in which there is nothing that belongs to sensation" (A20/B34). "Space, represented as *object* (as we are required to do in geometry), contains more than mere form of intuition" (B160a). See Immanuel Kant, *Critique of Pure Reason*, trans. Norman Kemp Smith (London: Macmillan, 1958).

Spinoza's Theory of
Metaphysical Individuation

Don Garrett

A theory of metaphysical individuation seeks to explain what constitutes an individual thing; what constitutes the persistent identity of the same individual thing through time; and what constitutes the numerical difference among two or more individual things. (By way of comparison, a theory of epistemological individuation seeks to explain how one knows something to be an individual thing; how one knows something to remain the same individual thing through time; and how one knows individual things to be numerically different from one another.) In a discussion of physical topics that occurs between *Ethics* IIP13 and IIP14, Spinoza briefly presents a striking and original theory of metaphysical individuation for a class of entities that he calls "Individuals."[1] Among the theory's most striking features is that identity and difference of *substance* play no role in it—this despite the centrality of the notion of substance in both other seventeenth-century discussions of metaphysical individuation and in Part I of the *Ethics* itself. Among the theory's most original features is that it explains the existence, persistence, and difference of an individual as a function of what Spinoza calls its "ratio of motion and rest" (*ratio motus et quietis*).

Striking and original as Spinoza's theory evidently is, however, it has also been the object of considerable puzzlement. For he says surprisingly little in the *Ethics* about several crucial questions: what he means by the term 'motion and rest'; what he conceives "fixed ratios" of motion and rest to be; what the scope of the term 'individual', and hence of the theory as a whole, is intended to be; and how, if at all, his discussion of individuals in Part II is related to his pivotal claim at IIIP6 that "each thing, as far as it can by its own power [*quantum in se est*], strives to persevere in its being," a claim that serves as the foundation for both his psychology and his ethical theory. Many readers have concluded that Spinoza's theory is incoherent, unreasonable, narrow, and/or irrelevant. In the first section of this chapter, I will describe Spinoza's theory of metaphysical individuation as he presents it in Part

II of the *Ethics*. In the remaining four sections, I will consider, in order, the four crucial questions about the theory just posed. In doing so, I will argue that, despite the brevity of Spinoza's presentation, it is possible to determine the answers to these questions with a reasonable degree of probability; and I will argue that the resulting theory is a coherent, reasonable, inclusive, and powerful one.

INDIVIDUATION AND 'INDIVIDUALS'

Part II of the *Ethics* is entitled "On the Nature and Origin of the Mind." In the Scholium to IIP13, however, Spinoza proposes to present some general facts about the nature of the human body, so that we can know "the excellence of one mind over the others, and also the cause why we have only a completely confused knowledge of our Body, and many other things which I shall deduce . . . in the following [propositions]." The presentation that then follows—sometimes called the "Physical Digression"—contains, in all, five "Axioms," one "Definition," seven "Lemmas," and six "Postulates." The Digression divides naturally into three parts: first, Axioms 1' and 2' [following Curley's numbering convention], Lemmas 1–3, and Axioms 1" and 2", all concerning bodies in general, including the "simplest bodies" (*corpora simplicissima*); next, the Definition, Axiom 3", and Lemmas 4–7 plus a scholium to Lemma 7, all concerning composite bodies; and finally, Postulates 1–6, all concerning the human body in particular. Of these various elements, Lemma 1, the Definition, and Lemmas 4–7 bear most directly on the topic of individuation.

Lemma 1, which immediately follows Axioms 1' and 2', states that "bodies are distinguished from one another by reason of motion and rest, speed and slowness, and not by reason of substance." The demonstration of this lemma does not cite either of the two preceding axioms, even though Axiom 1'—"all bodies either move or are at rest"—arguably states a precondition for its truth. Instead, the claim that bodies are distinguished from one another by reason of motion and rest is said to be "known through itself," while the claim that bodies are not distinguished by reason of substance is said to be evident from both IP5 and IP8, and "more clearly evident" from IP15S. Spinoza cites these three passages presumably because each entails—when taken together with IIP2's claim that extension is an attribute—that there can only be *one* extended substance. After two further lemmas and a pair of additional axioms, Spinoza then offers his Definition of the term 'individual':

Definition: When a number of bodies, whether of the same or of different size, are so constrained by other bodies that they lie upon one another, or if they so move, whether with the same degree or different degrees of speed, that they communicate their motions to each other in a certain fixed manner, we shall say that those bodies are united with one another and that they all together compose one body or Individual, which is distinguished from the others by this union of bodies.

After one further axiom, Spinoza then presents four lemmas that describe the changes an individual can undergo while still "retaining its nature, without any change of form." Specifically, it can undergo the replacement of some of the bodies composing it by others of the same nature (Lemma 4); it can undergo an increase or decrease of parts, so long as the parts increase or decrease in a proportion that allows them to retain the same ratio of motion and rest as before (Lemma 5); it can undergo a change of direction of some of its parts, so long as the parts can continue their motions and communicate them to each other in the same ratio as before (Lemma 6); and it can move in any direction or be at rest, so long as the parts retain their motions and communicate them as before (Lemma 7). In each case, Spinoza's demonstration of the lemma is fundamentally the same: the "nature" or "form" of the individual is, by the Definition, constituted by a "certain fixed ratio of motion and rest," in accordance with which the parts "communicate their motions to one another"; hence, an individual's nature or form can withstand any change that does not alter this ratio. It is notable that in no case does the demonstration appeal to any of the preceding axioms, nor, indeed, to anything except the Definition of 'individual' and (in the case of the demonstration of Lemma 4) Lemma 1. Finally, in the Scholium to Lemma 7, Spinoza distinguishes between levels of composition:

Schol.: By this, then, we see how a composite Individual can be affected in many ways, and still preserve its nature. So far we have conceived an individual which is composed only of bodies which are distinguished from one another only by motion and rest, speed and slowness, i.e., which is composed of the simplest bodies. But if we should now conceive of another, composed of a number of Individuals of a different nature, we shall find that it can be affected in a great many other ways, and still preserve its nature. For since each part of it is composed of a number of bodies, each part will therefore

(L7) be able without any change of its nature, to move now more quickly, and consequently communicate its motion more quickly or more slowly to the others.

But if we should further conceive a third kind of Individual, composed of [many individuals] of this second kind, we shall find that it can be affected in many other ways, without any change of its form. And if we proceed in this way to infinity, we shall easily conceive that the whole of nature is one Individual, whose parts, i.e., all bodies, vary in infinite ways, without any change of the whole Individual.

It might be suggested that to interpret these brief passages as outlining a theory of metaphysical individuation is to overread them. Might not some or all of Spinoza's remarks about bodies "being distinguished from one another by reason of motion and rest" rather than "by reason of substance," about individuals "retaining their natures, without change of form," and about individuals being "distinguished from others by this union of bodies" be regarded instead merely as a contribution to a theory of *epistemological* individuation, in the sense specified earlier? So construed, Spinoza would simply be proposing the existence of mechanistic explanations of how the discernible characteristics that we employ to identify, reidentify, and distinguish individuals actually arise, without commitment to any specific theory of metaphysical individuation.

There can be little doubt that Spinoza *does* endorse the view that there are mechanistic explanations of the discernible characteristics of individuals (Epistle 6). There are three reasons, however, for thinking that he intends more than just this in the Physical Digression. First, even read in isolation, the Digression is more naturally interpreted as offering a theory of metaphysical individuation than as merely contributing to a theory of epistemological individuation. In particular, the Definition of 'individual'—and the very choice of the term 'definition' for it—strongly implies that Spinoza is describing what *makes* something an individual, and not merely what makes something be *recognized* as an individual. Second, his discussion of personal identity at IVP39D and IV39S (which cites the definition of 'individual') identifies an individual's loss of nature or form with its *destruction* (see also IV Preface). Hence, it is clear that Spinoza's claims in Lemmas 4–7 about the ability of individuals to retain their "natures" or "forms" (claims that are of course also derived from the definition) are intended as a contribution to a *metaphysical* theory of individuation. Finally, in Appendix II.14 of his earlier *Short Treatise on God, Man, and His Well-*

Being, Spinoza quite explicitly offers fixed ratios of motion and rest as the principle of metaphysical individuation, in all of its aspects, for all individual corporeal things. Thus he writes:

> [14] Here, then, we shall suppose as a thing proven, that there is no other mode in extension than motion and rest, and that each particular corporeal thing is *nothing but* a certain proportion of motion and rest, so much so that if there were nothing in extension except motion alone, or nothing except rest alone, *there could not be,* or be indicated, in the whole of extension, *any particular thing.* The human body, then, is nothing but a certain proportion of motion and rest. (emphasis added)[2]

And there is no evidence that Spinoza later intended to withdraw the metaphysical role that this earlier passage clearly assigns to ratios of motion and rest—whatever he may conceive those ratios to be.

Thus, it is reasonable to interpret the Physical Digression following IIP13 as providing the outlines of a theory of metaphysical individuation. Moreover, this theory stands in marked contrast to at least one theory of metaphysical individuation naturally suggested by the writings of Descartes and others. For on that seemingly Cartesian theory, the only individual things are substances, and substance *always* plays the crucial role in individuation. Something is an individual thing, according to that theory, in virtue of being a substance supporting modes, qualities, or attributes; it remains identical through time simply in virtue of being the numerically same underlying substance; and two entities constitute numerically different individual things simply in virtue of being numerically different substances.[3]

In contrast, Spinoza maintains that there is only one substance (IP14 and C1). Thus, if he is nonetheless to affirm a real plurality of individual things, he must reject each of the doctrines just described; and so he does in Part II of the *Ethics.* The Definition implies that individuals are bodies, which, by IID1 (the Definition of 'body'), are not substances but rather modes of substance. (The phrase of the definition translated as "one body or individual" is *unum corpus, sive Individuum. Sive* has the sense not of disjunction but rather of "in other words" or "that is to say.") Something is an individual, according to the Definition, in virtue of having parts that communicate their motions in a "certain fixed ratio" (*certa quadam ratione*). These individuals remain identical through time, Lemmas 4–7 conclude, in virtue of retaining this same fixed ratio of motion and rest. Finally, Lemma 1 entails that

individuals are, like all bodies, distinguished from one another "by reason of motion and rest" and not by reason of substance; more specifically, according to the Definition, two entities constitute different
"individuals" in virtue of their being (numerically) different "unions of
bodies," where this "union" is itself constituted simply by the fixed
ratio of motion and rest among the component bodies.

MOTION AND REST

According to Spinoza, it is not 'substance' but 'motion and rest' that
serves as the principle of individuation for individuals and, indeed, for
all bodies. Yet the meaning of this term is not at all obvious. Most of
the passages of the *Ethics* that refer to motion and rest—including a significant number in the Physical Digression—appear to treat motion and
rest in a relatively ordinary way, as two different and contrary characteristics of particular bodies or individuals, consisting in their change
or retention, respectively, of spatial relations. As we have seen, however, the *Short Treatise* describes a hypothetical situation in which there
would be motion (or rest, but not both) without the existence of any
particular things at all; and this seems to imply that motion and rest are
two different and contrary characteristics not of particular bodies or
individuals, but of the one extended substance itself. Furthermore, in
IP21 Spinoza describes certain "eternal and infinite" modes that follow
immediately "from the absolute nature of any of God's attributes"; and
in Epistle 64, he specifies that motion and rest is an example, for the
attribute of extension, of such an immediate infinite mode. Yet this
characterization seems to imply that motion and rest is somehow a single pervasive feature of the one extended substance.

Nor is this all. As we have seen, Lemma 1 states that all bodies are
"distinguished by reason of motion and rest," and the Scholium to
Lemma 7 states that the "simplest bodies" (*corpora simplicissima*) are
"distinguished from one another *only* by motion and rest" (emphasis
added; the latter claim also occurs in the paragraph just prior to the
Definition). Yet as Jonathan Bennett points out, these two passages
threaten Spinoza's theory with incoherency if they are interpreted as
referring to motion and rest in the ordinary sense (as characteristics of
extended bodies consisting in their change or retention, respectively,
of spatial relations). For how can motion and rest give rise to the metaphysical distinction of numerically different bodies if motion and rest
themselves cannot exist except as characteristics *of* different bodies?
Moreover, if at the ultimate level there is no qualitative diversity other

than differences of such motion and rest by which bodies can be distinguished, then it seems that the extended world must be entirely homogeneous at any single moment, so that there cannot be any synchronic variety at all.[4] And it will then be difficult to conceive of mere motion and rest as producing any distinction of bodies—or, indeed, of any real motion as having actually taken place—through time either, since the extended world will always *remain* an entirely homogeneous and seemingly undifferentiated whole from one moment to another. Thus, it seems that motion and rest, as ordinarily understood, cannot coherently do the job that Spinoza's theory seems to assign them.

This interpretive situation is difficult, but not hopeless. Spinoza wrote his first published work, *Principles of Cartesian Philosophy* (cited henceforth as "PP"), as an explication of Descartes's philosophy, not as a presentation of his own. As such, it contains a number of doctrines with which Spinoza clearly disagrees—for example, the doctrine that individual bodies are "really distinct" in the technical Cartesian sense that entails their being different substances from each other (PP IIP8S). (The Preface to the work, written by Lodewijk Meyer, mentions other examples.) The work is, nevertheless, a useful guide to Spinoza's own understanding and use of the standard Cartesian terminology from which his own terminology is often derived; and it is particularly helpful in the present case.

In Part II of that work, Spinoza, following Descartes, defines 'local motion' as "the transfer of one part of matter, or one body, from the vicinity of those bodies that touch it immediately, and are considered as resting, to the vicinity of others" (PP IID8). However, in a note to the definition, he distinguishes this "transfer" from the "force or action" that moves the thing said to be in motion; and he also uses the term 'motion' for this force (e.g., PP IIP22). The quantity of this force is the "quantity of motion"; this is also a crucial magnitude of Cartesian physics, where it is equivalent to mass (or volume) times velocity. Spinoza asserts, in accordance with this Cartesian doctrine, that the quantity of motion is greater in a body of greater size than in a body of lesser size but equal speed (PP IIP21); and that it is greater in a body with greater speed than in a body of lesser speed but equal size (PP IIP21). A body has not only a quantity of motion, but also a quantity of rest, which varies inversely to its quantity of motion (PP IIP22 and C1; see also *Short Treatise* Appendix II.15); and when one body transfers a portion of its motion to a second, the second body at the same time transfers an equal portion of its rest to the first (PP IIP18 and D). Force considered as quantity of motion can be distinguished from force considered as quantity of rest: "Note that here, by force in moving bodies, we understand a quantity of motion. . . . But in bodies at rest we understand by force of resisting a quantity of rest" (PP II22S). Nevertheless, in another way, these two forces or quantities can, it seems, ultimately be considered manifestations of the *same* force:

> It is commonly thought that this force or action is required only for motion, and not for rest. But those who so think are thoroughly deceived. For as is known through itself, the force which is needed to impart certain degrees of motion to a body at rest is also required to take away those certain degrees of motion from the body so that it is wholly at rest. (PP IID8S)

Given these features of Spinoza's use of 'motion and rest' in *Principles of Cartesian Philosophy*, it becomes possible to reconcile his uses of the term elsewhere. For it now becomes comprehensible how he could see not only motion-and-rest as a force that constitutes a single pervasive feature of the extended universe—as his apparent claim that motion and rest is an immediate infinite mode of extension implics—but also as one that manifests itself in two different and complementary ways, as quantity of motion (in varying degrees) and as quantity of rest (in inversely varying degrees). (Descartes, too, speaks of "quantity of motion" as "force" or "power,"[5] although he resists giving it the ontological status needed to make it function as a true explanation of local motion; this resistance is related both to the role of God's will in the behavior of bodies and to Descartes's desire to treat local motion as relative. No such resistance need be attributed to Spinoza, however. On the contrary, the passages already cited strongly suggest that he *does* treat quantity of motion and quantity of rest as a force that explains local motion and rest.) Furthermore, these dual quantities of force need not be distributed to a plurality of individual substances, but rather could be distributed differentially throughout the one extended medium that is Spinoza's extended substance. This differential distribution of the dual manifestations of force would, of course, introduce synchronic diversity into his one extended substance, for even at a single time one region of the extended substance might contain greater force as quantity of motion and correspondingly lesser force as quantity of rest than another. From this diversity, in turn, there might arise the distinction among different bodies, as required by Lemma 1.

In particular, the "simplest bodies," which are said to be "distinguished from one another *only* by motion and rest" (Lemma 7 Scholium), might be supposed to be, at any given moment, constituted of those regions of the one extended substance that are, at that time, entirely homogeneous with respect to the distribution of quantity of motion (and, correlatively, quantity of rest). They might, in effect, *be* such homogeneities. And the changing positions—what Spinoza calls the "local motion"—of these simplest bodies might be constituted simply by the changing distributions of these homogeneities in the force of motion-and-rest, changing distributions that are required by what he elsewhere calls "the laws of motion and rest" (e.g., IIP2S).

Bennett's discussion of what he calls Spinoza's "field metaphysics" provides a very useful account of how this constitution might work: the spatiotemporal path of bodies would be a function of momentary qualitative variety together with the continuous temporal "passage" of certain aspects of this momentary qualitative variety through contiguous regions of an extended medium. Much as the spatiotemporal path of a "thaw" through the countryside is determined by the continuous temporal passage of certain qualitative features through the medium of the countryside, so the path of a body will be determined by the passage of certain qualitative features through the one extended substance.[6] But whereas Bennett implies that the qualitative features on whose variety the field metaphysics depends must be unknown for Spinoza, and are called "motion and rest" probably through confusion with the behavior of the individuals to which they give rise, I have suggested that Spinoza does have at least some conception of the nature of these underlying features—as a force manifesting itself (in varying proportions) as the quantity of motion and quantity of rest familiar from Cartesian physics—and that his use of the term 'motion and rest' for them is thus coherently related to his other uses of that term to designate the '*local* motion' and '*local* rest' of particular bodies. For what Spinoza calls the "local" motion or rest of the simplest bodies will be both the consequence of, and a measure of, the force or quantity of motion (and correlative quantity of rest) that belongs to them and, indeed, constitutes them.

It is worth noting that, on this account, the particular quantities of motion and of rest constituting a simplest body need not remain the same throughout its spatiotemporal path, even if the size or volume of the body itself does not change; it will suffice that the path be continuous and that distribution of quantity of motion—and corresponding quantity of rest—remain homogeneous throughout the body. And indeed, the second axiom of the Digression asserts that "each body moves now more slowly, now more quickly," while the Demonstration of Lemma 2 asserts that this is a respect in which all bodies agree. It is also worth noting that, on this account, a single simplest body may change sizes (and hence also that different simplest bodies may be of different sizes). But this changeability seems in any event required by the conjunction of Lemma 5, which states that the parts composing an individual may "become greater or less," with the Scholium to Lemma 7, which states that in the preceding lemmas "we have conceived an Individual . . . composed of the simplest bodies."

Given the existence of simplest bodies, Spinoza's individuals will just be, as the Definition states—composites of such simple bodies, composites that maintain a fixed ratio of this same force of motion and rest among their parts, even as their particular component parts change. Some of the characteristics of these composites will be derived from characteristics of their constitutive fixed ratio, while other characteristics will be derived from other, more variable, aspects of the motion and rest of their component parts—just as suggested by the Scholium to Lemma 7.

In this way, then, 'motion and rest' can refer sometimes to *local* motion and rest, sometimes to the closely related underlying force(s) of motion and rest that produce local motion and rest, and sometimes—since the former are a function of the latter—to either one indifferently. At the same time, motion and rest, as forces, can be conceived as directly characterizing the one extended substance, and also as being possessed by the simple and composite bodies that they serve to constitute and whose local motion they explain, in accordance with the laws of motion and rest. This provides one account of how motion and rest could consistently be said to be (1) an infinite mode, and hence a single pervasive feature of the one extended substance; (2) two different features of the one extended substance; (3) two different features of particular bodies; (4) that which ultimately distinguishes all bodies; and (5) the only respect in which simple bodies are distinguished from one another. This account is naturally suggested by Spinoza's use of the terms 'motion' and 'rest' in *Principles of Cartesian Philosophy*; and it is difficult to see what other account could so fully explain his various uses of those terms. Thus, I conclude that it is the most probable interpretation. If it is correct, then Spinoza's conception of motion and rest as a principle of individuation is an eminently coherent one.

FIXED RATIOS

Although the preceding account provides a likely interpretation of what the fixed ratios of motion and rest that constitute the forms of individuals are ratios *of*, it does not yet say what the ratios themselves *are*. Some commentators have claimed that Spinoza is referring to the specific mathematical ratio between an individual's own quantity of motion and its own quantity of rest; and this ratio, in turn, is often identified with the mathematical ratio between the sum of the quantities of motion of the individual's parts and the sum of the quantities of rest of the individual's parts.[7] The Preface to the Second Part of the *Short Treatise* strongly suggests that Spinoza has just such a specific mathematical ratio in mind:

> So if such a body has and preserves its proportion—say of 1 to 3—the soul and the body will be like ours now are; they will, of course, be constantly subject to change, but not to such a great change that it goes beyond the limits of from 1 to 3. . . . But if other bodies act on ours with such force that the proportion of motion (to rest) cannot remain 1 to 3, that is death, and a destruction of the soul.

There are, however, a number of difficulties with this proposed interpretation. For example, according to *Principles of Cartesian Philosophy*, when a body is accelerated (say, by impact with another body), its quantity of motion thereby increases *and* its quantity of rest decreases, other things being equal (PP IIP22 and C1), thus greatly altering the ratio between the two. Yet individuals can generally survive acceleration, just as Lemma 7, and also the second axiom of the Digression, imply. It will not help to suggest that when acceleration increases the total quantity of motion of an individual, the quantity of rest of its parts will almost always increase proportionately. For according to *Principles of Cartesian Philosophy*, a body can only acquire rest from another body giving up rest (PP IIP18); and it is not easy to see how or why other bodies should be counted on to give up precisely the correct quantity of rest in every case of an individual's acceleration. Yet these doctrines from *Principles of Cartesian Philosophy* are almost certainly principles that Spinoza himself would accept. They are practically constitutive of the concepts of 'quantity of motion' and 'quantity of rest'; and they are both involved in his derivation of Descartes's seven laws of motion (PP IIPP24–31), all but one of which he accepts (Epistle 32).[8]

Second, Spinoza indicates in his correspondence with Oldenburg (Epistles 6 and 13) that the difference between water and ice (and between nitre and spirit of nitre) is one of the amount of "agitation" of the parts. He should thus be at least willing to consider the possibility that lesser differences in temperature—differences that do not yet produce such radical changes as that between liquid water and solid ice— also involve different degrees of agitation of the parts. Moreover, he appears to agree with Boyle's claim that heat is "nothing but a various and nimble motion of the minute particles of bodies" (see note 24 in the Curley edition). And *Short Treatise* Appendix II.15 offers a related account of heat perception. But from this view of heat, it follows that the ratio of the quantity of motion of the parts to the quantity of rest of the parts would change very considerably when an individual became even slightly warmer; in fact, however, individuals can evidently survive even some quite considerable changes of temperature. It might be replied that the parts agitated in heating are not the primary *parts* of the individual itself, but only *parts* of its parts (or parts of those parts, etc.). If, however, the ratio of motion and rest of an individual is to be identified with the mathematical ratio of the sum of the quantities of motion of its parts to the sum of the quantities of rest of its parts, then presumably the quantities of motion and rest of the primary parts are, by the same token, to be identified with the sum of the quantities of motion and rest of all of *their* parts, and so on.

Alexandre Matheron offers a proposal that might overcome both of these objections.[9] If we can construe the motion of a body as composed of one or more different motions, then we might regard only some of the motions of the parts of an individual as contributing to the relevant sum of quantities of motion. The particular motions of parts resulting from acceleration of the individual as a whole, or from its increase in temperature, might then be excluded. This proposal, while helpful, is not without problems of its own. In the first place, it is not obvious how this proposal should treat the quantities of rest that also go to make up the ratio. (Matheron himself explicitly identifies the quantity of rest with mass, but this seems not to take into account the requirement that quantity of rest vary inversely with velocity.) Furthermore, if that problem were solved, it seems likely that any collection of bodies (of constant size) could be then construed as "preserving the same ratio of motion to rest" by abstracting out all motions whatever. Even if we put both of these problems aside, however, there remain difficulties with the original interpretation that Matheron's proposal does not touch.

For example, organic individuals can, it seems, lose one or more parts (a strand of hair, a tooth, a hand, or a leg) without losing their identity. These parts must either have the same mathematical ratio of motion to rest as the individual as a whole (for whatever motions are relevant for determining this ratio), or else a different ratio. But if the ratio is different, then the loss would presumably result in a change in the mathematical ratio of motion to rest of the remaining individual, and hence a change in its form and identity, contrary to the appearance that the individual can persist through such a loss. If, on the other hand, the ratio is the same, that entails the strange conclusion that a man has the same nature or form as a strand of hair, a tooth, a hand, or a leg. Since Spinoza claims at the end of the Preface to Part IV that a horse would be destroyed if it were changed into an insect or man only on the grounds that it would thereby lose its form, it would also follow that a man might be changed into a strand of hair, a tooth, a hand, or a leg *without* thereby losing his identity. Of course, it might be replied to this that the relevant mathematical ratio of motion to rest allows for a certain margin of variation. And certainly, the larger the margin of variation, the less likely it is that the loss of a single part will result in a loss of form. But no matter how large the margin, if the individual happens already to be near one of its limits, a very slight loss (say, of a single strand of hair) might still be enough to make the difference. Furthermore, the larger the margin is, the more likely it becomes that a man, for example, could after all share the same form as one of his parts.

Finally, and most important, even if it were true that every individual somehow retains the same mathematical ratio of motion to rest for its entire duration, it is difficult to see how Spinoza could think himself to be in a position to know this fact. If this principle were merely an arbitrary stipulation of what is to be meant by the term 'individual', then of course the problem would not arise. But Spinoza intends the term 'individual' to apply at least to human beings and animals (including horses, fish, and insects) (E IIIP57S). By what argument can he be assured that the total mathematical ratio of motion to rest in these organisms never changes outside narrow bounds, so that increased motion in some parts is always compensated by properly proportional increased rest in others? Matheron provides a nice example: in running, the muscles are stimulated and the brain dulled, while in intoxication the brain is stimulated and the muscles dulled.[10] But to suppose that such compensations *always* occur, and occur in the right proportion, can only be sheer speculation. And the same epistemological problem also has a converse expression. Spinoza claims, as just noted, that a horse would be destroyed by transformation into an insect or a man; but by what argument can he be assured that the quantity of motion to rest of the parts of a horse is always different from the mathematical ratio of the quantity of motion to rest of the parts of a man or an insect? Once again, increasing the margin of variability of the mathematical ratio partially alleviates the first version of the problem only at the price of greatly exacerbating the latter.

Thus, if Spinoza is committed to requiring definite mathematical ratios of quantity of motion to quantity of rest as the forms of individuals, then he is committed to an implausible and unreasonable position. However, it is possible to give a less restrictive interpretation of the term 'fixed ratio of motion and rest'. For the Latin term *ratio* is not nearly so specific as the English term 'ratio'; it can mean simply "pattern" or "relation." Thus, Samuel Shirley's translation, for example, proposes 'relation' or 'mutual relation of motion-and-rest'; R. H. M. Elwes gives 'relation' or 'mutual relations of motion and rest'; and W. H. White and A. H. Sterling offer 'proportion' or 'kind of motion and rest'.[11] Accordingly, Bennett treats the phrase 'ratio of motion and rest' as designating simply a "coherence of organization"; the term 'fixed ratio', he suggests, is "just a placeholder for a detailed analysis which (Spinoza) had not worked out, perhaps because it might involve a detailed anatomical and physiological theory of organisms which he knew was not yet available."[12]Knowledge of the specific character of the relations of motion and rest among the parts composing particular kinds of individuals does, no doubt, require detailed knowledge of a kind Spinoza is not prepared to provide. That fact does not, however, rob the phrase 'ratio of motion and rest' of all content, nor would Bennett suppose that it does. Given the requirement of the definition and Lemmas that the parts continue to "communicate" their motions to one another in a given "fixed" manner, we can interpret the definition as imposing at least two minimal conditions on individuals when it appeals to ratios of motion and rest: first, an individual must consist of parts whose quantities of motion and rest do not vary entirely independently of the motion and rest of the remainder of the parts; and second, the manner in which the motion and rest of these parts is interrelated must conform to some enduring pattern—even though the identity, size, number, position, direction, and motion of the parts playing these roles may change. Presumably any such pattern *could* ideally be expressed by a mathematical formula describing the relations of quantities of motion and rest among parts that must be preserved; but the formula need not be so simple as a fixed ratio of quantity of motion to quantity of rest. On the other hand, a fixed ratio of quantity of motion to quantity of rest would be one such pattern. Evidently, it is just such a ratio that characterizes the individual constituting the "whole of nature," described in the Scholium to Lemma 7, since Spinoza writes in Epistle 62 that "there is preserved in all together, that is, in the whole universe, the same ratio of motion *to* rest" (*eadem ratione motus ad quietis*; my translation). (The preservation of this mathematical ratio is, of course, required by Descartes's principles of the conservation of motion and conservation of rest [PP IIP13].) Spinoza's use in the *Short Treatise* of the example of "3 to 1" to describe the ratio of motion and rest characterizing a human body may be understood, not as a serious hypothesis about the nature of the human body, but simply as an arbitrary example of a pattern, chosen from the simplest kind of pattern available.

This less restrictive interpretation, according to which ratios of motion and rest are simply fixed patterns of communicated motion and rest among parts, can thus accommodate everything that Spinoza says about fixed ratios of motion and rest. It also ascribes to him views that he would be far more likely to accept than those that must be ascribed on the alternative interpretation. I conclude, therefore, that it is the more likely interpretation; at the same time, it also renders the resulting theory of metaphysical individuation far more reasonable.

THE SCOPE OF 'INDIVIDUAL'

I have argued that, on the most plausible interpretation, Spinoza's conception of ratios of motion and rest provides a coherent and reasonable content to the theory of metaphysical individuation he proposes in the Physical Digression. Still unresolved, however, is the question of the theory's scope and completeness. In particular, it may be questioned whether the theory applies to substances; to infinite modes; and to such finite modes as minds, inorganic objects, and the "simplest bodies" mentioned in Lemma 7—and, if it does not, whether those restrictions undermine the completeness of the theory.

There is a very broad sense in which substances may be considered individual things. Thus, in *Ethics* IP8S, Spinoza sets forth a principle concerning "individuals" ("no definition involves or expresses any certain number of individuals") that he then explicitly applies to substances. (The 1677 Dutch translation[13] adds the explanatory note that "by individuals are understood particulars which belong under a genus," presumably in order to distinguish this sense of the term from that introduced in Part II.) But, while a substance may be an individual thing in this broad sense, it cannot be an individual in the sense defined in the Physical Digression, for two reasons. First, as already noted, the definition speaks of *unum corpus, sive Individuum* (see also Lemma 4), thereby implying that individuals are bodies, and hence (by ID1) *modes* of substance. Second, the definition requires that individuals be composed of parts, whereas substances (by IP12S and IP15S; see also Epistle 12) cannot be composed of parts.

But although a substance is not an individual in the sense defined, this is not a serious lacuna in Spinoza's theory of metaphysical individuation; for to the extent that such a theory is needed for substances, it can easily be inferred from Part I of the *Ethics*. Presumably, to the extent that a substance is an individual thing, it is so simply in virtue of its being a substance. A substance persists as the same individual thing simply by continuing to instantiate its definition, a definition that captures its nature or essence (IP8S). There cannot be more than one substance instantiating that definition (IP8S), and any substance that does so exists necessarily and so cannot fail to exist eternally with that nature or essence (IP7 and ID8). Finally, Spinoza's monism—the doctrine that there is only one substance (IP14 and C1)—obviates the problem of distinguishing substances, either metaphysically or epistemologically. Hence he writes at IP10S: "If someone now asks by what sign we shall be able to distinguish the diversity of substances, let him read the following propositions, which show that in Nature there exists only one substance, and that it is absolutely infinite. So that sign would be sought in vain."[14]

The Scholium to Lemma 7 states that "the whole of Nature is one Individual, whose parts, i.e., all bodies, vary in infinite ways, without any change of the whole Individual." Since Spinoza also identifies nature with God, the only substance, in the recurrent phrase 'God or Nature' (*Deus sive Natura*), it may thus appear that a substance *must*, after all, be an individual. However, as Spinoza's distinction between *Natura naturans* and *Natura natura* at IP29S indicates, the sense in which "nature" is identical with God is only one sense of that term. After citing motion and rest as an immediate infinite mode in Epistle 64, Spinoza continues by citing as an example of a mediate infinite mode: "the face of the whole Universe (*facies totius Universi*), which, although it varies in infinite modes, yet remains always the same; on this subject see Scholium 7 to the Lemma before Proposition XIV, Part II." The reference to the Scholium of Lemma 7 leaves little doubt that the individual identified there as the "whole of Nature" is the "face of the whole Universe" of Epistle 64 and hence an infinite mode of substance, rather than a substance in its own right. Yet, on the other hand, Spinoza also seemingly implies that infinite modes *cannot* be individuals. For he claims in the Demonstration of Lemma 3 that "bodies (by IID1) are singular things"; and singular things, by IID7, are "things that are finite and have a determinate existence." Thus, if all individuals are bodies, it will follow that all individuals are finite. And as we have seen, the Definition's reference to one "body or Individual" (*corpus, sive Individuum*) implies that all individuals *are* bodies. Thus, either the "whole of Nature" must be regarded simply as an exception to this implication, or else the Definition must be regarded as using the phrase *corpus, sive*

Individuum to broaden slightly the sense of 'body', so as to include at least one infinite mode.

Could any other infinite modes be individuals as well? As already noted, Individuals are by definition composed of bodies; and any compound of bodies that lacked some bodies as members could hardly be "infinite," in Spinoza's sense of that term, which means "unlimited" (ID2). This is confirmed by the demonstrations of IPP21-23, which treat infinite modes as pervasive throughout the attribute of which they are modes.[15] Thus, no other infinite mode could be an individual, unless it shared all of the same parts as the "whole of Nature." The possibility of different individuals sharing the same parts is a topic to which I will return; but in any case, any infinite modes that do not have all bodies as parts must be pervasive features of substance that are not compounds of bodies at all. But although such infinite modes will thus not be individuals, this is not a serious limitation on the scope of Spinoza's theory of individuation. For such infinite modes are also unlikely to be anything that would ordinarily be construed as individual things; they will instead be such universal entities as general features of an attribute as a whole, laws of nature, and eternal essences of things.[16]

Because the definition specifies that individuals are composed of bodies, they are by definition extended things. Nevertheless, IIP7S states that a mode of extension and the idea of that mode are identical; and according to IIP21D, this entails that "the Mind and the Body, are one and the same Individual." And in fact, throughout the remainder of the *Ethics* Spinoza consistently identifies human beings—whether conceived under thought or extension—as individuals. Moreover, in IIA3, he writes of different *ideas* as being "in the same Individual." Thus, it seems that, for Spinoza, things are individuals not only insofar as they are extended but also insofar as they are thinking. Presumably, then, he restricts the Definition to extension only because it occurs in a discussion that is devoted explicitly to bodies and extension, rather than to minds and thought. Spinoza does not offer a theory of metaphysical individuation for individuals insofar as they are thinking; but given the parallelism of the attributes and the identity of ideas with their objects (IIP7 and S), it is not difficult to infer what that theory would be: a thinking thing is an individual in virtue of being the idea of a composite body with a fixed ratio of motion and rest; it persists as the same individual through time in virtue of being the idea of the same composite body, constituted by the same fixed ratio of motion and rest; and it is distinguished from another thinking individual in virtue of being the idea of a (numerically) different union of bodies, where each such union is constituted by a fixed ratio of motion and rest.

Spinoza states explicitly that human beings are individuals; and IIIP57S implies that animals are also individuals. Postulate 1 entails that the organs of the human body, and even the primary parts of the organs of the human body and *their* primary parts, are individuals. Moreover, it appears that a group of human beings can also be an individual, as Spinoza indicates at IVP19S:

> For if, for example, two individuals of entirely the same nature are joined to one another, they compose an individual twice as powerful as each one. . . . Man, I say, can wish for nothing more helpful to the preservation of his being than that all should so agree in all things that the Minds and Bodies of all would compose, as it were, one Mind and one Body.

If a group of persons can be an individual, of course, then it follows that an individual can be spatially discontinuous. This need not violate the requirement that motion and rest be communicated among the parts in a fixed pattern, however, for the parts may communicate motion and rest to one another by various media that are not themselves parts of the individual. In the case Spinoza is envisaging, human beings who live in accordance with reason have natures that agree with one another, or have a great deal in common. To the extent that such individuals are in (say, written or spoken) communication with one another, they tend to maintain one another in existence, and to maintain one another in the reasonable nature that they share. Hence the motion and rest of the parts of one such person consistently help determine the motion and rest of the parts of the others in a given fixed pattern—namely, that pattern characteristic of reasonable persons.

Although persons and animals are clearly identified as individuals, it is less obvious whether nonliving things, such as rocks or planets, tables or books, can be individuals. Thus Bennett, for example, while not positively asserting that only living things can be individuals, writes that 'individuals' means "something like 'organisms'" for Spinoza; that "the paradigmatic individuals are organisms"; and that Spinoza usually reserves the term 'individuals' for "things having organic unity—organisms or parts of organisms such as organs and cells."[17]

There are several reasons for thinking that Spinoza *does* intend the class of individuals to include ordinary nonliving things. As we have seen, the whole of nature is an individual, even though it is not obviously a living thing in the ordinary sense. Spinoza's use of the phrase 'body or Individual' (*corpus, sive Individuum*) in the definition implies not only that every individual is a body, but also that every body is an individual. Moreover, he claims at IIP13S that all individuals are animate "in varying degrees"; if every body is indeed an individual, this suggests that the living/nonliving distinction itself may be only a matter of degree for him. (See also his definition of 'life' as "the force through which things persist in their being" at *Principles of Cartesian Philosophy*, Appendix ("Metaphysical Thoughts"), Part II, Chapter 6; this, together with IIIP6, entails that every thing has life.) Perhaps most important, though, nonliving things do in fact generally satisfy the definition of 'individual' as we have interpreted it. To take a simple example: although some pages of a book may move a certain distance, in a certain direction, without moving the rest of the book, there is a definite limit to such motion; when part of a book is moved beyond this limit in a given direction, the other parts are compelled to move as well, by a communication of motion among the parts in a manner that remains constant throughout the duration of the book's existence. There is thus a definite fixed pattern to the relation of motion and rest among its parts involving mutual dependence of motions; and the same holds for other ordinary nonliving individual things.

Is there any reason to suppose that nonliving things are *not* individuals for Spinoza? One reason, of course, is Spinoza's failure to mention them explicitly as individuals. However, this failure is easily explained given that Spinoza's ultimate concern in the *Ethics* is for human beings, and that the topic of "individuals" is introduced primarily for the light it can shed on the relation between the human mind and the human body.

A more complicated reason, however, may be found in IVP39S, where Spinoza makes it clear that when the human body dies and is transformed into a corpse, this constitutes the destruction of the human body as an individual. For if such nonliving things as rocks and books are individuals, then so presumably is the corpse, since the parts of the corpse maintain fixed mutual relations of motion and rest among themselves of much the same kind as those maintained by the parts of a rock or a book. Furthermore, it seems reasonable to say that the individual that is the corpse does not come into existence at death, but rather is the *continuation* of an individual that also existed *before* death, since these fixed mutual relations of motion and rest (supplemented, to be sure, by others of a more organic kind) already held prior to death. Yet the parts of this seeming-individual were the same as those of the living human body; hence, unless two individuals can consist of the same parts at the same time, there follows the contradictory conclusion that death both is and is not the destruction of the individual that is the human body. One way to avoid this contradiction would be to deny that the corpse is an individual at all; and if the corpse is not an individual, consistency would seem to require that other nonliving objects, such as rocks and books, not be individuals either.[18]

This is not, however, the only way to avoid the contradiction. For one thing, Spinoza might well hold that the individual that is now the corpse did not exist prior to death. For although the pattern of motion and rest that now characterizes its parts also characterized them before, it did so only as a part of a larger and hence different pattern of motion and rest constituting the life of the human being. Alternatively, Spinoza might well deny the principle that two different individuals cannot be composed of the same parts at the same time. In IVP39S, he writes that:

> I understand the Body to die when its parts are so disposed that they acquire a different proportion of motion and rest to one another. For I dare not deny that—even though the circulation of the blood is maintained, as well as the other (signs) on account of which the Body is thought to be alive—the human Body can nevertheless be changed into another nature entirely different from its own. For no reason compels me to maintain that the Body does not die unless it is changed into a corpse.
>
> And, indeed, experience seems to urge a different conclusion. Sometimes a man undergoes such changes that I should hardly have said he was the same man. I have heard stories, for example, of a Spanish Poet who suffered an illness; though he recovered, he was left so oblivious to his past life that he did not believe the tales and tragedies he had written were his own. He could surely have been taken for a grown-up infant if he had also forgotten his native language.
>
> If this seems incredible, what shall we say of infants? A man of advanced years believes their nature to be so different from his own that he could not be persuaded that he was ever an infant, if he did not make this conjecture concerning himself from others. But rather than provide the superstitious with material for raising new questions, I prefer to leave this discussion unfinished.

In this deliberately indeterminate passage, Spinoza's language seems to imply both that the Spanish poet is the same individual who wrote the tales and tragedies ("oblivious to *his* past life") and that he evidently is not ("indeed, experience seems to urge a different conclusion . . . a man undergoes such changes that I should hardly have said he was the same man"). Similarly, Spinoza implies both that men of advanced years are not the same individuals they were as infants (by writing with seeming approval of the difficulty of being persuaded of an identity, given the great difference of nature involved), and also that they are the same individuals (by suggesting that one's observation of others shows that such an identity nevertheless does hold). One possible interpretation of the passage is that, in such cases as that of the Spanish poet, there is an individual that does continue, constituted by the particular fixed ratio of motion and rest involved in continuation of the same animal functions, and another individual that does not, one for which the more complex fixed pattern of motion and rest involved in retaining memory and similarity of higher mental functioning is essential.

I therefore conclude that there are several strong reasons to suppose that ordinary nonliving things in general *are* individuals for Spinoza, and no strong reasons to suppose that they are not. Still, even if ordinary nonliving things are individuals for Spinoza, it may appear obvious that at least one class of nonliving things cannot be—namely, the "simplest bodies" (*corpora simplicissima*) mentioned prior to the definition and in the Scholium to Lemma 7. For according to the definition, individuals are composite bodies; and according to the Scholium, individuals of the lowest level of composition are themselves composed of simplest bodies. Despite this appearance, however, Matheron suggests that we may regard simplest bodies as "composite" bodies with only one part.[19] They would thus constitute a subset of the class of individuals of the lowest level of composition. Of course, if the fixed ratio of motion and rest constituting the form of such an individual were interpreted as a mathematical ratio of motion *to* rest, this would entail—as Matheron observes—that simplest bodies could not survive a change of speed (at least, unaccompanied by a corresponding change of size). And this consequence is contrary to the demonstration of Lemma 2, which states that "all bodies agree in that . . . they can move now more slowly, now more quickly, and absolutely, that now they move, now they are at rest." On the less restrictive interpretation of 'fixed ratios', however, the fixed ratio may consist simply in the continued homogeneity of the distribution of force as quantity of motion and of (corresponding) force as quantity of rest throughout these simplest bodies.

This way of treating the fixed ratio of motion and rest of simplest bodies suggests, in turn, another way of construing those bodies as satisfying the definition: we may regard them as being composed of smaller simplest bodies all of which share a completely uniform distribution of force as quantity of motion and of (corresponding) force as quantity of rest. For by 'simplest bodies' Spinoza need not mean "bodies that are absolutely simple," but only "bodies of the simplest kind there are." If the universe contained ultimate simple atoms, of course, then composites of those simplest bodies could not themselves be bodies of the simplest kind. Atoms, however, are incompatible with Cartesian science as Spinoza presents it (PP IIP5). And if every body can be construed as a compound of other bodies, which are themselves compounds of other bodies, and so on, then the simplest bodies will be those that are internally homogeneous. Subregions of such bodies will, of course, themselves be homogeneous, and hence may *also* be construed as simplest bodies.

There are thus at least two ways of interpreting simplest bodies as individuals. Such an interpretation is desirable, for as already noted, the Definition implies that all bodies are individuals. But even if the simplest bodies are not individuals, this would still not be a fatal objection to the completeness of Spinoza's theory of metaphysical individuation. For we have already seen, in the second section of this chapter, how he can account for the identity, persistence, and distinction of simplest bodies as bodies distinguished "*only* by motion and rest," even without the supposition that they are themselves individuals in the sense he defines.

Spinoza's ontology contains only substances (in fact, of course, only one substance) and modes (IP6C); modes, in turn, are either infinite or finite. I have argued that, although substances are not individuals in Spinoza's sense, this fact does not constitute a serious limitation on the scope of his theory of metaphysical individuation. I have also argued that the only infinite modes that could be regarded as individual things are individuals for him and hence fall within the scope of the theory. Furthermore, I have argued that all bodies, including non-living and "simplest" bodies, are also individuals for him, and hence also within the scope of the theory. Since all finite modes of extension are bodies (ID1), and since (as I argued) the ideas of individuals are also individuals, it follows that all finite modes of the attributes of extension and thought are included within the scope of his theory. Of course, Spinoza also allows for at least the possibility of other attributes of substance (ID6, IP11) with other modes. Nevertheless, since his account of the human mind entails that we cannot have any knowledge of such additional attributes (IIP13), his silence on the individuation of their modes cannot be regarded as a serious limitation. Thus, I conclude that Spinoza's theory of metaphysical individuation is not only coherent and reasonable, but also broadly inclusive.[20]

INDIVIDUALS AND SELF-PRESERVATION

At least as striking and original as the theory of metaphysical individuation presented in *Ethics* Part II is the application that Spinoza appears
to make of fundamental considerations about the nature of individual
things in *Ethics* Part III. At IIIP4, he appeals simply to the general concept of 'the definition of a thing' to argue for the proposition that "no
thing can be destroyed except through an external cause":

> Dem.: This Proposition is evident through itself. For the defi-
> nition of any thing affirms, and does not deny, the thing's
> essence, or it posits the thing's essence, and does not take it
> away. So while we attend only to the thing itself, and not to
> external causes, we shall not be able to find anything in it
> which can destroy it, q.e.d.

From IIIP4, he derives IIIP5, the claim that "things are of a contrary
nature, i.e., cannot be in the same subject, insofar as one can destroy
the other":

> Dem.: For if they could agree with one another, or be in the
> same subject at once, then there could be something in the
> same subject which could destroy it, which (by P4) is absurd.
> Therefore, things etc., q.e.d.

And finally, he appeals to both IIIP4 and IIIP5 in his demonstration of
IIIP6, the pivotal claim that "each thing, as far as it can by its own
power, strives to persevere in its being":

> Dem.: For singular things are modes by which God's attrib-
> utes are expressed in a certain and determinate way (by
> IP25C), that is, (by IP34), things that express, in a certain and
> determinate way, God's power, by which God is and acts. And
> no thing has anything in itself by which it can be destroyed, or
> which takes its existence away (by P4). On the contrary, it is
> opposed to everything which can take its existence away (by
> P5). Therefore, as far as it can, and it lies in itself, it strives to
> persevere in its being, q.e.d.

IIIP6, in turn, provides the foundation both of his psychology and of
the ethical theory for which the *Ethics* is named.
  But how—if at all—is the argument at IIIPP4–6 related to the the-

ory of metaphysical individuation presented in the Physical Digression of Part II? Spinoza himself makes no formal connection between the Part II theory of individuation and the Part III argument for the doctrine of self-preservation that he bases in large measure on the concept of 'the definition of a thing'. Accordingly, it can easily appear that the theory presented in Part II, though perhaps interesting, is largely irrelevant to the overall structure of the *Ethics*.[21]

But although the argument of IIIPP4–6 does not formally appeal to any part of the theory of metaphysical individuation found in the Physical Digression, that theory nevertheless has a crucial bearing on the argument and its final conclusion, in at least two ways. First, the rejection of substance as a principle of individuation helps to motivate and to render more plausible Spinoza's attempt to deduce strong conclusions about the behavior of individual things simply from the fact of their *being* individual things. From the claim that a thing is a Cartesian substance, nothing whatever follows about its *behavior*—it follows only that it has qualities and is capable of existing without dependence on any other thing except God. Thus, consider Descartes's own closest correlate to IIIP6: his claim at *Principles of Philosophy* II.37 that "each and every thing, in so far as it can, always continues in the same state," to which he adds the remark that "nothing can by its own nature tend towards its . . . own destruction." He deduces this claim not from the nature of individual things, but rather from God's (volitional) immutability. In contrast, Spinoza argues in effect at IIIPP4–6 that nothing can *be* an individual thing unless it tends to persevere in its own existence. While a full evaluation of that argument is beyond the scope of the present chapter,[22] Spinoza's rejection of substance as a principle of individuation at the very least clears the way for an alternative conception of individuality, one from which such a powerful conclusion about individual things might be derived. (There is an interesting comparison between, on the one hand, the way in which Spinoza derives a proposition closely related to the just-cited Cartesian metaphysical claim of *Principles* II.37, but without employing the Cartesian premise of God's volitional immutability; and, on the other hand, the way in which Spinoza appropriates the Cartesian epistemological principle that "clear and distinct ideas are true," but without employing the Cartesian premise of God's volitional nondeception.[23])

Second, the theory of metaphysical individuation presented in the Physical Digression serves to confirm the conclusion of IIIP6 by providing a plausible instantiation of it. That is, it describes a very large class of individual things (namely, the class of individuals—which is, I have argued, a very large class indeed) that arguably will tend to persevere in their own existence. For individuals, by definition, have as their form or nature a fixed ratio or pattern, in which motion and rest can continue to be communicated. The maintenance of this continuing ratio can thus be understood as the proper activity of the individual that has this form or nature. The disruption of this ratio, in contrast, can always be understood as the intervention of something not strictly pertaining to the individual's own form or nature, and hence as external to it. The theory thus provides specific content to the otherwise empty conception of the 'self' that every self-preserving thing endeavors to preserve;[24] and it shows how the distinction between an individual thing's *own* nature or essence, on the one hand, and that which is "external" to it, on the other, can be applied.

In both of these ways, then—by motivating and rendering more plausible the argument of IIIPP4–6, and by instantiating and thus confirming its conclusion—Spinoza's theory of individuation makes an important contribution to his larger ethical project. At the same time, the theory also bears directly, of course, on the question of personal identity (IVP39S), on the relation of the mind and the body, and on the philosophy of physics. I conclude that it is a theory of considerable importance and power in Spinoza's overall philosophy.

In this chapter, I have tried to provide the most likely interpretation of Spinoza's theory of metaphysical individuation. I have also argued that that theory has a number of important virtues: consistency, reasonableness, inclusivity, and power. It is important to emphasize, therefore, that I have *not* argued that the theory is true. Although the theory has many virtues, it can hardly be true just as it stands, since both the specific Cartesian physics and the resulting physical conceptions of motion and rest on which it relies are now in many ways out of date. Yet despite this fact, readers of the *Ethics* are often struck by a sense that modern science will eventually lead us to something very much like Spinoza's approach to individuation.[25] This need not be as surprising as it may initially seem. For Spinoza's replacement of substance by motion and rest as the principle of metaphysical individuation is the result of his deep reflection on the best science of his time— a science that, though distant, is still largely continuous with our own. Ironically enough, and yet appropriately too, the specific features of his theory that render it most outdated are thus the direct result of a method that renders it most modern—a method that is most worthy of emulation.

NOTES

1. *The Collected Works of Spinoza*, vol. 1, ed. and trans. Edwin Curley (Princeton: Princeton University Press, 1985). All quotations are from this translation unless otherwise indicated. The standard Latin edition is *Spinoza Opera*, 4 vols., ed. Carl Gebhardt (Heidelberg: Carl Winter, 1925). For Spinoza's later correspondence, see also *The Correspondence of Spinoza*, trans. and ed. A. Wolf (London: George Allen and Unwin, 1928).

2. This approach to individuation also occurs in the preface to the second part of the *Short Treatise on God, Man, and His Well-Being*: "Each and every particular thing that comes to exist becomes such through motion and rest. The same is true of all modes in the substantial extension we call body. The differences between [one body and another) arise only from the different proportions of motion and rest, by which this one is so, and not so, is this and not that."

3. This is the most natural reading of such passages as *Meditation* II and *Principles of Philosophy* I 51-64, among others, in which Descartes gives individual bodies as examples of substances. See *The Philosophical Writings of Descartes*, 2 vols., ed. John Cottingham, Robert Stoothoff, and Dugald Murdoch (Cambridge: Cambridge University Press, 1985). It is, of course, widely questioned whether Descartes *consistently* treats individual bodies or "parts of matter" as substances. In particular, Descartes's synopsis of the *Meditations* is often read as implying that only body in general is a substance, and that particular bodies are not. It is worth noting that Spinoza himself presents Descartes as committed to the view that individual bodies and parts of matter are *"really distinct"* from one another (PP IIP8S), which entails that they are different substances. I have also ignored any complications resulting from Descartes's doctrine that the human mind and body constitute a substantial union.

4. Jonathan Bennett, *A Study of Spinoza's Ethics* (Indianapolis: Hackett, 1984), pp. 108-9.

5. See Descartes, *Principles of Philosophy* I.65 and II.43-44 in Cotttingham, Stoothoff, and Murdoch, *Philosophical Writings*.

6. Bennett, *Spinoza's Ethics*, chapter 4. In a paper presented to the Pacific Division of the American Philosophical Association in 1987, Edwin Curley usefully distinguishes two aspects or levels of Bennett's "field metaphysics": first, an attempt to understand individual extended things as consequences of local diversity in the characteristics of a single extended substance; and second, an attempt to somehow reduce propositions whose logical subjects are regions of the extended substance to propositions about substance that do not refer to its regions. Spinoza is, I believe, committed by what he says about motion and rest and its role in individuation to the first of these projects. I am not convinced that he is committed by anything he says to the second of these two projects; at any rate, I am not concerned with it here.

7. David R. Lachterman, "The Physics of Spinoza's Ethics," in *Spinoza: New Perspectives*, ed. Robert W. Shahan and J. I. Biro (Norman: University of Oklahoma Press, 1978), pp. 71–111, especially pp. 85–86; and Martial Guéroult, *Spinoza II: L'âme* (Paris: Aubier 1974), Chapter 6. See also Alexandre Matheron, *Individu et communauté chez Spinoza* (Paris: Les éditions de Minuit, 1969), Chapter 3, which is somewhat more skeptical of this interpretation as applied to the *Ethics*.

8. In Epistle 32, Spinoza corrects Oldenburg's suggestion that he rejects Descartes's other laws of motion. He also states that "there is preserved in all together, that is, in the whole universe, the same ratio of motion to rest" (*eadem ratione motus ad quietis*; my translation), which would certainly be the case if the total quantity of motion and the total quantity of rest were conserved. Leibniz reports showing Spinoza, during their interview in the last year of Spinoza's life, the error of Descartes's principle of the conservation of total quantity of motion. (It is force as mass times acceleration that is conserved, not mass times velocity.) Guéroult shows that his interpretation of the 'fixed ratios of motion and rest' preserved by the individuals of the *Ethics* is generally incompatible with the Cartesian principle of the conservation of motion (Guéroult, *Spinoza II*, Appendix 8). I take this to be a reason to reject Guéroult's account.

9. Matheron, *Individu et communauté*, pp. 38–43.

10. Ibid., p. 40.

11. *The Ethics and Selected Letters*, trans. Samuel Shirley, ed. Seymour Feldman (Indianapolis: Hackett, 1982); *Ethics*, trans. W. H. White and A. H. Sterling (Oxford: Clarendon Press, 1927); and *The Chief Works of Spinoza*, vol. 2, trans. R. H. M. Elwes (London: George Bell and Sons, 1909).

12. Bennett, *Spinoza's Ethics*, p. 232.

13. *De Nagelate Schriften van B. D. S.* (Amsterdam, 1677), published by Spinoza's friends. It is uncertain to what extent Spinoza reviewed the translation prior to his death.

14. The crucial premise in Spinoza's proof of monism is IP5, which states that there cannot be two or more substances of the same attribute. I discuss his argument for this claim in "*Ethics* IP5: Shared Attributes and the Grounds of Spinoza's Monism," in *Essays in Honor of Jonathan Bennett*, ed. Mark Kulstad and Jan Cover (Indianapolis: Hackett, 1990), pp. 69–107. I argue there that Spinoza's unwillingness to allow substances to share attributes is in large part a consequence of his view that all metaphysical differences must be epistemologically conceivable, and that attribute-sharing would violate this requirement.

15. For fuller discussion of this point, see my "Spinoza's Necessitarianism," in *God and Nature: Spinoza's Metaphysics*, vol. 1, ed. Yirmiyahu Yovel (Leiden: Brill, 1991).

16. See Edwin Curley, *Spinoza's Metaphysics* (Cambridge, Mass.: Harvard University Press, 1969), Chapter 2. It should be noted that Spinoza's own use of the term 'universal' is more restricted—see IIP40S1.

17. Bennett, *Spinoza's Ethics,* pp. 33, 107, 321, respectively.

18. Guéroult, *Spinoza II,* Appendix 6, argues that the corpse is not an individual; however, Guéroult is guided by a more restrictive interpretation of 'fixed ratios of motion and rest'.

19. Matheron, *Individu et communauté,* p. 51.

20. IID7 states: "By singular things I understand things that are finite and have a determinate existence. And if a number of individuals so concur in one action that together they are all the cause of one effect, I consider them, all, to that extent, one singular thing." The concept of a 'singular thing', unlike that of a 'body' or a 'mind', thus potentially applies across all attributes. The second sentence of the definition may also seem to suggest that there are extended singular things that are not individuals. For it seems that a number of individuals may concur in producing an effect without entering into any fixed pattern of motion and rest among themselves; and it is implausible to regard such collections of individuals as true individual things in their own right. Spinoza is better interpreted simply as engaging in a terminological maneuver. Thus, for example, he can say in Lemma 3 that each body is "determined to motion and rest by another singular thing," when in fact the determination of the motion and rest of a given body is generally due to a very large number of different bodies that do not themselves compose any single individual thing.

21. Among commentators who have stressed at least some important relation of the Physical Digression to IIIP6 are Matheron and Lachterman.

22. For several challenging objections to the argument, see Bennett, *Spinoza's Ethics,* Chapter 10; for responses to these objections, see Alan Donagan, *Spinoza* (Chicago: University of Chicago Press, 1988), 8.1–8.2; Edwin Curley, *Behind the Geometrical Method* (Princeton: Princeton University Press, 1988), pp. 108–12; and Henry Allison, *Benedict de Spinoza: An Introduction,* rev. ed. (New Haven: Yale University Press, 1987), pp. 131–34.

23. For an account of the latter, see my "Truth, Method, and Correspondence in Spinoza and Leibniz," *Studia Spinozana* 6 (1990), 13–43.

24. See Bennett, *Spinoza's Ethics,* p. 250. Bennett argues that ratios of motion and rest cannot solve the problem of the emptiness of "self-preservation" as a criterion of individuality, because such ratios "concern diachronic counting of individuals, whereas we are asking about synchronic counting." I take it that Spinoza would reply that we can distinguish individuals at a given moment only by taking account of how that momentary state of the universe contributes, under the laws of motion and rest, to the preservation of such fixed ratios.

25. Stuart Hampshire, *Spinoza* (New York: Penguin, 1951), p. 72; Bennett, *Spinoza's Ethics,* Chapter 4.

Locke on Identity:
The Scheme of Simple
and Compounded Things

Martha Brandt Bolton

LOCKE'S PERSPECTIVES ON THE TOPIC OF INDIVIDUATION

illiam Molyneux's suggestion that Locke might write a treatise on "what the schools call logic and metaphysics" seems to have been the stimulus for the chapter "Identity and Diversity," which Locke added to the second edition of the *Essay* (1694).[1] When pressed on topics he had in mind, Molyneux mentioned two: the principle of individuation and eternal truths.[2] Locke was familiar with Scholastic metaphysics texts in use at Oxford, such as those by Christoph Scheibler and Richard Crakanthorpe.[3] Although traditional texts express some views similar to points in Locke's account of individuation, the dissimilarities are far more striking. Locke recast the problem in terms set by the modern mechanist physics, with which he was affiliated, and his own new way of ideas.

In some Scholastic texts Locke would have known, the 'problem of individuation' arises from the Aristotelian doctrine that the essences or forms of individual substances are, at the same time, species essences (universals). That is, roughly, the form of Socrates constitutes both the individual substance and the species man (the "species substance," Crakanthorpe calls it). One problem is to explain the difference between an individual and its species given that both have the same form.[4] In contrast, Locke takes the notion of an individual substance to be primitive; what needs explanation is generality, species or kinds. According to Locke, whatever exists is particular, and nothing in a particular is correctly regarded as universal. This goes for qualities, modes, and relations, as well as the individual substances to which they belong. As he puts it:

103

General and Universal, belong not to the real existence of Things; but *are the Inventions and Creatures of the Understanding*, made by it for its own use, *and concern only Signs*, whether Words, or *Ideas*. . . . When therefore we quit Particulars, the Generals that rest, are only Creatures of our own making, their general Nature being nothing but the Capacity they are put into by the Understanding, of signifying or representing many particulars. For the signification they have, is nothing but a relation, that by the mind of Man is added to them. (III, iii, 11)

There is more to Locke's account of general ideas and their relation to particular ideas and particular things; but what it is to be a particular, as opposed to a universal, is primitive for Locke.

When Locke refers to the *principium individuationis*, he means the principle that distinguishes one individual from every other. That issue, too, was discussed under this title in some Scholastic texts known to Locke. They consider it in the framework of Aristotelian hylomorphism. The leading contenders for what distinguishes an individual are: its matter, its form, and both.[5] In contrast, Locke's account is suited for mechanist physics, which rejects Aristotelian matter and form. Locke appeals to spatiotemporal place to individuate things, a theory that is incomplete without an account of what it is for the same individual to exist at different times. That topic was not often addressed in metaphysics texts, but it receives the bulk of Locke's attention. There were other topical reasons for his interest in it.

One is that it extends Locke's critique of claims to know the essences of substances, and thinking substances in particular. The doctrine that it is essential to a mind to think, urged by Descartes among others, came in for special criticism in the first edition of the *Essay* (II, i, 9–19). It is unlikely we have thoughts we cannot recall even immediately afterward, Locke argued, and we have no recollection from periods of dreamless sleep (see especially II, i, 14–15, 18–19). Moreover, if our souls have thoughts we are wholly unable to retain, they might just as well be thoughts of other men (see especially II, i, 11–12). Descartes identified *himself* with a perpetually thinking substance, but Locke argued that such a substance has some thoughts Descartes could hardly recognize as his own.

Locke's interest in personal identity seems also to derive from the doctrine of general resurrection (see 340:4–7, 344:8–12, 347:6–12). The Christian doctrine raised some problems concerning identity that were intensely discussed in the middle decades of the seventeenth century. These earlier debates had cooled when Locke took up the issue of identity.[6] But he was certainly aware of points made in that context. According to the "orthodox" interpretation of the New Testament, advocated by the Roman Church and many Anglicans, we will be resurrected with souls and bodies that are numerically identical to those we have in this life.

As for the soul, the "orthodox" view insisted that it is an immaterial substance and thus naturally indestructible. One dispute was over the soul's state in the interim between death and resurrection: whether it is disembodied, resides in some indestructible part of the body, or transmigrates from one living body to another. In midcentury, the hottest topic concerned whether the soul is preserved in an active state, as the "orthodox" maintained. Some advocated that souls subside into inactivity and unconsciousness between bodily death and resurrection, a view that had been advocated by Martin Luther. In the furor this opinion raised, Henry More observed that even if persistence of an inactive soul were possible, it could not ensure memory and a sense of self.[7]

Bodily resurrection raised different problems. A difficulty posed by cannibalism was often mentioned. As Kenelm Digby put it: "If a Cannibal should feed upon my body, and convert it into the substance of his, can both of us rise again with the same bodys we enjoy here?"[8] Digby's reply reveals his views about persistence of bodies in general. He maintains that no material thing can remain the same for more than a moment unless it has an immaterial form; and there are no forms except rational souls. This leaves plants and nonhuman animals without the ability to persist over time. But it enables Digby to use a theory, roughly based on Thomas Aquinas, to account for the persistence of human bodies in this life and at resurrection. Digby argues that matter taken apart from form is nothing but a capacity to receive all forms equally. So matter in its own right has no individuation or identity. When matter is united with a form (for Digby, a rational soul), the persistence of the man and the body of the man depends entirely upon persistence of that particular soul. So if the soul is merely united with matter at the resurrection, it will have a body identical to its body in this life.[9]

A solution to the cannibal conundrum based on an alternative theory of matter was offered by Robert Boyle. On his view, matter is divided into corpuscles that have identities in their own right. Corpuscles coalesce into compound bodies, but they retain identity and can, in principle, be recovered from any compound into which they enter. For Boyle, the problem about bodily identity is not that matter is amorphous, but rather that the particles that compose a living body are continually being lost and replaced. He notes that we suppose our bodies remain numerically the same, but ventures no account of the basis for this opinion (although he does agree with Digby that rational souls are the only immaterial forms). Boyle concludes we can reasonably suppose that our resurrected bodies will be reconstituted from intact remains of our earthly bodies, particles we have sloughed off, and whatever further corpuscles may be required. For such a body has a claim to be identical to one's earthly body comparable to that of the earthly body to retain its identity through time.[10]

Locke, writing more than twenty-five years later, makes no effort to defend strict identity of the resurrected body (see 340:5–8, 347:10). But he is concerned to explicate the identities of human and nonhuman living things. This was a topical issue in its own right. Digby and Boyle, who considered the numerical sameness of bodies problematic, were both affiliated with mechanism. This new natural philosophy posed some questions about the status and persistence of material things. In very general terms, the mechanist program aimed to explain all phenomena of the material world by nothing but insensible particles of matter, their sizes, shapes, motions, collisions, and arrangements. Mechanists shared two doctrines that are especially relevant to the identity of things like plants and animals. The first is that matter or material particles are substances in their own right (for example, they retain identity).[11] The mechanists thus rejected two main Scholastic doctrines: that plants and animals are the paradigms of substances, and that substances are constituted by matter and form, two mutually dependent principles. In mechanist metaphysics, plants and animals are dependent on material substance(s) whose existence is entirely independent of theirs.[12] Locke favored Boyle's corpuscular mechanism,[13] on which gross material things are aggregates of atoms or corpuscles each of which has an identity in its own right.

The second relevant mechanist tenet is that material things have no immaterial forms (except the rational soul, according to some). This opposed traditional Scholastics and important non-Scholastic students of the "animal oeconomy," such as William Harvey and Jean Baptiste Van Helmont.[14] They argued that an immaterial form or agent is needed to explain how mere aggregates of particles in motion come to be vital processes. The immaterial form or agent was sometimes invoked for the additional purpose of grounding a metaphysical account of substantial 'unity': why a multitude of parts constitutes one thing and why that thing retains identity over time.

Mechanists thus tended to be sensitive to the charge that they lacked resources to account for the nonaccidental unity, persistence, and "substantiality" of sensible material things.[15] Of all the mechanist philosophers prior to Locke, Hobbes offered the most detailed and cogent account of the identities of material things.[16] But although Locke's account has some affinity with that of Hobbes, the latter rejected the atomist theory favored by Locke.

Among atomists, Gassendi's expositor Bernier explicitly considers the problem: how can things that are generated and destroyed, for example, living things, be substances, have identity and unity, if they have no immaterial forms? He replies that compounds are *effectivement substances*. They have "a true subsistence, because [their] parts subsist by themselves and conjointly, and they remain joined and adhering together in a certain manner."[17] In other words, a living thing persists, because its parts and their configuration remain intact throughout its life. This seems to conflict with Gassendi's account of the animal soul, which he takes to be the source of animal life. He holds that the soul is analogous to a flame, whose parts are continually being consumed and replaced.[18] If the soul does not retain its particles, it is not clear that there are any parts of an animal that remain in it throughout its life.

The corpuscularian, Boyle, briefly rebuts the charge that on his view all things are *entia per accidens* by claiming that the shape, situation, and motion of particles in a body are *ordinatur per se et intrinsece* to form a natural body; further, many parts are united into one body by the "contrivance" and "juxtaposition" of the parts.[19] Concerning the identity of natural bodies, Boyle points out that expert opinions differ and suggests the question is at least to some degree conventional.[20] In short, the mechanist philosophers with whom Locke affiliated provided no satisfactory account of what seems obvious, that plants and animals remain numerically the same through the course of their lives.

This background illuminates the aim and structure of Locke's chapter on "Identity and Diversity." He is, of course, pursuing the suggestion that identity of substance may not be sufficient (or even necessary) for persistence of self. But he also aims to account for the identity of living things in a mechanist and atomist universe. As we will see, Locke has an ingenious scheme for handling the identity of *compound* material things and it supplies the answer to a number of vexing problems about his theory of identity, including personal identity.

INDIVIDUATION AT A MOMENT

Locke approaches the *principium individuationis* by first explaining what distinguishes an individual from all other individuals at a given moment in time. This is only a start, since the *principium* must distinguish an individual from all others throughout its career. Accordingly Locke moves on in the third section and the rest of the chapter to considerations of diachronic identity. But we need first to consider individuation at a moment.

Locke proposes two basic principles: (A) it is impossible for two individuals of the same kind to exist in the same place at the same time and (B) it is impossible for one individual to exist in two places at the same time.[21] There are two main sorts of questions about these principles: how Locke supports them in the framework of his systematic philosophy, and how he accommodates certain cases that might seem to be counterexamples. We will look briefly at the first before turning to the second.

If individuals are to be distinguished on the basis of the places and times at which they exist, how are places and times to be distinguished? The idea of place, Locke explains, is the idea of the distance between one body and two or more other bodies (II, xiii, 7). Thus, for example, the place of a chessman is determined by its respective distances from two or more points on the chessboard, or its distances from two or more points on the shore, and so on. Locke observes that it makes no sense to say that the whole universe is in a place (II, xiii, 10), a point to which we will shortly return. As for time, it is measured relative to the succession of the states of something taken to be regular, for example, the succession of ideas in one's mind or, more suitably, the revolutions of the earth around the sun (II, xiv, 12, 19). So for Locke, bodies are individuated by their places and places are individuated by distance relations to bodies. Further, times are determined by changes in a persistent body, while a necessary condition of the persistence of a body, its individuation, is explicated by the times at which it exists (as we will see). This is circular, but it is not clear that it is viciously so.

One consideration that suggests there may be a problem is that some passages in the *Essay* give a sort of metaphysical priority to substances (for example, bodies) over their relations (especially II, xxv, 8). The interpretation of these texts requires care. There is, however, some temptation to think Locke meant that the relational properties of substances are determined by, or as we might say, strongly supervene on, the nonrelational modifications of those substances. In that case, it seems that individual substances must be distinguished on the basis of something more fundamental than their mutual positions. The contrary doctrine of Locke, that bodies are distinguished by their mutual relations of distance at a time, would fit better with the theory that at least some relations among substances are primitive, or that they have no determining foundations in their *relata*. Such an account of spatial relations is suggested, in any case, by the corpuscularian philosophy Locke favored. For the reality of gross material things depends not only on the reality of atoms, but also on that of their mutual arrangements, and atoms apparently offer no foundation for their positions or orientations in space. If held in conjunction with an appropriate theory of spatiotemporal relations, as far as I can see, the circularity in Locke's account of individuation is benign.

In support of thesis (A), Locke argued that the supposition that two individuals exist in the same place at the same time implies a contradiction:

> For Example, could two Bodies be in the same place at the same time; then those two parcels of Matter must be one and the same, take them great or little; nay, all Bodies must be one and the same. For by the same reason that two particles of Matter may be in one place, all Bodies may be in one place: Which, when it can be supposed, takes away the distinction of Identity and Diversity, of one and more, and renders it ridiculous. But it being a contradiction, that two or more should be one, Identity and Diversity are relations and ways of comparing well founded, and of use to the Understanding. (II, xxvii, 2)

It may be that Locke intended to exploit the point that it is not possible that the universe has a place. The line of reasoning would be that if two bodies can cohabit a place, then there is nothing to prevent all bodies cohabiting the same place, but that is impossible for no place can be assigned to the totality of things. However, this argument seems vulnerable to the charge of fallacious generalization, because there *is* a reason why all bodies could not be in one place. It is difficult to say just what the argument in this passage is. In any case, however, given Locke's definition of place, the supposition that two bodies are in the same place at the same time yields the contradiction that two places might be the same. This is because some places that are different when referred to one pair of bodies will be identical when referred to a pair of bodies that are in the same place.[22]

We can turn now to questions about how thesis (A) is meant to handle cases that might seem to be counterexamples. Several such questions can be raised, but the following is especially pertinent.[23] An animal and the matter of which it is composed are both material things and they exist in the same place at the same time; why does Locke think this is not a counterexample to thesis (A)? On a theory of matter like Digby's, the answer is that the matter of an animal is not an individual, and thus not an individual existing in the same place as the animal. (Of course, for Digby, neither matter nor a nonhuman animal is a true individual.) But Locke maintains that particles of matter have identities in their own right. So for Locke, there are two viable options for making the animal and the collection of its particles consistent with thesis (A). He can hold either (i) that the animal is identical to the collection of corpuscles that compose it at a given time (the aggregate and the animal are not distinct individuals), or (ii) that the corpuscles and the animal are *different* individuals that belong to *different* kinds.

Answer (i) implies that the animal lasts for only a moment. For Locke supposes that its particles are in continual flux and that the aggregate ceases to be numerically the same whenever it gains or loses a particle (see II, xxvii, 3). As it turns out, however, Locke thinks an animal continues numerically the same when its constituent particles change (see II, xxvii, 3). So he opts for (ii), the view that an animal and the aggregate of its constituents at a given time are *different* individuals that are officially in *different* kinds.[24] We may say both are 'material things', but material things cannot count as an official kind.

Section 2 (II, xxvii) gives some guidance concerning what counts as a kind. Thesis (A) is applied to kinds of substances, as well as to modes and relations. Locke says here that we have ideas of exactly three sorts of substances: God, finite intelligences, and bodies. He goes on to explain that two substances in the same kind cannot be in the same place at the same time although two substances in different kinds can cohabit a place (e.g., God and a body, a finite intelligence and a body). Here the example of a body is a "Particle of Matter, to which no Addition or Subtraction of Matter [is] made" (329:8–9). No two *such* bodies can cohabit a place, Locke argues.

Now we just saw that Locke's doctrines require him to say that if bodies is a kind that includes aggregates of particles, it cannot also include animals. For an animal and its constituent particles must be different individuals that share no official kind. But Locke applies the term 'body' to atomic particles, aggregates of particles, and living things (see e.g., II, xxvii, 3). So the term cannot name a kind for purposes of thesis (A). What *does* count as an official kind in the corporeal realm? The answer comes to the fore in section 3, where Locke introduces a distinction among "simple substances and modes . . . and compounded ones." As his examples indicate, the substances mentioned in section 2 are *simple* substances: God, simple finite intelligences, atoms, and aggregates of atoms, since no matter is added nor subtracted from them. Living bodies are in a different "kind," because they are *com-*

pounded.[25] This gives us the general description of Locke's metaphysical scheme: there are simple things (e.g., particles and aggregates of particles), and compounded things (e.g., animals); simple and compounded things are in officially different kinds and they can exist in the same place at the same time.

Locke's categories of individuals include modes and relations, as well as substances. It remains to say something about the individuation of modes and relations. This is crucial to later points in Locke's discussion, but he is cryptic about it: "All other things being but Modes or Relations ultimately terminated in Substances, the Identity and Diversity of each particular Existence of them too will be by the same way determined" (II, xxvii, 2). "[T]he same way" apparently refers to thesis (A). It is the only principle for determining "Identity and Diversity" previously stated or mentioned in the passage.[26] Locke seems to be saying that modes, like substances, "must necessarily each of them exclude any of the same kind out of the same place" (329:12–13). Locke supposes a mode can be assigned a place, because he takes a mode of a thing to be a particular (versus universal) (see, e.g., III, iii, 1 and 6). An example of a mode is a length of one yard.[27] Two yardsticks have two numerically different lengths although both lengths are exactly the same kind. Locke's remark that modes "terminate in substances" is meant to bring out that individual modes are located in the places of the things whose attributes they are.

Lockes' rule for counting particular modes provides a way of dealing with an odd sort of case that arises in his metaphysical scheme, namely, the co-specific *modes* of two individuals that occupy the same spatiotemporal place. An example might be the weight of an elephant at a moment and the weight of the aggregate of particles that compose the elephant at that time. Both the animal and the aggregate *have* a weight; and there seems no basis for denying that weight is the same *kind* of modification in each case. Now Locke could count particular weights by the things that have them, one for the elephant, another for the aggregate. But instead he proposes to count them by kind and spatiotemporal place. By this rule, there is one particular weight in the place where the elephant is and it belongs both to the animal and its mass of particles.

This sharing of particular modifications may be unorthodox, but it is well suited to Locke's commitment to mechanism. On that hypothesis, all sensible qualities are (or are reducible to) joint modifications of insensible particles.[28] It is clear that both the elephant-weight and the aggregate-weight are (reducible to) a combination of exactly the same modifications of exactly same particles. It would be bizarre to say that each particle has two numerically different weights, or that there are numerically distinct combined weights of those particles. But if there is only one combined weight and both the elephant and the aggregate have a weight reducible to it, then the animal-weight and the aggregate-weight are numerically the same. The mechanist reduction of qualities provides Locke with a strong motivation for holding that modes are individuated by thesis (A), and that one particular mode belongs both to a compound and the aggregate that constitutes it at a time. As we will see, this is a crucial element in Locke's metaphysical scheme.

"SUCH AS IS THE IDEA . . . SUCH MUST BE THE *IDENTITY*"

Locke first explicates the identities of simple things, an atom and a mass of atoms, and then goes on to compounded ones, an oak, a horse, a human being. In this section, we will consider his repeated claims to the effect that identity is determined by the kind of thing to which it is applied. The next section takes up the identities of simples and compounds.

There is a pattern to Locke's accounts of the conditions under which things in various kinds pesist. He first explains what a thing of the kind in question is; in Lockean terms, that is to explain what the *idea* of such a thing is. He then derives an account of its persistence on the basis of the idea. He places great importance on this procedure: "[F]or such as is the *Idea* belonging to that Name, such must be the *Identity*: Which if it had been a little more carefully attended to, would possibly have prevented a great deal of that Confusion, which often occurs about this Matter, with no small seeming Difficulties" (II, xxvii, 7; and also see 328:5–7, 27–30, 330:26–31, 335:9–10, 348:4–10). As critics have said,[29] it is unclear how the idea of a kind is supposed to dictate identity, and some of Locke's efforts to explain it seem merely trivial.

Consider this account of the persistence of an atom:

Let us suppose an Atom, *i.e.* a continued body under one immutable Superficies, existing in a determined time and place: 'tis evident, that, considered in any instant of its Existence, it is, in that instant, the same with it self. For being, at that instant, what it is, and nothing else, it is the same, and so must continue, as long as its Existence is continued: for so long it will be the same, and no other. (II, xxvii, 3)

Later on, summarizing what he describes as a "rule" for identity over time, Locke writes in a similar way:

whatever Substance begins to exist, it must, during its Existence, necessarily be the same: Whatever Composition of Substances begin to exist, during the union of those Substances, the concrete must be the same: Whatsoever Mode begins to exist, during its Existence, it is the same: And so if the Composition be of distinct Substances, and different Modes, the same Rule holds. (II, xxvii, 28)

These passages seem merely to belabor the obvious point that an individual persists just as long as *it* continues the same. But I suggest that when Locke purports to explain numerical identity by saying that a thing remains "the same," he is not offering the tautology that the thing continues *numerically* the same, but rather explaining that *something* continues *specifically* the same. He seems to take as primitive the notion of existence continuing from a place and time at which an atom exists. We can supposedly identify an atom at a certain place and time and consider what is continued from that place. The thesis is that as long as what continues is in the species atom, and only so long, the numerically same atom persists.

The account of the identity of an oak follows a similar pattern:

an Oak . . . [is] such a disposition of [Particles of Matter] as constitutes the parts of an Oak; and such an Organization of those parts, as is fit to receive, and distribute nourishment, so as to continue, and frame the Wood, Bark, and Leaves, *etc.* of an Oak, in which consists the vegetable Life. That being then one Plant, which has such an Organization of Parts in one coherent Body, partaking of one Common Life, it continues to be the same Plant, as long as it partakes of the same Life, though that Life be communicated to new Particles of Matter vitally united to the living Plant, in a like continued Organization, conformable to that sort of Plants. (II, xxvii, 4)

An oak, identified at a place and time, persists as long as something is continuous with it and what continues is in the species oak (has parts so organized that they perform the life-functions distinctive of oaks).

If we have understood the accounts of atoms and oaks correctly, Locke determines the diachronic identity of an individual by reference to its place of existence at a time, its kind, and the continued existence of something in that kind. Since kinds are determined by general ideas, this method is what Locke has in mind in passages such as this:

> But to conceive, and judge of [identity] aright, we must consider what *Idea* the Word it is applied to stands for: It being one thing to be the same *Substance*, another the same *Man*, and a third the same *Person*, if *Person*, *Man*, and *Substance*, are three Names standing for three different *Ideas*; for such as is the *Idea* belonging to that Name, such must be the *Identity*. (II, xxvii, 7; also see 330:29–31, 348:4–10)

Among substance, man, and person, one relevant difference is the distinction between simple and compounded things. We can now turn to that.

SIMPLE VERSUS COMPOUNDED MATERIAL THINGS

Diachronic identity seems easier to grasp in the case of simples than compounds, Locke says. Atoms provide an example of the identity of simple substances. Finite intelligences are also simple substances but nothing is said about their identity (a point we will mention later). An atom, i.e., "a continued body under one immutable superficies," is naturally indestructible according to the atomist theory. In nature, the matter of an atom cannot exist in a place or at a time in which the atom does not; nor can the atom exist at one time without the matter it has at some other time. So we can say that an atom has no parts. By 'a part' of x, I mean an individual that (1) occupies some or all of the place occupied by x at some time, (2) is numerically different from x, and (3) is among the individuals to which some sensible qualities, powers, operations, or acts of x can be reduced.[30]

A mass, or set of atoms in mutual proximity, is another simple substance: "And whilst [those atoms] exist united together . . . the Mass must be the same Mass, or the same Body. . . . But if one of these Atoms be taken away, or one new one added, it is no longer the same Mass, or the same Body" (330:16–20). A mass has parts, the individual atoms of which it is composed (330:18), but an atom and a mass of atoms are similar with respect to their diachronic identities. Neither persists under change in parts; an atom has no parts, and a mass cannot survive unless its parts remain numerically the same. This sort of diachronic identity is distinctive of simple things.

Oaks and horses are paradigms of compounded things. With

them, "the variation of great parcels of Matter alters not the Identity" (330:23–24). In these cases, "there may be a manifest change of the parts: So that truly they are not either of them the same Masses of Matter, though they be truly one of them the same Oak, and the other the same Horse" (330:27–29). Here Locke invites us to think of the oak as a series of numerically different masses of matter. Each time the tree gains or loses a particle, it is constituted by a numerically different mass of atoms. Of course, the oak is an individual distinct from each of these masses, for the oak exists at times when each of the successive masses has been destroyed or has not yet been formed by the flux of particles. It is distinctive of a compound to be a sequence of numerically different individuals, which are in some way mutually coordinated.

Consider an oak at a moment in time. It has a variety of sensible qualities and is engaged in vital processes; there is a mass of particles that forms the oak at this time, which also has sensible qualities and inner motions. For instance, the oak has a grey-brown color and rising sap; so does the aggregate that forms the oak. In general, we can say that if the oak has a quality that is reducible to a joint modification of its particles, then the aggregate also has that quality. We have seen how Locke analyzes this duplication of individuals and their modifications. The particular grey-brown color (or rising sap) that pertains to the oak is in the same place as the grey-brown color of the aggregate that (temporarily) forms the oak. By Locke's rule, there is only one grey-brown color, and it belongs to both the oak and the aggregate.

Now consider the oak over a period of years. The tree is a succession of different masses of particles, but what of the oak's qualities and operations? Mechanists typically rejected the theory that a quality can literally be passed from one subject to another.[31] Locke presumably agrees that the weight or color of a mass of particles is a particular that ceases to exist when the mass does. Now he also holds that the grey-brown color of the oak at a given time is numerically identical with the color of the aggregate that composes it at that time. It follows that the tree has numerically different grey-brown colors whenever its constituents change. The color we ascribe to the oak over time is a series of numerically distinct individual colors, each belonging to a different mass of particles. The colors of the masses are simple modes, and the color that belongs to the oak as its particles come and go is a compound mode.

This metaphysical scheme of simple and compound remains in place when Locke turns from the identity of living things to that of persons.

PERSONAL IDENTITY

According to Locke, a person is "a thinking intelligent Being, that has reason and reflection, and can consider it self as it self, the same thinking thing in different times and places" (335:10–13). This is based on Locke's view on the nature of thought, in general, according to which all thoughts are essentially self-consciously entertained (see 335:11–19, 338:3–6). What is at issue is the identity of that to which one ascribes one's mental states.

Identity of self or person is said to be determined by consciousness: "And as far as this consciousness can be extended backwards to any past Action or Thought, so far reaches the Identity of that *Person*; it is the same *self* now it was then; and 'tis the same *self* with this present one that now reflects on it, that that Action was done" (II, xxvii, 9). The notion of a 'consciousness extended backwards' is a well-known locus of difficulty. I will argue that it is not the capacity to remember, but it is built up out of that concept. A memory-theory appears to be open to Butler's devastating charge of circularity,[32] and numerous critics have charged that Locke's theory of personal identity fails for other reasons, as well. As we will see, many of these problems disappear when we attend to the way persons are treated in the scheme of simples and compounds.

Locke wants, above all, to maintain that personal identity and identity of substance are conceptually distinct: "It not being considered in this case, whether the same *self* be continued in the same, or divers Substances" (335:19–21). In actual fact, Locke supposes, the identity of a person may well be grounded in identity of substance. But his core thesis is that it is conceptually possible that a person should persist without persistence of substance. When Locke uses the term 'substance' in this context, he surely means one of the simple substances specified in section 2: either bodies (that neither gain nor lose matter) or finite intelligences. Locke's scheme also includes compounds or series-beings such as animals. His initial argument for the core thesis consists of suggesting that the identity of persons may be modeled on that of animals:

Different Substances, by the same consciousness (where they do partake in it) being united into one Person; as well as different Bodies, by the same Life are united into one Animal, whose *Identity* is preserved, in that change of Substances, by the unity of one continued Life. For it being the same consciousness that makes a Man be himself to himself, *personal*

> *Identity* depends on that only, whether it be annexed only to
> one individual Substance, or can be continued in a succession
> of several Substances. (II, xxvii, 10)

If the identity of persons is like that of animals, then persons are compound things.

Whether or not persons are strictly series-beings, Locke makes a point of saying that persons persist in change of parts. As he puts it, the parts of our bodies that are "vitally united to this same thinking conscious self, so that we feel when they are touch'd, and are affected by, and conscious of good or harm that happens to them, are a part of our *selves*" (336:34–37). The bodily parts of a person obviously change. Or, as Locke says: "the *Substance*, whereof *personal self* consisted at one time, may be varied ... without the change of personal *Identity*" (337:6–7). This shows that Lockean persons cannot be classified as simples in his metaphysical scheme. But Locke mostly ignores complexity in persons due to bodily parts per se focussing instead on the *thinking* ingredient(s) in the aggregates that constitute a person.

He is agnostic about "the Nature of that thinking thing, that is in us, and which we look on as our *selves*" (347:16–18). But he catalogues the relevant options in terms of the distinction between simples and compounds as shown by an offhand remark: "*Self* is that conscious thinking thing, (whatever Substance, made up of whether Spiritual, or Material, Simple, or Compounded, it matters not)" (341:14–16). He explicitly states four hypotheses but makes no definitive choice among them. (1) The first is the materialist theory: "Thought [is placed] in a purely material, animal, Constitution, void of an immaterial Substance" (337:14–15). According to the other hypotheses, thinking things are immaterial substances. This affords three additional possibilities: (2) that "two thinking substances may make but one Person" (338:25–26), the same consciousness being "transferr'd from one thinking Substance to another" (338:24); (3) that "the same immaterial Substance remaining, there may be two distinct Persons," the substance being "stripp'd of all the consciousness of its past Existence" (338:28–33); and (4) that a person is the same if and only if the immaterial substance is the same. This clearly fits the Lockean scheme. According to the materialist theory and hypothesis (2) what thinks in a person is a compound, a *series* of masses of particles or immaterial simple substances; on the other two hypotheses, (3) and (4), what thinks in a person is one (immaterial) simple substance.

Now Locke holds that *persons* think. How are persons and the thoughts of persons related to the thinking things described in these hypotheses? Locke is not offering theories about nonthinking mental entities or ones that have some unspecified role in a theoretical account of cognition. The entities in these hypotheses are things *that think*. They are repeatedly so described: "Substances . . . that do think" (337:30–31); "the . . . Substance, which thinks" (337:10–11); "thinking Substance" (e.g., 337:29, 33, 338:5). Moreover, an immaterial substance is said to be "conscious of the Actions of its past Duration" (338:31–32); to have "memory or consciousness of past Actions" (346:16; also 344:34–35); to "perform . . . Operations of Thinking and Memory" (347:20), and, most strikingly, to be the "agent" of acts performed by persons (338:7–9).[33] In other words, the hypothetical thinking things, whether animal constitution or immaterial substance, *duplicate* the cognitive activities of persons.

This duplication has been the source of much misunderstanding. Commentators tend either to overlook the fact that persons and substances have the same cognitive capacities[34] or to think it collapses Locke's distinction between substance and person. The former ignores Locke's clear and repeated statements to the effect that immaterial substances do think (if they exist). The latter, the conflation of persons and substances, sets Locke up for objections. In particular, the passage on transferred consciousness has been a lightning rod for alleged refutations of Locke's theory of personal identity. I want to look at this passage in more detail.

PERSONS AS COMPOUNDED THINGS

Locke's exposition of hypothesis (2) appeals to our ignorance of the capacities immaterial substances may have (if they exist):

> why one intellectual Substance may not have represented to it, as done by it self, what it never did, and was perhaps done by some other Agent, why I say such a representation may not possibly be without reality of Matter of Fact, as well as several representations in Dreams are, which yet, whilst dreaming, we take for true, will be difficult to conclude from the Nature of things. (II, xxvii, 13)

Nevertheless, Locke argues, we can hardly suppose this to be the case:

> And that it never is so, will by us, till we have clearer views of the Nature of thinking Substances, be best resolv'd into the

Goodness of God, who as far as the Happiness or Misery of any of his sensible Creatures is concerned in it, will not by a fatal Error of theirs transfer from one to another, that consciousness, which draws Reward or Punishment with it. (II, xxvii, 13)

The "fatal error" is ours. Perhaps it is sin that brings it about that punishment is rightly inflicted on conscious beings. Certainly the error is not to believe that one is the person who did the acts to which one can extend consciousness. Locke makes no retreat from the doctrine that personal identity rests with sameness of consciousness, "that consciousness, which draws Reward or Punishment with it" (338:18). But he does say we can trust to God's goodness not to allow consciousness to be transferred among different thinking substances. This is apparently Locke's reason for concluding later in the chapter that the "more probable" hypothesis is that a consciousness is "the Affection of" *one immaterial* substance (345:26). (The materialist hypothesis also posits transfer of consciousness from one thinking substance to another; see 338:19–21.)

Several long-standing objections against this argument for the core thesis assume that Locke is committed to identifying persons and substances because both are thinking things. One traces its origin to Thomas Reid, who argued that because Locke says that persons are "intelligent beings," he cannot consistently suppose, as he does, that the same person might not be the same intelligent being.[35] Following Reid, Sidney Shoemaker argued that since persons are by definition thinking things, and thinking things are substances, Locke contradicts himself when he says that the same person might not be the same substance.[36] A different charge was made by Antony Flew, followed by others.[37] In our passage, Locke says that a substance may regard itself as having done an act that was done by a different agent. Apparently assuming that such a substance satisfies Locke's definition of person, Flew takes the passage to say, in effect, that a person can be conscious of having done an act that was done by another person—a flat contradiction of Locke's account of personal identity. The same assumption lies behind another objection made by Flew, Allison, Mabbot and others.[38] In an effort to establish his core thesis, Locke recklessly proposed that a substance (assumed to be a person) may take itself to have done acts it did not do. Then seeing that were this to happen it would violate his account of personal identity, Locke ineptly invoked God to ensure that his theory is never actually breached. All these objections assume Locke cannot sustain his vaunted distinction between persons and thinking substances.

Locke does define a person as a "thinking intelligent being" with certain specific capacities, and proceeds to entertain the hypothesis that "what thinks in us" is one or more substances that have these same capacities. This is the duplication we noted earlier. Still, the notions of person and thinking substance determine things that fit differently in Locke's metaphysical scheme. The theoretical notion of a thinking substance is one of the simple substances from II, xxvii, 2: either a body that neither gains nor loses parts or a finite intelligence (see section 2 above). In contrast, the definition of a person specifies a thinking thing without mentioning whether a person is a simple or a compound being. And we know that a person, as opposed to what may think in a person, *is* compound, because persons survive addition and loss of bodily parts.

Nevertheless there may seem to be a ground for the Reid–Shoemaker–Flew opinion that Locke's distinction between persons and substances collapses. For thinking substances do duplicate the activities of persons. Whenever a person forms a thought, there is a simple thinking substance that forms that thought. At the same time, Locke holds it possible that the person and substance are distinct individuals with distinct identities. This is strikingly illustrated when Locke declares that different *substances* may be the agents of acts that are correctly ascribed to one *person*. Consider the question, is it possible that numerically one act should be done by two distinct individuals? If not, then the person and the substance who perform the same act *must* be the same individual, despite Locke's claim to the contrary.

Locke's response is clear from our discussion of compound things such as plants and animals. According to hypothesis (2), a person's body is a series of aggregates of material parts and, more important, the thinking thing in these aggregates is a series of immaterial substances. A person forms a thought of x (at a given time), only if the simple substance that is part of the person (at that time) forms a thought of x. How are we to individuate acts of thinking? Locke's rule is thesis (A): it is not possible for two modes of the same kind to be in the same place at the same time. There is one individual thought of x and it is correctly ascribed both to the person and the simple substance, which are nevertheless different individuals. Double ascription does not collapse the simple substance-person distinction. It simply follows from the hypothesis that a person is a compound on the model of an animal.

The duplication of thinking things does generate some complications for an account of what words such as 'I' and 'self' are used to refer to. On a narrow account, both are used exclusively to refer to persons; but *that* view creates problems for Locke.[39] For Locke maintains that all acts of thought are self-conscious. Both persons and simple thinking substances perform acts of thinking and acts of expressing their thoughts in words. So Locke is committed to saying that thinking substances, as well as persons, are conscious of them*selves* and capable of using the word 'self' to express this consciousness. In the transfer of consciousness passage, he makes just this assumption. It is possible, he says, that ". . . one intellectual Substance may . . . have represented to it, as done by itself, what it never did, and was perhaps done by some other Agent . . ." (338: 7–9). Here 'itself' refers to the simple substance, for the point is that the substance (versus person) did not do an act represented to it as done by itself. Although this underscores a complication involved in reference to (and thought about) oneself on hypothesis (i), I do not think it reveals a confusion on Locke's part. The difficulties can be avoided by rejecting the narrow account in favor of one on which words like 'self' can refer to several different sorts of things, including thinking substances, as well as persons, and the context of use determines which. This is clearly the view Locke endorses. He himself points out that a man can use 'I' to refer to a man or a person and we can be mislead about personal identity if we do not "take notice of what the Word *I* is applied to" (II, xxvii, 20).

Perhaps the duplication of *selves* helps solve one of the main puzzles about the transfer of consciousness passage. Why does Locke suppose God's goodness assures us that persons are not series-beings? It seems natural to think it turns on the justice of divine reward and punishment. After all, if a person is a series-being, then when she is held accountable at resurrection, she may be constituted by a simple substance that performed none of her offensive acts. Now, as we have seen, if a person experiences punishment (at a given time), so does the thinking substance that constitutes the person (at that time); so punishing a series-person *seems* unjust. But if this is Locke's opinion in our passage, it conflicts with what he says elsewhere. He insists repeatedly that identity of *person*, alone, determines responsibility: "In this *personal Identity* is founded all the Right and Justice of Reward and Punishment; Happiness and Misery, being that, for which every one is concerned for *himself*, not mattering what becomes of any Substance, not joined to, or affected with that consciousness" (II, xxvii, 18; also see IV, iii, 6). Some commentators have concluded that in the crucial transfer of consciousness case, Locke abandons the doctrine that persons (versus substances) are accountable.[40] But there is another answer.

Locke actually appeals to divine benevolence, not justice. The suggestion is that a world in which persons are formed by one thinking substance is *better* than one in which persons are sequential. If Locke

supposes the one is better than the other because it is more just, then
he does equivocate on his doctrine of personal accountability. But he
might have had a different reason for his evaluation of the alternatives.
Here is one suggestion based on the duplication of conscious individuals one can refer to as 'self'. Locke is well aware of the special concern
one has for the happiness of oneself (see II, xxvii, 26). But how is a
series-person to consider its own happiness and act accordingly? The
person's interests may well diverge from those of the thinking substance that is in the person at a given time (consider ultimate reward
and punishment). In such cases, informed practical deliberation pits
the happiness of a simple substance against that of the person it temporarily constitutes. During their association, any thought or act of the
substance is thereby a thought or act of the person; so action informed
by what is in both agents' interests may often be impossible. The choice
between a world where persons coincide with substances and one in
which persons are series-beings is, then, a choice between a world
where conscious agents can, in general, pursue what is genuinely con-
ducive to their happiness and one in which this is not possible. This
might well explain why Locke takes the former to be better than the latter.

   The fact that simple substances duplicate the cognitive capacities
of persons sheds some light on the circularity alleged against Locke's
theory of personal identity. The notion of 'consciousness extended
backward' is naturally taken to be a notion of memory (accommodated
to the possibility of consciousness transfer).[41] The problem is that we
seem to need the notion of personal identity to properly explicate the
notion of memory. Recall Bertrand Russell's example of paramnesia,
George IV appropriated Nelson's victory at Waterloo. It can seem to a
person that he remembers doing deeds, which he did not do and thus
cannot *remember* doing. We might handle this by saying that a person
remembers doing A only if (i) it seems to her that she remembers doing
A and (ii) she *did* A. But (ii) uses the notion of personal identity. So
Locke's account of personal identity appears to be open to the charge
of vicious circularity.[42]

   For Locke, simple thinking substances are parts of persons, not to
be identified with persons. But the cognitive acts and capacities of persons are identified with those of their component simple substances. So
a person (at a time) can represent herself as having done something only
if the simple substance that constitutes the person (at that time) can represent itself as having done it. Now no suspicion of circularity stands in
the way of Locke's supposing that simple substances have memory.
These substances are either aggregates of particles that form an "animal

constitution" or immaterial finite intelligences. A material simple substance can remember an act, we might say, only if the animal it temporarily constitutes did that act. (A man [versus person] can remember
and forget [see II, xxvii, 20].) This is not circular, because the identities
of animals are determined by continuity of life without regard for memory. An immaterial substance also is presumed to have an identity independent of memory. It might be "wholly stripp'd of all the consciousness
of its past Existence, and lose it beyond the power of ever retrieving
again," Locke suggests (338:32–34). The way is open, then, to define a
person's ability to "extend consciousness" to a past action in terms of a
simple thinking thing's ability to remember that act.

   This is easy on two of Locke's hypotheses, (3) and (4). We can simply say that a person can "extend consciousness" to act *A* if and only if
the immaterial thinking substance that is part of the person can
remember doing *A*. On the materialist hypothesis, what thinks in a person is an "animal constitution"; on the assumption that a person coincides exactly with one animal (for example, a man), a person "extends
consciousness" to an act if and only if the coincident animal can
remember doing that act. Hypotheses that posit transfer of consciousness have to be handled somewhat differently. The basic idea is that a
person's ability to "extend consciousness" is defined in terms of her
ability to represent herself as having done those acts that could (prior
to total stripping of consciousness) be remembered by the thinking
substances that are successive parts of the person. So a series-person
now has thinking substance *S* as a part and formerly had thinking substance *T* as a part if and only if *S* can now represent itself as having
done all those acts[43] such that *T* could remember doing them (at some
earlier time prior to stripping of *T*'s consciousness).

   Locke's account of personal identity is not, I have argued, circular
in the way it is often thought to be. But it is freed of that charge at the
cost of providing accounts of the identities of theoretical thinking
things. He does explicate the identities of aggregates of particles and
animals, but not that of a finite intelligences. He takes their identity for
granted, and it is far from clear how one might give an account of it. To
do so in terms of connections among psychological states risks circularity, once again. So reliance on the problematic identity of immaterial
substance shows as a weakness in Locke's account, once the familiar
circularity charge has been removed.

   In any case, one advantage of recognizing Locke's metaphysical
scheme is that it explains why he was not concerned about circularity
of a sort that seemed to Sargeant, Butler, Reid, and many others obviously to undermine his theory of personal identity. He was thinking all

along in terms of a model on which the cognitive acts and abilities ascribed to a person are acts and abilities that belong to a thinking thing whose definition and identity is different from that of the person.

CONCLUSION

Locke's foray into "what the Schools call metaphysics" produced a highly systematic treatment of individuation and identity. Its apparatus consists mainly of three basic principles: thesis (A) (applied to substances and modes), the rule that a particular exists as long as something continues specifically the same, and the metaphysical scheme of simples and compounded substances and modes. These principles have considerable power. Locke uses them to give accounts of identity that satisfy the diverse topical interests we mentioned at the start.

The apparatus was surely designed, in the first instance, to deal with identity of material things in the framework of mechanism. For the principles apply most naturally to living things, as understood on the corpuscular hypothesis. I have tried to suggest that Aristotelian metaphysics afforded ways of reconciling the flux of matter and the persistence of material things, which were jettisoned by the mechanists, who gave to matter or material particles the status of substances. In the new metaphysics, gross material things are individuals different from, and asymmetrically dependent upon, material substance(s). The challenge for Locke was to explain the substance-like role gross material things have in our experience-based conception of the world. His solution is to build the identity of individuals whose parts are in flux upon the strict identity of individuals that persist without change of parts; hence, thesis (A) and the scheme of simples and compounds. Part of the role of substance is to be the subject of modifications. Locke is concerned about the individuation and identity of modifications, as well as the identities of things that bear them. I have argued that modes are handled by the same apparatus as substantial things. Thus some individual modes belong simultaneously to two distinct individual subjects; and there are series-modes, which belong to series-beings, as well as simple modes that belong to simple substances. This unorthodox doctrine, too, is strongly motivated by Locke's mechanism. For it accommodates the strict reduction of sensible qualities to mechanical affections of insensible particles; and it adheres to the mechanists' insistence that modifications cannot be passed from one subject to another.

Thinking things come into the scope of Locke's apparatus, because he assimilates them to material things in certain ways that do not compromise his agnosticism on their nature. He endorses the non-Cartesian view that thinking things occupy regions of space. Moreover, the mechanist model of reduction is adapted to cognitive phenomena, in as much as Locke takes the cognitive acts and process of persons to be (reducible to) modifications of simple substances, distinct from persons, postulated by theory.

Locke actually says very little in the *Essay* on the controversial topic of general resurrection. But certain implications are clear. We cannot be resurrected after death with the numerically same bodies we have in life. And resurrected persons will extend consciousness to what they are held accountable for, whatever their interim state and whether or not they retain the same simple thinking agents. Locke's early critics were preoccupied with rebutting these implications for personal resurrection, and much recent discussion of Locke on identity has focused exclusively on personal identity. His treatment of personal identity must, however, be understood in the context of a metaphysical scheme motivated by atomistic mechanism.[44]

NOTES

1. *The Works of John Locke*, 10 vols., 10th ed. (London: T. Davison, 1801), 9: 298, 326, 350.

2. Locke embellished his first edition remarks on *aeternae veritates* by a few sentences added to IV, xi, 14 in the second edition (638:30–639:5). All citations and quotations from the *Essay* are from the edition of Peter H. Nidditch (Oxford: Clarendon Press, 1975). Where it is appropriate to cite small portions of a section of the text, I use the format: page number: line number. Otherwise, I use the standard format: book number, chapter number, section number.

3. *Inter alia.* See W. Henry Kenney, *John Locke and the Oxford Training in Logic and Metaphysics* (Ph.D. diss., St. Louis University, 1959). As Kenney notes, Locke berates Scheibler in "Some Thoughts concerning Education," sec. 94.

4. E.g., Richard Crakanthorpe, *Introductio in metaphysicam* (Oxford: I. Lichfield and I. Short: Oxford, 1619), p. 385, who refers his readers to discussions by Fonseca and Zabarella.

5. E.g., Christoph Scheibler, *Metaphysica* (Oxford: H. Hall and G. West, 1665), pp. 96–97. Scheibler lists as other possible bases of individuation: Aquinas' *materia signata*, accidents, and existence; but he opts for form plus matter.

6. Nevertheless, the unorthodox view Locke ventures came under attack soon after it appeared in 1694; see, e.g., Thomas Beconsall, "The doctrine of the general resurrection: wherein the identity of the rising body is asserted against the Socinians and scepticks" (Oxford: L. Lichfield for G. Wesp, 1697).

7. Henry More, *Psychodia Platonica*, "Antipsychopannicia," cant. I, especially verses 8–11 (*The Complete Poems of Henry More*, ed. Alexander Grosart [Edinburgh: Edinburgh University Press, 1878], p. 104). On the 'mortalism' controversy, see Norman Burns, *Christian Mortalism from Tyndale to Milton* (Cambridge: Harvard University Press, 1972).

8. Kenelm Digby, *A Discourse Concerning the Vegetation of Plants* (London: J. Dakins, 1661), p. 86.

9. Descartes had urged a similar account of the earthly identity of the bodies of human beings in his letter to Mesland, 9 February 1645, in *Descartes: Philosophical Letters*, trans. Anthony Kenny (Oxford: Clarendon Press, 1970), p. 156.

10. Robert Boyle, "Some Physico-Theological Considerations about the Possibility of the Resurrection" (1675), in *Selected Philosophical Papers of Robert Boyle*, ed. M. A. Stewart (Manchester: Manchester University Press, 1979), pp. 192–208.

11. See, e.g., Descartes, *Principles of Philosophy*, trans. John Cottingham, Robert Stoothoff, and Dugald Murdoch (Cambridge: Cambridge University Press, 1984), pt. I, prins. 52–54; Hobbes, *De corpore*, ed. William Molesworth (reprint of ed. 1839, Scientia Aalen, 1962), pt. II, chapter 8, sec. 1; François Bernier, *Abrégé de Gassendi* (Lyon: Annison and Pousel, 1678), pt. II, pp. 346–52 and *passim*; Boyle, "The Origin of Forms and Qualities," in *Selected Papers*, pp. 18, 50.

12. The main mechanist thinkers differed markedly in their views on the relation between material substance(s) and things like plants and animals. The main difference is between atomistic views, held by Gassendi and assumed by Boyle, and views on which matter is infinitely divisible, held by Descartes and Hobbes (in later work). The latter philosophers tend to say that there is only one material substance and that plants, animals, and other bodies are, roughly, modifications of that substance (Descartes) or parts of it (Hobbes). The status of bodies, their individuation, and their identity are especially problematic in the Cartesian philosophy; see Geneviève Rodis-Lewis, *L'individualité selon Descartes* (Paris: J. Vrin, 1950).

13. Locke was neither a slavish nor a dogmatic adherent of the 'corpuscularian Hypothesis'; see especially IV, iii, 16.

14. See Walter Pagel, "The Reaction to Aristotle in Seventeenth-Century Biological Thought," in *Science, Medicine, and History*, ed. E. A. Underwood (Oxford: Oxford University Press, 1953), 1: 498–509.

15. The issue surfaces in discussion of the traditional doctrine of generation, corruption, and alteration, which mechanists are called upon to explain without recourse to creation or destruction of substance or substantial form. In addition to Bernier and Boyle (mentioned below), see Walter Charleton, *Physiologia Epicuro-Gassendo-Charletoniana* (New York: Johnson Reprint Corp., 1966), ed. London, 1654, p. 417; and the Cartesian, Pierre-Sylvain Régis, *Le cours entier de philosophie* (Amsterdam: Huguetan, 1691), Physics, I, ii, 1.

16. See Hobbes, *De corpore*, pt. II, chapter 9, sec. 7.

17. Bernier, *Abrégé de Gassendi*, pt. II. p. 356.

18. Ibid., pt. V, pp. 456–65.

19. Boyle, *Selected Papers*, pp. 58, 66. For a summary of Boyle's treatment of a variety of arguments in support of immaterial forms, see Peter Alexander, *Ideas, Qualities and Corpuscles* (Cambridge: Cambridge University Press, 1985), pp. 54–59.

20. E.g., Boyle, *Selected Papers*, pp. 44–46, 193–94.

21. Locke derives a thesis from (A) and (B): "That therefore that had one beginning is the same thing, and that which had a different beginning in time and place from that, is not the same but divers" (328:25–27). This is sometimes interpreted as: (i) it is impossible for one thing to come into existence at two *different times* (see ,e.g., Vere Chappell, "Locke and Relative Identity," *History of Philosophy Quarterly* 6 [1989]: 73). But if the thesis is to follow from (A) and (B), as Locke indicates, it must be read as: (ii) it is impossible for one thing to come into existence in *two places* at the *same time*. For thesis (B) affords no account of identity or diversity for individuals that exist at *different* times. A similar point is made by Joshua Hoffman, "Locke on Whether a Thing Can Have Two Beginnings of Existence," *Ratio* 22 (1980): 106–11.

22. Locke says a place is individuated by its respective distances from two or more bodies. This is not strictly correct (as R. I Aaron noted in *John Locke* [London: Oxford University Press, 1937], p. 154, note 2). The reasoning just sketched can be adapted to an amended definition of place in Euclidean space.

23. Here are some others: (1) What sort of general term is to count as naming a *kind* for purposes of thesis (A)? Apparently we need to rule out non-specific terms such as 'thing', 'being', 'substance'; if they name official kinds, then thesis (A) conflicts with Locke's explicit doctrine that two substances of different kinds can exist in the same place at the same time (329:10–11). Are there further restrictions, beyond those considered above, on official kinds? (2) Does (A) prohibit partial spatial overlap between individuals in the same kind or only complete overlap? (3) How does (A) accommodate a whole and one of its parts if both belong to the same official kind, in case that ever occurs, as it might, for example, with organisms or machines? These are questions I am not going to try to pursue here.

24. The claim that they are different individuals is *not* supported by thesis (B) (see above, note 21). For according to Locke, it is not possible that an animal and the aggregate of particles that constitutes it should exist in different places at the *same* time; the aggregate loses its identity as soon as one of its members is lost. So if the aggregate were dissolved and then its member particles regrouped, the resulting aggregate would not be numerically identical to the original one.

The claim that the animal and aggregate are different individuals is supported by an intuitively acceptable principle (that Locke did not state, as far as I know). That is thesis (C): if there is a time at which individual *a* exists and individual *b* does not, then *a* is not identical to *b*.

It might be objected that (C) is unacceptable to Locke, because it implies that a new individual is produced by every change. For example, suppose a woman becomes a wife; there is a time at which the woman exists and the wife does not, so according to thesis (C) the woman is not identical to the wife. But this result is blocked by Locke's substance-modification ontology. On a Lockean analysis, the woman is a substance and being a wife is a modification (relation) whose existence depends on that of the woman. The *modification* does not exist before the ceremony and does after. But the woman who has the modification does not begin to exist when she acquires it.

25. Are they compounded substances or modes? William Alston and Jonathan Bennett, in "Locke on People and Substances," *Philosophical Review* 97 (1988): 25–29, maintain that in II, xxvii, Locke applies the term 'substance' to atoms and immaterial thinking things, but not to animals, plants, or persons as (they claim) he does elsewhere in the *Essay*. On their view, the exhaustive list of kinds of substances in II, xxvii, 2 *excludes* compounded things. It is not clear that this is correct, because Locke labels corporeal substances 'bodies' and applies that term to living things, as well as to particles and aggregates. But here I do not want to take a stand on the question of whether Locke gives a meaning to the term 'substance' that limits its application to simple substances, as opposed to compounds. The question whether Locke posits both simple and compounded substances is discussed by Vere Chappel, "Locke on the Ontology of Matter, Living Things and Persons," *Philosophical Studies* 60 (1990), pp. 19–32 and William Uzgalis, "Relative Identity and Locke's Principle of Individuation," *History of Philosophy Quarterly* 7 (1990), pp. 283–97.

26. One might think Locke means to say that modes and relations are individuated by the substances to which they belong. This is unworkable as a reading of the passage, because the text in no way indicates *how* substances might be supposed to individuate modes. Here are three different proposals: (i) it is impossible that two modes of the same kind should belong to the same substance at the same time; (ii) it is impossible that one mode should belong to two substances at different times; (iii) it is impossible that one mode should belong to two subjects at the same time. None of these principles is suggested by the remark that modes are "terminated in Substances," and none is genuinely available in the passage as a referent of the phrase "by the same way determined." I think, however, Locke would agree with (i) and (ii), but not (iii).

27. What Locke says about modes generally goes for relations as well. He is casual about the distinction, and even places some modifications in both categories, for example, time and place (II, xxvi, 3; II, xiii, 7; II, xiv, 1).

28. The exact notion of reduction Boyle or other mechanists may have had in mind is difficult to determine. For a detailed discussion of some of these issues, see Alexander, pp. 71–82 and 150–67.

29. See, e.g., Alston and Bennett, "Locke on People and Substances," pp. 32–33.

30. Lockes' views imply that conditions (i) and (ii) can be satisfied by things not related as whole and part, for example, a body and a finite intelligence.

31. See Boyle, *Selected Papers,* pp. 21–23; Descartes, "Sixth Replies," Cottingham, et. al., v. II, p. 293; and especially Leibniz, *New Essays,* trans. Peter Remnant and Jonathan Bennett (Cambridge: Cambridge University Press, 1981), pp. 231–32.

32. Joseph Butler, "On Personal Identity," in *The Analogy of Religion* (London: G. Bell, 1889). A similar complaint was made earlier by John Sargeant in *Solid Philosophy Asserted* (New York: Garland, 1984), reprint of ed. 1697, p. 265.

33. Some commentators say Locke resorts to vague expressions to refer to the relation between "what thinks in us" (substances) and persons and that this shows that he has no precise view of the relation between persons and substances. See Janice Thomas, "On a Supposed Inconsistency in Locke's Account of Personal Identity," *Locke Newsletter* 10 (1970): 17–79; and Udo Theil, "Locke's Concept of Person," in *John Locke: Symposium Wolfenbuttel 1979,* ed. Reinhard Brandt (Berlin: de Gruyter, 1981). In fact, Locke's language is reasonably precise and entirely appropriate to his position. The *appearance* of vagueness may be due to failure to distinguish the substance-person relation from the substance-consciousness relation. When referring to the relation between *person* and substance, Locke uses locutions such as: a person is "placed in" (342:5), "consists of" (341:7), and is "made up of" (341:9, 15, 345:8) one or more substances; or one substance may be "part of" different persons (346:12). These expressions invoke the metaphysical scheme according to which a person does have (spatial) parts which include (*inter alia*) one or more thinking substances. When Locke refers to the relation between *consciousness* and substance, his language is very different. Locke takes consciousness to be an affect of a thinking thing or, perhaps, a concomitant of the activity of thinking. When referring to the substance-consciousness relation, he says, consciousness is "annexed to" (338:1, 344:30), "annexed to and the affection of" (345:26), "adheres to" (347:11), and is "owing to" (344:27) one or more substances; and substance is "affected with" consciousness (342:2). Such expressions are typically used by Locke and his contemporaries to refer to the relation between a substance and its modifications.

34. See Thomas, Theil, and also compare Kenneth Winkler, "Locke on Personal Identity," *Journal of the History of Philosophy* 29 (1991): 220.

35. *Essays on the Intellectual Powers of Man* (Cambridge: MIT Press, 1969), Essay III, chapter vi (pp. 356–57).

36. *Self-Knowledge and Self-Identity* (Ithaca: Cornell University Press, 1963), p. 46.

37. "Locke and the Problem of Personal Identity," in *Locke and Berkeley*, ed. C. B. Martin and D. M. Armstrong (Garden City: Doubleday, 1968), pp. 163–64; also Henry E. Allison, "Locke's Theory of Personal Identity: A Reexamination" in *Locke on Human Understanding*, ed. I. C. Tipton (Oxford: Oxford University Press, 1977), p. 119.

38. J. D. Mabbot, *John Locke* (London: Macmillan, 1973), p. 62.

39. Compare Shoemaker, *Self-Knowledge and Self-Identity*, pp. 45–55.

40. See Allison, "Locke's Theory," pp. 107, 119; J. L. Mackie, *Problems from Locke* (Oxford: Clarendon Press, 1976), p. 184; Harold Noonan, "Locke on Personal Identity," *Philosophy* 53 (1978): 343–51; Susan Mendus, "Personal Identity and Moral Responsibility," *Locke Newsletter* 9 (1978): 75–89.

41. Section 13 has sometimes been taken to show that Locke's account does not base personal identity on memory, but merely on an ability to represent oneself as having done an action (without objective conditions on that ability); see Eric Matthews, "Descartes and Locke on the Concept of a Person," *Locke Newsletter* 8 (1977): 9–34. Some passages lend plausibility to this view (II, xxvii, 16 and 337:35–37); but others indicate more clearly that 'extended consciousness' is to be understood as a kind of memory (336:21–23, 17–24).

42. There have been some relatively recent attempts to argue that a psychological account of personal identity can be defended against the circularity charge: John Perry, "Personal Identity, Memory, and the Problem of Circularity" in *Personal Identity*, ed. John Perry (Berkeley: University of California Press, 1975); Sidney Shoemaker, "Persons and Their Pasts," in Sidney Shoemaker, *Identity, Cause and Mind* (Cambridge: Cambridge University Press, 1984); Derek Parfit, *Reasons and Persons* (Oxford: Oxford University Press, 1986), sec. 80.

43. Here I am supposing that transfer of consciousness is complete (versus fragmentary). Locke places no constraints on what is transferred or how, and alternative requirements have significantly different implications for personal identity. For example, consider accounts that define consciousness transfer in terms of a causal process, as opposed to defining it in terms of psychological content alone; or, those that allow (partial or complete) fusion and/or fission of the contents of different consciousnesses, as opposed to those that do not. The requirement imposed here seems natural, because it distinguishes transfer of consciousness from the standard cases of paramnesia.

44. Shorter versions of this paper were read at the Locke commemorative symposium at the Pacific division APA meeting in 1990 and the University of Mexico in 1991. I am grateful for the discussions that took place there. Thanks also to Shaun Nichols for discussions of Locke on personal identity.

Berkeley, Individuation, and Physical Objects

Daniel Flage

Many contemporary metaphysicians maintain that sortal identity and spatiotemporal continuity are among the necessary conditions for the numerical identity and individuation of physical objects.[1] Since Locke and Hume also tied the *principium individuationis* to the question of numerical identity,[2] we might do well to ask whether Berkeley's account of the numerical identity and individuation of ordinary physical objects rests on considerations of sortal identity and spatiotemporal continuity. I believe that, within strict limits, it does. To show this, I begin by considering various senses of 'identity' and distinguishing between two kinds of numerical identity. Next, I turn to the epistemic question of the criteria by which an individual person claims to know that a certain collection of ideas as a time t_1 is one thing and is the same thing at t_2, or if you prefer, the question of how an individual person bundles ideas into ordinary objects that are identical through time. Finally, I consider whether Berkeleian ordinary objects are 'public', whether and in what sense the bundle of ideas I call a particular tree is identical with the bundle of ideas that another person identifies as the same tree.

IDENTITIES

Before considering the individuation of Berkeleian physical objects, we should draw some distinctions between senses of 'identity' and the application of those senses of 'identity' to Berkeley's philosophy. In the eighteenth century the question of the individuation of objects was posed in terms of the numerical identity of a presumptive object through time.[3] Let us call this "transtemporal numerical identity." To understand the implications of this general position for Berkeley's philosophy, we must look briefly at Berkeley's account of time and the implications of this account vis-à-vis judgments of transtemporal numerical identity.[4]

133

Not all Berkeleian objects are 'in' time, or, at least, not all Berkeleian objects are 'in' time in the same sense. While Locke holds that the succession of ideas in a mind provides one's primary notion of duration,[5] Berkeley contends that time itself is nothing but the succession of ideas in a (finite) mind. This is a point raised numerous times in the *Philosophical Commentaries* (*PC* 4, 16, 39, 118, 167, 590, 647; cf. *PC* 13)[6] and is stated explicitly in his Correspondence with Samuel Johnson: "a succession of ideas I take to constitute time and not to be only a sensible measure thereof, as Mr. Locke and others think" (*CJ* 4.2). This passage shows that ideas are the fundamental components of time and suggests that they are the basic units for measuring temporal duration. The latter point comes to the fore in *Principles* 98, where Berkeley suggests that the flow of ideas in a mind is uniform (see also *DHP* 1:192), argues that time is nothing but the succession of ideas in a mind, and concludes that "the duration of any finite spirit must be estimated by the number of ideas or actions succeeding each other in the same finite spirit" (*PHK* 98). By identifying ideas with indivisible temporal points, Berkeley attempts to avoid Zeno's paradoxes of time in the same way that positing minimum sensibles avoids Zeno's paradoxes of space (*PHK* 132–34; *NTV* 54, 62, 80–88).[7] But this solution to the paradoxes comes at a price. On Berkeley's account, time is "private" (radically subjective), "Each Person's time being measured to him by his own ideas" (*PC* 590).[8] Properly, there is no external standard of time: my times and your times are distinct.[9]

Berkeley's account of time has important consequences for discussions of identity. First, insofar as an idea is a minimum unit of time, no ideas in one's mind are subject to true judgments of transtemporal numerical identity. Since Berkeley holds that ideas are inherently individual (*PC* 318 and 366; *PHK* Intro., 12 and 15), this entails that transtemporal numerical identity is not a metaphysically necessary condition for the individuation of ideas. Second, since time is radically subjective, none of the ideas in my mind properly can be said to "occur at the same time" as any ideas in some other finite mind.[10] Nonetheless, it is at least possible that one or more of the ideas in my mind is numerically identical with one or more ideas in some other mind, and Berkeley seems to hold that all the ideas in my mind are numerically identical with some of the ideas in God's mind (see *DHP* 2:212, 3:230–31, 235; *PHK* 29).[11] Such a notion of 'numerical identity' must be independent of time. To give a name to this atemporal sense of 'numerical identity', that is, the numerical identity of ideas across minds, let us call it "transnoetic numerical identity." In the fourth section of this chapter we shall ask whether claims of transnoetic numerical identity are true with respect to any minds other than that of an individual human being and God.

Just as ideas are inherently individuals, so are minds (*PC* 318 and 666; *PHK* Intro. 12 and 15). While individual ideas (as the components of [a] time) are not subject to judgments of transtemporal numerical identity, there is a sense in which minds are subject to judgments of transtemporal numerical identity. While minds *as such* are not 'in' time, but time (a succession of ideas) is 'in' a mind, minds can be reidentified on the basis of the veracious memories one has. As Berkeley notes in his brief discussion of the Lockean account of personal identity, a veracious memory is a sufficient, but not a necessary, condition for judging that one is the same person (mind or spirit; see *PHK* 27) that formerly was conscious of a certain idea. Berkeley recognizes that identity is a transitive relation. Consequently, if at time t_3 one remembers some idea i_1 that occurred at an earlier time t_2, one is identical with the person who had i_1 at t_2, and if at t_2 one remembered an idea i_2 that had occurred at an earlier time t_1, one is also identical with the person who had i_2, even if one does not remember i_2 at time t_3 (*A* 7.8). The fact that Berkeley takes time to be 'in' a mind, and, therefore that temporal predicates are ascribable to minds only in virtue of the succession of ideas in them, entails that there are no temporal gaps in the existence of a mind. While Locke distinguishes between the discontinuous existence of a person and the continuous existence of a substance,[12] Berkeley's account of time allows him to claim that there is no time at which a person *qua* mind is nonexistent. This position is not without its own paradoxes, of course, for it entails that "resurrection follows the next moment to death" (*CJ* 4.2; *PC* 590). As we shall see below, the subjective nature of Berkeleian time implies that temporal continuity is applicable to ordinary physical objects in only a hypothetical sense.

Claims of numerical identity must be distinguished from claims of sortal or specific identity. Claims of sortal identity are based upon resemblance and, in anything but a trivial sense, presuppose numerical distinctness (see *PHK* Intro.; *PC* 192). As we shall see, claims of sortal identity are at the heart of Berkeley's account of the individuation of physical objects.

SORTAL IDENTITY AND PHYSICAL OBJECTS

Minds and ideas are Berkeley's ontological primitives (fundamental entities). Objects of both kinds are inherently individuals. Physical objects are composed of ideas (*PHK* 1), and, as such, they are ontologically secondary, that is, they are collections of ideas. Nonetheless, Berkeley seems to accept the commonsense position that physical objects are epistemically prior to ideas, that is, one claims to know that there are physical objects before one claims either that there are ideas or that physical objects are analyzed in terms of ideas.[13] In turning to the question of the individuation of ordinary objects, we must distinguish the epistemic issues of the discernibility of an ordinary object at a time and its reidentification at a later time from the ontological issue of what makes an individual ordinary object an individual object. Regarding the ontological issue, the individuality of an ordinary object partially depends on the individuality of the ideas that are 'gathered together' to form an object. Of primary ontological interest is the question of the transnoetic identity of ideas among finite minds, since, given the analysis of physical objects in terms of ideas, the truth of the presumption that there is a single, publicly observable realm of physical objects depends on the transnoetic numerial identity of ideas.[14] In this section and the next I focus on the epistemic issues of individuation and criteria for reidentification. I also raise the question of how individual ideas are bundled into ordinary objects. The issue I consider in this section is the role of sortal identity in judgments of the transtemporal numerical identity of physical objects.

Consider a claim of transtemporal numerical identity: a at t_1 is numerically identical with b at t_2. If the claim is true, or even intelligible, a must be one thing (a unit) and b must be the same thing. A judgment that a relation of numerical identity obtains presupposes the unity of its *relata*, that is, that each of the *relata* is considered as one thing,[15] and recognizing this supports the presumption that Berkeley deemed sortal identity a necessary condition for the transtemporal numerical identity of physical objects.

Berkeley discusses the notion of unity in the context of his criticisms of the primary/secondary qualities distinction. He repeatedly claims that the notions of unity and number are "creatures of the mind" and that, apart from the specification of what is to count as a unit, numerical judgments are unintelligible. Responding to Locke's contention that number is a primary quality existing as such in objects,[16] Berkeley remarks:

> number (however some may reckon it amongst the primary qualities) is nothing fixed and settled, really existing in things themselves. It is entirely the creature of the mind, considering either an idea by itself or any combination of ideas to which it gives one name, and so makes it pass for a unit. According as

the mind variously combines its ideas, the unit varies; and as the unit, so the number, which is only a collection of units, doth also vary. We call a window one, a chimney one; and yet a house in which there are many windows and many chimneys, has an equal right to be called one; and many houses go to the making of one city. In these and the like instances, it is evident the *unit* constantly relates to the particular draughts the mind makes of its idea, to which it affixes names, wherein it includes more or less, as best suits its own ends and purposes. Whatever, therefore, the mind considers as one, that is a unit. Every combination of ideas is considered as one thing by the mind, and in token thereof is marked by one name. Now, this naming and combining together of ideas is perfectly arbitrary, and done by the mind in such sort as experience shows it to be most convenient—without which our ideas had never been collected into such distinct combinations as they now are. (*NTV* 109; see also *PHK* 12, 119–20, *PC* 104, 110, 325, 545, 759, 763, 765, 767–68)

Berkeley held that number is a collection of units, but the notion of a unit is sortal-relative. It is for this reason that 'one thing' can be composed of many other things, each of which is unitary, although the kind of unit pertaining to the whole is sortally different from that pertaining to any part. By bringing objects under sortal terms it is possible to count objects as objects of a sort. Since Berkeley divided the world into kinds (assigned sortal terms) on the basis of resemblances among objects (*PHK* Intro. 11–12; *DHP* 3:245),[17] and given that both *relata* in a judgment of numerical identity are conceived as units, this *suggests* that Berkeley considered sortal identity a necessary condition for numerical identity.

Further evidence that Berkeley considered sortal identity a necessary condition for numerical identity in general and the numerical identity of physical objects in particular can be found in the *Philosophical commentaries*. There Berkeley wrote, "No identity other than perfect likeness in any individuals besides persons" (*PC* 192). At the least, this passage indicates that sortal identity pertains to physical objects. If this is Berkeley's point, then it is reasonable to contend that sortal identity is a necessary condition for the transtemporal numerical identity of physical objects. But the passage also might suggest that *only* sortal identity pertains to physical objects and that not even transnoetic numerical identity pertains to ideas. If one reads it in the second way, it implies that, contrary to common sense, no judgments of transtemporal numerical identity are true and, contrary to Berkeley's published writings, none of God's ideas are numerically identical with those in a finite mind. Given these consequences of the second reading of the passage together with the fact that, in his published writings, Berkeley is willing to allow that there is a sense in which collections of ideas constitute 'one thing' (*PHK* 1; *DHP* 3:245), it seems reasonable to suggest that he took sortal identity to be a necessary condition for the transtemporal numerical identity of physical objects.

SPATIOTEMPORAL CONTINUITY

Physical objects are composed of ideas of the several senses (*PHK* 1). We have seen that Berkeley seems to hold that a judgment of sortal identity is a necessary condition for a judgment of the transtemporal numerical identity, and therefore the individuation, of physical objects. Is spatiotemporal continuity also a necessary condition for a true judgment of the numerical identity of a physical object? One might cite entry 194 of the *Philosophical Commentaries* as providing a negative answer to that question. There Berkeley writes: "On account of my doctrine the identity of finite substances must consist in something else than continued existence, or relation to determin'd time and place of beginning to exist. The existence of our thoughts (wch being combin'd make all substances) being frequently interrupted, & they having divers beginnings, & endings" (*PC* 194). This suggests that insofar as our thoughts "of" objects are interrupted, the existence of those objects is interrupted, and, therefore, discontinuous. Hence, spatiotemporal continuity cannot pertain to physical objects.

But the evidence from the *Philosophical Commentaries* is not wholly consistent. A scant nine entries earlier Berkeley had written: "Colours in ye dark do exist really *i.e.* were there light or as soon as light comes we shall see them provides we open our eyes. & that whether we will or no" (*PC* 185a). This suggests that qualitative components of physical objects exist even when one is not oneself perceiving them. To answer the question of the spatiotemporal continuity of physical objects I examine Berkeley's discussions of 'real things'. Throughout this discussion I am concerned with 'my objects' insofar as I leave open questions of the transnoetic identity of ideas and, therefore, physical objects among finite minds. Recognizing that 'my objects' cannot properly be spatiotemporally continuous since they are discontinuous in appearance, I argue that there is a presumption of spatiotemporal continuity and that the 'time' in which my objects exist is a hypothetical time.

Berkeley's discussion of the distinction between real things and imaginary things occurs at *Principles* 29-34.[18] It is, at least in part, an account of the distinction between *ideas* of sense and *ideas* of the imagination, although it provides clues to the analysis of ordinary physical objects. Berkeley says that ideas of the sense are independent of one's own will; the mind is passive in perceiving ideas of sense (*PHK* 29). Further,

> The ideas of sense are more strong, lively, and distinct than those of the imagination; they have likewise a steadiness, order, and coherence, and are not excited at random, as those which are the effects of the human will often are, but in a regular train or series. . . . Now the set rules or established methods, wherein the mind we depend on excites in us the ideas of sense, are called *Laws of Nature*: and these we learn by experience, which teach us that such and such ideas are attended with such and such other ideas, in the ordinary course of things. (*PHK* 30)

> The ideas imprinted on the senses by the Author of Nature are called *real things*; and those excited in the imagination being less regular, vivid and constant, are more properly termed *ideas*, or *images of things*, which they copy or represent. But then our sensations, be they never so vivid and distinct, are nevertheless *ideas*, that is, they exist in the mind, or are perceived by it, as truly as the ideas of its own framing. The ideas of sense are allowed to have more reality in them, that is to be more strong, orderly, and coherent than the creatures of the mind; but this is no less argument that they exist without the mind. They are also less dependent on spirit, or thinking substance which perceives them, in that they are excited by the will of another and more powerful spirit: yet still they are *ideas*, and no *idea*, whether it be strong or faint, can exist otherwise than in a mind perceiving it. (*PHK* 33)

> What therefore becomes of sun, moon, and stars? What must we think of houses, rivers, mountains, trees, stones; nay, even of our own bodies? Are all these but so many chimeras and illusions on the fancy? To all which, and whatever else of the same sort may be objected, I answer, that by the principles premised, we are not deprived of any one thing in Nature. Whatever we see, feel, hear, or any wise conceive or under-

stand, remains as secure as ever. There is a *rerum natura*, and
the distinction between realities and chimeras retains its full
force. This is evident from *Sect.* 29, 30, and 33, where we have
shown what is meant by *real things* in opposition to *chimeras*,
or ideas of our own framing; but then they both equally exist
in the mind, and in that sense are alike *ideas* (*PHK* 34; see also
DHP 3:235, 249, *PC* 305, 535)

I quote these passages at length because it is important to recognize
that Berkeley seems to be drawing two distinctions, namely, between
ideas of sensation and ideas of the imagination, and between real things
and imaginary things. If one focuses strictly on considerations of passiv-
ity (*PHK* 29), strength, liveliness, and distinctness (*PHK* 30), these alone
will not provide the basis for deeming a collection of ideas part of the
rerum natura (realm of real objects). It is consistent with Berkeley's philosophy to suggest that God might provide one with a vision of the New
Jerusalem, that one's mind is passive during the vision, and that all the
ideas involved are strong, lively, and distinct. Hence, the ideas involved
in one's vision are ideas of sensation rather than ideas of the imagination. Nonetheless, this would not suffice to suggest that the New
Jerusalem one perceives in one's vision is part of the natural realm (a
real object), since Berkeley consistently identifies real objects with what
we ordinarily consider to be physical objects (see *DHP* 3:249, 250ff.).
While being a collection of ideas of sensation is a necessary condition
for being a real object, those ideas of sensation that constitute real
things possess "steadiness, order, and coherence," that is, they occur in
accordance with laws of nature. This implies at least that the behavior of
real things *qua* collections of ideas is in principle predictable and locatable within the larger realm of real things.[19] By considering the role of
laws of nature vis-à-vis physical objects, one can account for the common
presumption that physical objects are spatiotemporally continuous.

Consider a Berkeleian physical object. The object is real insofar as
it is composed solely of lawfully ordered ideas of sensation. Insofar as it
is discernible at a time and reidentified over time, it must be taken to
be a thing of a certain sort. So let us assume we are concerned with a
tree, specifically the tree I see outside my window. The issues we need
to consider are these. (1) How does one discern that a certain set of
ideas at a moment is a particular (individual) object (a tree)? (2) What
conditions are necessary for ascribing sortal identity to a real object?
(3) On what grounds does one ascribe transtemporal numerical identity to an object (succession of collections of ideas) and thereby individuate an ordinary object?

Berkeley does not address these issues directly, although part of his answer to (2) seems to be that the collection of ideas that I see now is similar to other collections of ideas I call trees. The crucial issue is (1), because it is only if one can discern a collection of ideas as an object (at a time) that one can either see the object as a tree (notice the resemblances between that object and others of the same sort) or reidentify that particular tree at a later time. Indeed, once we can answer (1), we shall have come some distance toward answering (2) and (3) and toward specifying the sense in which ordinary objects are spatiotemporally continuous. As a first step toward answering (1), let us consider Berkeley's discussion of creation.

In "Dialogue Three" Hylas asks Philonous whether his reduction of 'real things' to ideas is consistent with the scriptural account of creation. Philonous replies that so long as one calls the objects of our senses 'things' and one "does not attribute to them any absolute external existence, and I shall never quarrel with you for a word. The creation, therefore, I allow to have been a creation of *real* things" (*DHP* 3:251). When pressed regarding the supposed existence of sensible objects before the creation of created spirits, Philonous introduces the notion of existence relative to a finite mind (hypothetical existence). He says:

All ideas are eternally known by God, or, which is the same thing, have an eternal existence in his mind: but when things before imperceptible to creatures, are by a decree of God, made perceptible to them; then are they said to begin a relative existence, with respect to created minds. Upon reading therefore the Mosaic account of the Creation, I understand that the several parts of the world became gradually perceivable to finite spirits endowed with proper faculties; so that, whoever such were present, they were in truth perceived by them. (*DHP* 3:252)

This passage is premised on the assumption that finite nonhuman minds (angels) might have existed prior to the creation of human minds (*DHP* 3:251-52), but as Berkeley goes on to note, the sense of relative or hypothetical existence with which he is concerned is consistent with that ascribed to plants in a desert when no one is seeing them (*DHP* 3:252). Hence, as Berkeley frames the issue, creation prior to the creation of human minds is a creation of perceivable objects (ideas). The portion of the passage quoted on which I focus is the claim that "the several parts of the world become gradually perceivable to finite spirits *endowed with proper faculties*" (my emphasis). What does Berkeley mean by spirits "endowed with proper faculties"? It might mean simply that any finite spirit with functional perceptual faculties perceives ordinary objects in all their qualitative splendor. But there is a problem with such a reading. As Berkeley indicates at several points, the ideas of each of the sensible modes are distinct objects: one does not properly see and touch the same thing (*NTV* 49–50, 79, 103, 108, 111, 115, 119, 121, 127–46, 149; *PHK* 44; *DHP* 3:245; *A* 4:10–12; *TVV* 41–46). But in perceiving a rose one *takes* the objects of the several sensible modes to be constituents of *one thing*. Further, if one looks at a rose petal under a microscope, the idea one perceives is different from the petal perceived by the naked eye, yet those ideas also are taken to be continuants of the same flower (*DHP* 3:245–46). If Berkeley's allusion to "finite spirits endowed with proper faculties" was merely an allusion to the faculties of sense, it would not explain the tendency of human beings to take properly distinct objects of the several senses to constitute one thing. If Berkeley's concern with faculties is broader than this, that is, if his point is that the mind is created in such a way that it not only receives but organizes concomitant ideas to form complex ordinary physical objects, this would explain the tendency to organize experience in the way we actually organize it. But is there evidence that Berkeley so construed the role of human psychological faculties?

There is some, although admittedly inconclusive, evidence for such an organizational construal of 'faculties'. In the *Philosophical Commentaries* Berkeley claims, "There are innate ideas that is, Ideas created with us" (*PC* 649). In the early modern period the notion of an 'innate idea' was ambiguous, sometimes referring to something like an idea of an actual thing that is somehow present in the mind prior to experience, whether or not one is conscious of it, sometimes referring to a faculty or ability to form an idea.[20] While the mature Berkeley seems willing to reject innate ideas in the first sense (*S* 308), he acknowledges that the mind has innate dispositions to have certain kinds of ideas under certain circumstances (*A* 1:14; see also *PO* 25).[21] Further, since it is on the basis of a contingent relation that the ideas of the several sensible modalities are combined to form one thing,[22] and since Berkeley seems to hold that relations apart from their *relata* are actions of the mind (*PHK* 142), it seems reasonable to construe at least some of those 'faculties' with which a finite spirit is endowed as abilities or dispositions to organize experience in certain ways.[23]

If I am correct in suggesting that Berkeley explained the organization of ideas at a moment into, and thereby the discernibility of, ordinary objects on the basis of a certain psychological faculty, I have answered question (1). It is on the basis of such a faculty that the collection of ideas constituting the tree I now see from my study is one thing. In turning to (2), the question of sortal identity with respect to natural kinds, one might suggest that if one can discern that a certain collection of ideas is one thing and notice the resemblances between that collection and other collections of ideas, then one can use sortal terms and make judgments of sortal identity. But to be able to observe resemblances among momentary complex collections of ideas does not seem sufficient to allow one to ascribe sortal identity to real things. Most real things are taken to be continuants. If while sober and making observations in good light one saw what appeared to be a tree but which persisted for only a moment, one would not claim to have seen a (real) tree. As Berkeley notes in sections 31–34 of the *Principles*, real objects operate in accordance with natural laws. Natural laws are the will of the governing spirit (*PHK* 32). They give "us a sort of foresight, which enables us to regulate our actions for the benefit of life" (*PHK* 31). As Berkeley notes later in the *Principles*:

> There are certain general laws that run through the whole chain of natural effects: these are learned by the observation and study of Nature, and are by men applied as well to the framing artificial things for the use and ornament of life, as to the explaining of various phenomena: which explication consists only in shewing the conformity any particular phenomenon hath to the general Laws of Nature, or, which is the same thing, in discovering the *uniformity* there is in the production of natural effects; as will be evident to whoever shall attend to the several instances, wherein philosophers pretend to account for appearances. That there is a great and conspicuous use of these regular constant methods of working observed by the Supreme Agent, hath been shewn in *Sect.* 31. And it is no less visible, that a particular size, figure, motion and disposition of parts are necessary, though not absolutely to the producing any effect, yet to the producing it according to the standing mechanical Laws of Nature. (*PHK* 62)

> ideas are not any how and at random produced, there being a certain order and connexion between them, like to that of cause and effect: there are also several combinations of them, made in a very regular and artificial manner, which seem like so many instruments in the hand of Nature, that being as it were behind the scenes, have a secret operation in producing

those appearances which are seen on the theatre of the world, being themselves discernible only to the curious eye of the philosopher. But since one idea cannot be the cause of another, to what purpose is that connexion? And since those instruments, being barely *inefficacious perceptions* in the mind, are not subservient to the production of natural effects; it is demanded why they are made, or, in other words, what reason can be assigned why God should make us, upon a close inspection into his works, behold so great variety of ideas, so artfully laid together, and so much according to rule; it not being credible, that he would be at the expense (if one may so speak) of all that art and regularity to no purpose? (*PHK* 64)

Ideas in the *rerum natura* occur in accordance with divinely instituted laws. It is because ideas *qua* real things are lawfully ordered that, after a certain amount of experience, one can make predictions regarding, for example, those ideas of touch one can perceive concomitantly with certain visual ideas of a tree. One might discover that one can predict with considerable certainty that if one sees one's hand touching the trunk or branches of a tree, one will at the same time have a certain kind of tactile sensation. Indeed, if one did not have the appropriate kind of tactile sensation, one would conclude that it is not a real tree. For example, if one touched the branch of a Christmas tree and had the sort of tactile sensations one has when touching smooth, twisted wires, rather than the sort of tactile sensations one has when touching tree bark, one would conclude that the tree is artificial. It is the presumptive fact that God causes ideas of sensation in a regular order, that is, that there are laws of nature, which explains one's belief that 'real things' are composed of qualities perceivable by distinct senses and that they persist through time.

Since real things are composed of ideas of the several senses and are presumed to exist through time, the description of a natural kind involves not only resemblance claims regarding the ideas of a particular sense that constitute momentary phases of a thing of that kind; it also involves laws of nature specifying the kinds of ideas of the other senses that, under specifiable conditions, are perceived concomitantly with, for example, the ideas of sight. Further, natural objects 'behave' in characteristic ways. Hence, there are sets of natural laws that express the characteristic development of a thing of a kind and which explain any deviation from that characteristic development. I suggest that the Berkeleian notion of sortal identity as it pertains to natural kinds (and, *mutatis mutandis*, to artifacts) is to be understood in terms of the natural laws that 'govern' the composition and changes in those objects. If this is correct, then I have answered (2): real things are divided into sorts on the basis of natural laws. The tree I now see outside my window is a collection of ideas, and its 'behavior' is governed by natural laws, that is, insofar as it is a real thing persisting through time one can predict the kinds of ideas that will be bundled together to form the object.

Having answered (2), I am on my way to answering (3), the question of the criteria by which individual objects are reidentified through time. Consider the tree I see outside my window. I look at it for several moments, observing no change. Why do I claim that the tree I perceive now is the same tree I perceived several moments ago? It has behaved in the way one expects trees to behave. The ordinary development of a tree proceeds very slowly: unless acted upon by a natural force such as lightning, one would not expect to notice a difference in the tree over a period of a few moments. Once planted, trees do not move except by extraordinary means, and the tree appears to be in the same place it was several moments ago: it appears to be in the same position relative to the street and the stately maple across the street. Does this make a difference? It seems to. At one point in the *Philosophical Commentaries* Berkeley notes that the "Identity of Ideas may be taken in a Double sense either as including or excluding Identity of Circumstances, such as time, place, etc." (*PC* 568). If one remembers Berkeley's remark that "No identity other than perfect likeness in any individuals besides persons" (*PC* 192), the remark in entry *PC* 568 suggests that one reidentifies an object by means of its circumstances, for example, its spatial location. And, of course, it is well within the Lockean tradition to suggest that it is on the basis of "the circumstances of Time, and Place" that "determine them [objects] to this or that particular Existence."[24] Since the only way one can locate an extended object is relative to some other extended object (*PHK* 110–17), the only way to locate the tree I see from my window is relative to some other object. Although I might single out a certain collection of ideas at a moment that I call "the tree outside my window" and describe an exactly similar collection of ideas at a different moment in the same way, this alone will not explain my tendency to judge that the tree I see now is identical with the tree I saw a few moments ago. Such a judgment rests upon numerous resemblances in my visual field from moment to moment. At each moment I see (1) the edge of a window frame, (2) a tree outside of and to the right of the window frame, (3) a street, and (4) a maple tree on the far side of the street. Each of the objects in my present visual field resembles those of a moment ago, as do the spatial relations among the visual objects in my momentary visual fields.[25] It seems that it is on the basis of the resemblances among the complex tree-ideas I see from moment to moment in conjunction with the resemblances of other complex ideas (e.g. maple-tree-ideas, street-ideas, window frame-ideas) that retain the same relative location vis-à-vis my tree that I can identify successive sets of tree-ideas as the tree I see outside my window. Indeed, it seems that it is primarily on the basis of the exact similarity of appearance of spatial relations that one comes to recognize natural laws such as, "Except under extraordinary circumstances, trees once planted (or buildings, or anything whose location becomes a 'fixed' point of reference) do not change location."

Thus, with respect to 'fixed' ordinary objects, it seems that spatial continuity in the sense of retention of position relative to other 'fixed' objects is a necessary condition for judgments of the transtemporal numerical identity and individuation of objects. And with the appropriate sortal differences, including differences with respect to natural laws, the same considerations hold with respect to 'nonfixed' objects. If on two days I perceive a collection of ideas that I call a horse-drawn coach, a necessary condition for my judgments that I saw the same coach on the second day that I saw on the first would be an exact or, at least, a great similarity of the ideas. A sufficient condition would be tracing the relative position of the coach through that period of time, that is, actually perceiving collections of ideas (partially) constituting the coach throughout that period.[26] Thus, it seems that considerations of sortal identity and spatiotemporal continuity are sufficient conditions for judgments of the individuality of a Berkeleian ordinary physical object.

There are several things to notice here. First, I am concerned with the epistemic issue of the *judgment* of the individuality of an ordinary physical object. I reconstruct the way in which Berkeley would account for the commonsense judgment. But even if I have shown that judgments of individuality are consistent with presumptions of sortal identity and spatiotemporal continuity, considerations of the temporal continuity of ordinary objects properly violate Berkeley's account of time. Since Berkeleian time is 'private', that is, there are as many 'times' as there are finite minds, and since the absence of successive ideas is the absence of times, my *commonsense* presumption that ordinary objects are temporally continuous requires that they exist at times that I cannot properly deem times at all, for example, when I am in a deep sleep (when there is no succession of ideas in my mind).[27] This problem reflects a tension between Berkeley's account of time and the common account of a natural law. Natural laws of succession require a 'public' notion of time. Assume it is a natural law that acorns grow into oak trees; that is, whenever an acorn is planted in the ground it first sprouts, then becomes a sapling, then becomes an adult tree.[28] If this is a natural law, then it pertains to all oaks, whether or not they are perceived by a finite mind, and, hence, whether or not they are in anyone's time. But the law employs temporal predicates, and just as real objects that are unperceived by finite minds possess a relative or hypothetical existence (*DHP* 3:252), they also must exist in a hypothetical time: it is the succession of ideas that one would perceive if one continuously perceived, for example, the entire development of an oak tree from the sprouting of the acorn to the demise and, perhaps, the rotting away of the (now) ancient fallen oak.[29]

Second, given Berkeley's account of time, it is implausible to contend that spatiotemporal continuity is a metaphysically necessary condition for the existence of Berkeleian physical objects, and I have merely contended that it is an epistemically necessary condition for an individual's judgment that a certain set of collections of ideas is an individual.

Finally, while Berkeley claims that real things must be composed solely of ideas of sensation (see *PHK* 29–34, 41, 90; *DHP* 3:249), compositional considerations are not sufficient to explain the individuation of physical objects. It seems that Berkeleian real objects are merely epistemic creations: they are things formed by judgment. Nor should one find that surprising. Physical objects are ontologically secondary, and if the individuation of physical objects is strictly a function of judgment, this would have no serious ontological consequences.[30] If all human minds organize experience in approximately the same way, and Berkeley seems to have held that they do (see *A* 1:14, 7:4–5), there would be at least a very general agreement regarding the nature and existence of physical objects. If the nature and individuality of physical objects is a matter of convention insofar as it rests upon the tendencies of human beings to organize similar experience in similar ways,[31] one can understand why Berkeley deemed "fruitless the Distinction twixt real & nominal Essences" (*PC* 536): all essences are fundamentally nominal.[32]

Before concluding, I consider one more issue, namely, whether there is something more than a conventional sense in which finite spirits can claim to see "the same thing." To answer this question, I ask whether there is evidence for the transnoetic numerical identity of ideas among finite spirits.

THE PUBLICITY OF PHYSICAL OBJECTS

If one can claim that the physical objects perceived by distinct finite spirits are numerically identical in more than a conventional sense, then there must be transnoetic numerical identity of some of the ideas perceived by finite spirits. Does Berkeley claim that there is such identity? The answer seems to be negative, although his philosophical principles do not in principle preclude the transnoetic numerical identity of ideas.[33] In the "Third Dialogue," Hylas raises the issue of the transnoetic numerical identity of ideas. Hylas asks, "But the same idea which is in my mind, cannot be in yours, or in any other mind. Doth it not therefore follow from your principles, that no two can see the same thing? And is not this highly absurd?" (*DHP* 3:247). Philonous replies:

> If the term *same* be taken in the vulgar acceptation, it is certain (and not at all repugnant to the principles I maintain) that different persons may perceive the same thing; or the same thing or idea exist in different minds. Words are of arbitrary imposition; and since men are used to apply the word *same* where no distinction or variety is perceived, and I do not pretend to alter their perceptions, it follows, that as men have said before, *several saw the same thing*, so they may upon like occasions still continue to use the same phrase, without any deviation either from propriety of language, or the truth of things. But if the term *same* be used in the acceptation of philosophers, who pretend to an abstracted notion of identity, then according to their sundry definitions of this notion (for it is not yet agreed wherein that philosophical identity consists), it may or may not be possible for diverse persons to perceive the same thing. But whether philosophers shall think fit to call a thing the *same* or not, is, I conceive, of small importance. Let us suppose several men together, all endued with the same faculties, and consequently affected in like sort by their senses, who had yet never known language; they would without question agree in their perceptions. Though perhaps, when they came to the use of speech, some regarding the uniformness of what was perceived, might call it the *same* thing: others especially regarding the diversity of persons who perceived, might choose the denomination of different things. But who sees not that all the dispute is about a word? to wit, whether what is perceived by different persons, may yet have the term *same* applied to it? Or suppose a house, whose walls or outward shell remaining unaltered, the chambers are all pulled down, and new ones built in their place; and that you should call this the *same*, and I should say it was not the *same* house: would we not for all this perfectly agree in our thoughts of the house,

considered in it self? and would not all the difference consist in a sound? If you should say, we differed in our notions; for that you superadded to your idea of the house the simple abstracted idea of identity whereas, I did not; I would tell you I know not what you mean by that *abstracted idea of identity*; and should desire you to look into our own thoughts, and be sure you understood your self—Why so silent, Hylas? Are you not yet satisfied, men may dispute about identity and diversity, without any real difference in their thoughts and opinions, abstracted from names? (*DHP* 3:247–48)

Berkeley leaves open the question of the transnoetic numerical identity of ideas. Philonous does not reply to Hylas's contention that all the ideas in two finite minds are numerically distinct. He remarks merely that whether or not two persons see 'the same thing' depends on what one means by 'the same': the vulgar would claim that whoever looks out my window will see the same tree I see, while philosophers might not. Insofar as Philonous alludes to a positive notion of identity, he is concerned with sortal identity: "men are used to apply the word *same* where no distinction or varity is perceived." Following the vulgar, human beings see the same thing insofar as there is a close resemblance between the ideas human beings have when they claim to see 'the same' object. But, of course, and though it is not mentioned here, there also are differences due to the perspectives from which several persons 'perceive the same object'. Further, insofar as one is concerned with perceiving a thing of a sort, different perceivers will tend to gather more or fewer ideas together in perceiving an object of a kind (and explicating a sortal term (*PHK* 49]) due to the amount and kinds of experiences they have had. A botanist or a forester will 'see more' in the 'same' tree I see from my window insofar as he or she will see it as a thing having a certain kind of biological structure. If Berkeley rejected the nominal/real essence distinction in favor of nominal essences (*PC* 536), and if my remarks on how the mind unifies diverse ideas into ordinary objects are correct, then Berkeley would seem committed to the claim that the ordinary objects we perceive differ from one another at least to the extent that they have different (nominal) essences: what kinds of ideas are grouped together into forming what one takes to be a unitary thing of a kind differs with one's experience, and, therefore, the composition of that bundle of ideas I call the tree outside my window might differ 'essentially' from that of a botanist, on the one hand, and that of one of my young children, on the other, even though we all would claim to see the same tree. Nonetheless, as Locke grants regarding nominal essences of a thing of kind, the intersubjective similarities are sufficient for purposes of communication.

But this leaves open the question of the transnoetic numerical identity of some of the ideas composing 'my tree' and those composing 'your tree' when we claim to see the same tree. Are all Berkeleian ideas private, or public only insofar as they are also perceived by God, as many commentators suggest?[34] Perhaps. While the passage under consideration does not deny the transnoetic numerical identity of ideas, the sole reason it provides for claiming numerical identity is that "the vulgar speak that way." Nor should it be surprising that Berkeley provided no direct answer to the question. His argument for the *existence* of finite minds shows that the existence of finite minds other than one's own is probable, but by no means certain (*PHK* 145). And even if it were certain, it is unclear how one could know that ideas in two minds are numerically, rather than merely qualitatively identical. Indeed, with anything short of a 'God's-eye-view', there are no firm grounds for claiming the transnoetic *qualitative* identity of ideas. Nonetheless, Berkeley might well have said that even if the ideas in finite minds are numerically distinct, the presumption that ideas are similar from mind to mind is "sufficient for discourse, and serve[s] all our purposes in company, in the pulpit, on the theatre, and in the schools."[35]

CONCLUSIONS

In this chapter I have examined Berkeley's account of the individuation of ordinary physical objects. I have argued that his discussion of unity supports the contention that sortal identity is a necessary condition for the transtemporal numerical identity of physical objects. I also argued that although there is a tension between Berkeley's discussions of time and laws of nature, it is not unreasonable to suggest that the *presumption* of spatiotemporal continuity plays a significant role in the individuation of a physical object by a finite mind. In the case of the transnoetic numerical identity and individuation of physical objects, Berkeley seems content to suggest it is purely a matter of convention.[36]

NOTES

    1. See P. F. Strawson, *Individuals: An Essay in Descriptive Metaphysics* (Garden City, N.Y.: Doubleday Anchor Books, 1959), pp. 10–19; David Wiggins,

Daniel Flage 151

Identity and Spatio-Temporal Continuity (Oxford: Basil Blackwell, 1967); Eli Hirsch, *The Concept of Identity* (Oxford and New York: Oxford University Press, 1982); D. W. Hamlyn, *Metaphysics* (Cambridge: Cambridge University Press, 1984), pp. 69–75; but cf. Panayot Butchvarov, *Being Qua Being: A Theory of Identity, Existence, and Predication* (Bloomington and London: Indiana University Press, 1979), pp. 169–76. Further, even if one argues against the metaphysical importance of spatiotemporal contiguity, this does not entail that considerations of spatiotemporal contiguity are epistemically unimportant. See Jorge J. E. Gracia, *Individuality: An Essay on the Foundations of Metaphysics* (Albany: State University of New York Press, 1988), pp. 150–55, 184–91.

2. John Locke, *An Essay concerning Human Understanding*, ed. P. H. Nidditch (Oxford: Clarendon Press, 1975), 1.27.3, p. 330; David Hume, *A Treatise of Human Nature*, ed. L. A. Selby-Bigge, 2d rev. ed. by P. H. Nidditch (Oxford: Clarendon Press, 1978), p. 201. I leave open the question whether Locke's and Hume's concerns with the principle of individuation were primarily metaphysical or epistemological.

3. See Locke, *Essay* 1.27; Hume, *Treatise*, pp. 201, 219–21, 253–54. A reasonable way to read Locke's chapter on identity is as an examination of the necessary and sufficient conditions for the transtemporal numerical identity of different kinds of objects.

4. My objective is to state the tenets of Berkeley's theory of time; it is not my objective to evaluate that theory critically. For critical discussions and evaluations of Berkeley's account of time, see I. C. Tipton, *Berkeley: The Philosophy of Immaterialism* (London: Methuen, 1974), pp. 273–77; George Pitcher, *Berkeley*, "The Arguments of the Philosophers" (London: Routledge and Kegan Paul, 1977), pp. 206–11; A. C. Grayling, *Berkeley: The Central Arguments* (La Salle: Open Court, 1986), pp. 174–83.

5. Locke, *Essay*, 2.24.3–4, see also 2.24.21. As Tipton notes, the role Locke assigns to the succession of ideas is compatible with a theory of absolute time. See Tipton, *Berkeley*, p. 273.

6. References to Berkeley's works are to *The Works of George Berkeley, Bishop of Cloyne*, ed. A. A. Luce and T. E. Jessop, 9 vols. (London: Thomas Nelson and Sons, 1948–57), and are made parenthetically within the text of the paper. References to the *Philosophical Commentaries* (*PC*) are made by entry: references to *An Essay Towards a New Theory of Vision* (*NTV*), *Treatise concerning the Principles of Human Knowledge* (*PHK*), the *Alciphron* (*A*), *The Theory of Vision or Visual Language Shewing the Immediate Presence and Providence of a Deity Vindicated and Explained* (*TVV*), and *Passive Obedience* (*PO*) are made by section; references to the *Correspondence with Johnson* (*CJ*) are made by letter and section; and references to the *Three Dialogues between Hylas and Philonous* (*DHP*) are made by dialogue and page in volume 2 of the *Works*.

7. See also Hirsch, *The Concept of Identity*, pp. 156–62. Berkeley recognized, however, that his account raised its own puzzles and paradoxes. See *CJ* 4.2.

8. This passage might be open to a less radical interpretation, namely, that *as far as anyone knows* the train of ideas in one's own mind is numerically distinct from the train of ideas in anyone else's mind, and although each person's train of ideas is taken as the measure of time, the possibility that two minds share a numerically identical idea implies that it is at least possible that ideas in distinct minds can 'occur at the same time'. While we shall see below that Berkeley considered it logically possible for distinct minds to share numerically identical ideas, it is doubtful that he would allow that, in fact, ideas in distinct minds can 'occur at the same time'. It would not be sufficient to claim that an idea in two distinct minds 'occurs at the same time' if it were merely the case that two minds had a particular idea i_1, for it is the position of a particular idea relative to all other ideas in a mind that determines its temporal position. Hence, if two minds had some particular idea i_1, that idea could be said to 'occur at the same time' in both minds only if all the ideas in both minds were numerically identical and occurred in the same order. While such a state of affairs might be logically possible, Berkeley would seem to hold that, as a matter of fact, no two finite minds have all the same ideas occurring in the same order. Such a conclusion seems to follow from the laws of perspective (cf. the "First Dialogue").

9. This does not imply, however, that there is no conventional measure of time. Clocks still would be as reliable as ever, functioning in accordance with the laws of nature, and, consequently, Berkeley could suggest at *PHK* 97 that his servant would know what it meant to meet him somewhere at a certain time. As we shall see below, however, there is a tension between the account of time and common presumptions regarding laws of nature.

10. Since there is no succession of ideas in God's mind, God is atemporal (see *CJ* 4.2), and, consequently, there is no ultimate ontological basis for claims that ideas occur 'at the same time'.

11. See also Berkeley's recently discovered "Summary" of his metaphysics, quoted in David Berman, "Berkeley's Quad: The Question of Numerical Identity," *Idealistic Studies* 16 (1986): 41–42.

12. Locke, *Essay* 2.27.10.

13. On epistemic priority, see Hirsch, *The Concept of Identity*, 202–10.

14. Short of the transnoetic numerical identity of at least some ideas constituting a physical object there would seem to be no ontological grounds for claiming a numerical identity of complex objects perceived by different minds. I consider the question of transnoetic numerical identity in the final section of this chapter.

15. Hume recognized this fact but conflated the notions of unity and simplicity. See Hume, *Treatise*, p. 221; see also Hirsch, *The Concept of Identity*, pp. 236–63.

16. Locke, *Essay* 2.8.13, 2.8.17, see also 2.16.1.

17. Berkeley does not use the term 'resemblance' in his discussion of the division of the world into sorts, but since Berkeley recognized that there are "likenesses" among ideas (*PHK* 8), since resemblance plays a principal role in Locke's account of abstraction (see *Essay* 3.3.7–8), and since it is strictly Locke's account of the formation of an abstract idea that is the object of Berkeley's criticisms, it is reasonable to suggest that resemblance or, since physical objects are composed of ideas derived from several senses (*NTV* 108; *DHP* 3:245), a set of resemblances is the basis for the division of the world into sorts.

18. I am not interested in the arguments for the existence of God found in these passages. See Jonathan Bennett, *Locke, Berkeley, Hume: Central Themes* (Oxford: Clarendon Press, 1971), pp. 165–72; Jonathan Dancy, *Berkeley: An Introduction* (Oxford: Basil Blackwell, 1987), pp. 43ff.; David R. Raynor, "Berkeley's Ontology," *Dialogue* 26 (1987): 611–20.

19. Certain laws of nature would be in effect even in the case of a vision of the New Jerusalem; for example, there might be states of the eye or the brain that characteristically occur when having normal perceptual states. Nonetheless, it would seem that the New Jerusalem would not count as a real thing since it would not be lawfully related to other things constituting the natural realm. This presumes that the natural realm, the realm of real objects, and the realm of physical objects are identical. If my presumption is incorrect and one's idea of the New Jerusalem is, in some sense, a 'real thing', this will not affect the remainder of my discussion of physical object identity and individuation.

20. Descartes seems to use 'innate idea' in the latter sense in his *Notes Against a Programme (Comments on a Certain Broadsheet)*. See René Descartes, *Comments on a Certain Broadsheet*, in *The Philosophical Writings of Descartes*, trans. John Cottingham, Robert Stoothoff, and Duggald Murdoch, 2 vols. (Cambridge: Cambridge University Press, 1985), 2:303–4, 309; see also A. (B.) C., *The Theory of Rationale of Ideas, in a Letter to a Friend* (London: Thomas Howlett, 1727), pp. 13–14.

21. It is well within the empiricist tradition to contend that there are powers or dispositions to form ideas that are 'innate' in the mind. Even Locke made such a presumption in introducing the notion of a secondary quality. See Locke, *Essay* 2.8.8, 2.8.13; see also *Essay* 1.2.5.

22. Berkeley denied that there are necessary connections among ideas. See *PC* 884; *NTV* 45, 58, 62, 104; *PHK* 31; *A* 4:7; *TVV* 42.

23. See my *Berkeley's Doctrine of Notions: A Reconstruction Based on His Theory of Meaning* (London: Croom Helm, 1987), pp. 154–67. In his general discussion of identity, Eli Hirsch recently argues that the best explanation of the tendency to organize experience into units (objects) is on the basis of certain innate tendencies. See Hirsch, *The Concept of Identity*, Chapter 8.

24. Locke, *Essay*, 3.3.6.

25. It seems proper to claim that spatial relations can resemble one another, even if the relation itself is nothing more than an act of judgment. See my *Berkeley's Doctrine of Notions*, pp. 154–67.

26. There are conditions under which one actually perceiving the coach for an extended period would deny that exact similarity is a necessary condition for a judgment of numerical identity. If, for example, the black coach I saw at the beginning of my observation were taken into a shop, painted red, and had a different crest placed on its side, I would claim it was the same coach throughout the period, even though the similarity is less than exact.

27. Since God is atemporal insofar as there is no *succession* of ideas in God's mind (*CJ* 4.2), one cannot appeal to 'divine time' to set things right.

28. This is strictly for purposes of illustration, since, presumably, more acorns provide nourishment for squirrels or rot in the ground than develop into oaks.

29. This explains why, as Bennett has noticed, Berkeley has little concern with continuity. See Bennett, *Locke, Berkeley, Hume*, pp. 172–80.

30. This would seem to be a gross violation of common sense, and Berkeley claims to be a defender of common sense. But Berkeley's alliances with common sense (precritical presumptions about the world) are rather selective. While Berkeley claims that one perceives physical objects immediately in virtue of the fact that objects are composed of ideas and ideas are perceived immediately, he certainly parts with common sense in holding that physical objects are ontologically secondary. It would seem to be a general tenet of one's precritical common sense that, if anything exists, physical objects do.

31. In claiming that questions regarding the nature and individuation of objects is conventional, I mean *only* that common agreement on these issues arises due to the (unconscious) disposition in human beings to organize experience in approximately the same ways. I *do not* want to suggest that this organization is, in any sense, a matter of choice. See *PC* 185a.

32. Compare Berkeley's explication of the word 'die' (*PHK* 49).

33. See George S. Pappas, "Berkeley, Perception, and Common Sense," in *Berkeley: Critical and Interpretive Essays*, ed. Colin Turbayne (Minneapolis: University of Minnesota Press, 1982), p. 9.

34. See Pitcher, *Berkeley*, pp. 147–48; Grayling, *Berkeley*, p. 26.

35. Hume, *Treatise*, p. 603.

36. I wish to thank A. P. Martinich, Ronald J. Glass, and the editors of this volume for their helpful comments on earlier versions of this chapter.

Substance and Self in Locke and Hume

Fred Wilson

bjects, as we perceive them, are complex entities. Thus, I now perceive two objects: a red disc and a green disc. I recognize them as two, that is, distinguish one from the other, identifying them as different. But the two are not simply different, not simply two. They are rather, each of them, of a certain kind, or kinds. Thus, when I distinguish an object, there are, as it were, two parts to this act. There is, first, an identification of a sortal element, which determines the kind to which the object belongs, and, second, an indexical element, which identifies the particular object that in the context is being identified. As Aristotle put it, an individual object is a *this such*.[1] Given the traditional criterion of identity,

$$x = y : \longleftrightarrow : (f) (fx \longleftrightarrow fy),$$

where '$\rightarrow$' represents the material conditional and '$\longleftrightarrow$' the material biconditional, every individual will be a certain individual sort or *nature* or *essence*, or, more precisely, to distinguish this from the "real essences" that Aristotle also talked about, every individual will have a *definitional essence*.[2] This definitional essence is the sum of the properties, relational and nonrelational, which may truly be predicated of the object. The *such* in a *this such* is, ultimately, the definitional essence of the individual. The aspect—I speak as neutrally as possible—of a *this such* that is the *this* is that which makes the object the individual that it is; however one analyzes it, the *this* is that which individuates. At the same time, however, the *this* also accounts for the unity of the object. For the properties that form the definitional essence of the object are part of that essence only by virtue of being jointly individuated by the *this*. If the *this* individuates, it also unifies by tying the various properties together to form the complex that is the object.

Many objects endure through time. For such objects there will be features of the definitional essence such that we can identify the *this such now* with the *this such then*. For objects that endure through time,

155

there are features of the *such* that allow for reidentification of the object as *the same*. Thus, if the *this* has a unifying function, so too does the *such*, at least for those objects that endure through time.

Among the objects with which we are familiar are persons. Persons are individuals. But like all objects, they are also natured. Each person has a certain configuration of traits, that is, a configuration of passions, abilities, sentiments, and temperaments, dispositionally analyzed. This configuration is unique and constitutes, as we say, the person's character.[3] This unique character forms the nature of the individual; a person's name picks him or her out not only as an individual but also as having a certain character. This linkage of the individuality and the character of a person was noted by Hume when he pointed out that, for socialized persons, "our reputation, our character, our name are considerations of vast weight and importance" (T, p. 316).[4]

In the first instance a person's character determines his or her response to events and experiences; in the first instance it is one's character that determines one's responses to social and environmental conditions, rather than those conditions determining one's character.

But persons can also grow and develop. They can not only respond *in* character to events in their environment but their characters can themselves change in response to those events. Some persons, moreover, have the capacity to change their own characters; there can be *self-development*.[5] Those who can do the latter have a special character trait, that of being able to self-consciously monitor their own selves and change themselves in ways that they self-consciously determine. In this way, at least some persons are individuals who are responsible for themselves. They are not merely the subjects of desires, of passions, of mental and physical abilities, and of traits of character. They are also beings who are able to reflectively monitor themselves; they are able to pose the de jure question about whether the self they discover themselves to be is the sort of being they *ought* to be; and if they are not, they are able to modify their characters to conform to the standard that this moral desire sets for them. In Heidegger's terms, man is "das Seiende, dem es in seinem Sein um dieses selbst geht,"[6] that is, a person is the sort of individual for whom the question arises about what kind of being he or she is going to realize. Or, as Frankfurt has put it, there is in persons a "capacity for reflective self-evaluation . . . manifest in the formation of second-order desires," that is, desires to the effect that we want to be moved by certain desires, and in the formation of "second-order volitions," volitions determining which first-order desires move one to action.[7] A person is thus a self-determining individual, changing but unified as one person throughout the process of change.

This concept of a person is, as Amélie Rorty has put it, the idea of "a unified centre of choice and action, the unit of legal and theological responsibility." This concept of a person is central to Christian belief. Again as Rorty puts it, "If judgment summarizes a life, as it does in the Christian drama, then that life must have a unified location."[8] This concept had been wed for the medieval philosophers to the doctrine of substance that they inherited from the ancient world. This coupling of the two was effected by Boethius, who held that *persona . . . est naturae rationabilis indiuidua substantia*: a person is the individual substance of a rational nature.[9]

Hume accepts this picture of the self or person as a natured and unified individual, determined to be the sort of person he is by his own reflective self-consciousness. At the same time he rejects the substantialist account of the self that had been inherited by the modern world from the medieval world by way of Descartes. The substantialist tradition holds that each substance has a real essence, and this provides the criteria for reidentification of the substance over time. But Hume, following Locke, rejects this doctrine of real essences. Both bodies and persons are natured objects, but their unity and the criteria for identity over time derive neither from substances nor real essences. Hume, again following Locke, offers a very different account of the unity of bodies and of persons. In fact, in each case he argues that there is a conventional component which, in the case of persons is due to the concept of a person being, in Locke's terminology, a 'forensic' notion.

However, Hume's own picture of the self leaves him curiously dissatisfied. He is reasonably satisfied with his account of causation. He is reasonably satisfied with his account of body. But when it comes to the self, he is, as he records in the famous "Appendix" to the *Treatise*, unable to arrive at a conclusion that is philosophically satisfactory. The problem, in its basic outline, is clear enough. What Hume argues is that the self is a "bundle or collection of different perceptions which succeed one another with an inconceivable rapidity and are in a perpetual flux and motion" (T, p. 252). This seems incompatible with the idea that the self is a unity, and that that unity derives from a center of reflective self-consciousness. Unable to resolve the difficulty he is left dissatisfied.

Unlike many of his critics, however, Hume does not take this seemingly unresolvable inconsistency as a *reductio* of his position; more reasonably than those critics, he takes it instead as a problem that remains to be solved. His attitude is that one does not abandon a well-defended position at the least difficulty; rather, one puts it aside in the hope that eventually it will prove to be solvable. Or, perhaps, since this is philosophy, dissolvable.

The aim of this chapter is to examine in detail Hume's account of the self, and to attempt to resolve the problems that Hume himself discovered. Hume's account depends crucially upon his nonsubstantialist account of the identity of body, which has its origins in Locke, and upon Locke's suggestion that the concept of a person is a 'forensic' notion. For these reasons it will prove useful to begin with Locke in each case. We will argue, following John Stuart Mill, that if certain shortcomings in Hume's (and Locke's) notion of psychological analysis are removed, then the problems that Hume raised about his account of the self can be overcome. The result will be a consistently defensible view of the self. As will turn out, we shall conclude specifically that, upon this consistent Humean account, the concept of a person and of personal identity is determined by the utility it has in defining what it is to be a role player in our system of social conventions and artificial virtues.

MATERIAL SUBSTANCE FROM LOCKE TO HUME

The Aristotelian tradition grounded the difference between laws and accidental generalities in the real essences of things. These real essences are the natures of the substances into which ordinary things are analyzed. The real essences or natures are, according to the tradition, known either by abstraction (Aristotle) or by innate ideas (Plato, Descartes). Locke does not deny this tradition on its ontological side, but he does deny its epistemology: on the basis of an appeal to the empiricist's Principle of Acquaintance, Locke, in contrast to both Aristotle and Descartes, denies that we have any knowledge of the real essences of things; rather, all that we can do rationally is make the suppositions that substances (substrata) and real essences exist. The supposition that substrata exist is based on the principle, that Locke claims we know a priori, that properties must inhere in substances. And the supposition that real essences exist is based on the principle, which Locke also claims we know a priori, that every event has a cause, where the idea of cause involves the idea of necessary connection. This latter idea of necessary connection is derived from our awareness of it in the crucial case of volition. But we are aware of it in no other case; for other qualities, all that we are aware of is constant conjunction, with no necessary connection that would prevent us from supposing that one of the conjoined properties exists and the other does not. For this reason we should for our practical purposes ignore the whole issue of real essences and get on with the scientific task of exploring the matter-of-fact regularities that we observe among the sensible impressions of things.[10]

It is the empiricist thrust of Locke that Hume takes up and develops, criticizing both the notion of real essences and that of substances as substrata, and moving even further than Locke from the substance tradition.

Once the claim that we are acquainted with real essences was abandoned, philosophers were forced to find another basis for our ordinary distinction between laws and accidental generalities. And for those who followed Locke in insisting that philosophy must adopt the empirical Newtonian method, the criterion had to be one rooted in our ordinary sensible experience of things. This approach to laws and causation would be required even if one allowed, as Locke did, that even though we cannot know specifically what those essences or powers are, we can nonetheless infer *that* there are such real essences in things. But so long as one thought one could infer the existence of real essences, and also of substances, then there was no need to rethink the traditional account of predication and the traditional account of ordinary material objects. It might be necessary to supplement that account in order to show how we manage to cope with the world that we experience even though we have no knowledge of certain entities that are crucial for determining what occurs in it. These criteria for lawfulness and for real powers, and for predication, will be second-best, but they are necessary *faut de mieux*. But so long as the basic ideas of substance and real essence or power are held to be intelligible, these empirical criteria will continue to be reckoned second-best, and it will never be thought that any fundamental revision of our metaphysics of bodies will be required. When Hume went on to attack what Locke was still defending—though also declaring largely irrelevant—he was forced to undertake just this rethinking, and, in fact, to recharacterize as fundamental what earlier thinkers had thought of as "second-best."[11]

There are two aspects to Hume's critique. One deals with our idea of an objective unanalyzable real power or necessary connection; the other, with the causal principles that Locke thought could be known to be true a priori.

With respect to the idea of a real power, Hume accepts the Lockean critique of innate ideas (T, p. 160), thus eliminating the source that Henry More, and Descartes before him, had thought they had available when they claimed to have the idea of an objective real essence. While Locke does not attempt to ground the idea in perceptual experience, he does claim to find its source in volition; when we exercise our will we experience a necessary tie between cause and effect. Hume treats this case in detail in Book II, Part iii, and Book III, Part i of the *Treatise*,[12] and, especially in the *Appendix*, where he argues, on the basis of the principle that what is distinguishable is separable, that if a volition and the action that it causes are indeed separable in thought, then there is no perceivable necessary connection between them (T, pp. 632–33).

With respect to the second aspect, Hume applies the same distinguishability/separability principle to establish that there are no causal principles that can be known a priori. While Hume does not dispute the truth of the principle that every event has a cause (T, p. 82), he does argue that the principle is not self-evidently true; its truth is, rather, a matter of fact, a principle that we discover in our experience to be, so far as we can tell, true. The principle could not be self-evidently true because for any event it is always possible to conceive that it exists when other events do not (T, pp. 79–80).

With the elimination of real essence and necessary connection, the whole pattern of explanation shifts: no longer is explanation to be conceived in terms of unobserved real essences; it rather consists in subsumption under matter-of-fact generalities, those generalities that Locke points out we must in any case rely upon for the inferences that we must all make as we go about pursuing our this-worldly purposes, including the pursuit of matter-of-fact knowledge.

The implication of this is that the very concept of reason itself has undergone a radical change. In the substance tradition of Aristotle, reason is the capacity to grasp the reasons of things, that is, the forms or natures that explain why things are as they are. But once this concept of explanation in terms of simple natures has been rejected and subsequently replaced by the notion that explanation consists in showing that the fact to be explained is an instance of a regular pattern, it follows that *reason is the capacity to come to know regular patterns*. And, in turn, since all that we are acquainted with are individuals, not the patterns as such, reason consists in the capacity to infer from observed particulars to the general pattern. As Hume points out, given the separability of all particulars, inferences of this sort are always hazardous. This makes the new reason of Locke and Hume, that is, the reason of the empiricist, very different from the reason of the substance tradition. The latter had it, as in Aristotle and as in Descartes, that reason was infallible. Not so the reason of Hume. But as Hume also argues, this implies a general skepticism about the ability of reason to achieve knowledge only if one accepts the traditional standard of infallibility. But if one rejects substances and natures and the concept of reason that they determine, then why should one accept the cognitive standards that they employ? Why not accept, as

Hume recommends, a standard that fits the fallible reason, which is the only reason that we have?[13]

One thing should perhaps be emphasized. Hume does not prohibit inferences to unobserved, and perhaps unobservable, entities. He explains to us how the vulgar are content to say that a watch sometimes works, and sometimes does not. What happens, so far as the vulgar are concerned, is that this is a matter of chance. But the artisan knows better. From his experience in discovering causes, the artisan can infer that when the watch stops working there is an unobserved cause for why it stops; it is, perhaps, a speck of dust. The philosopher generalizes from this experience to the more general conclusion that every event has a cause (T, p. 132). Of course, such inferences to unknown causes cannot arise from the repeated experience of the cause being succeeded by the effect, for, *ex hypothesi*, the cause is not known. It is, rather, a case in which certain more general rules control the inferences that we make with less general rules (T, pp. 149–50), a case in which higher-level habits control the formation of lower-level habits (T, pp. 137–8). As Hume puts it, "our reasonings of this kind arise not *directly* from the habit, but in an *oblique* manner" (T, p. 133). Since these reasonings fully conform to the "rules by which to judge of causes" (T, p. 149), their conclusions that certain unknown causes exist are fully rational. What Hume excludes as unreasonable are not inferences to unobserved events but only inferences to entities of which we can form no idea, and in particular inference to substances and to real essences and necessary connections.

The argument against substances is the same as the argument against objective necessary connections: we are not presented with such entities in experience. We have no impression of an entity with a continued existence, that is, a continuant (T, pp. 191–92); the only entities with which we are acquainted are "perishing" (T, p. 194). Locke agreed with this; the substance or continuant was something that we "supposed" was there, that is, inferred was there. But since he had (he thought) reason to suppose that it was in fact there, Locke could continue to hold that ordinary perceptual objects consisted of properties inhering in a substance. For Locke, then, predication represented what it did for Aristotle, the tie of inherence. But for Hume, since we have no acquaintance in experience with substances, then from his basic principle that we have no ideas without antecedent impressions it follows that ordinary bodies are what they appear to be, namely, collections consisting of the properties or attributes that are predicated of them. As he puts it in the *Treatise*, "the idea of a substance . . . is nothing but a collection of simple ideas" (T, p. 16); or, as he puts it in the

Abstract,[14] "our idea of any body, a peach, for instance, is only that of a particular taste, colour, figure, size, consistence, etc." (p. 25).

But even if there is no continuant, ordinary objects or bodies are taken, Hume tells us (T, p. 188), to have a continued existence, even when not perceived, and an existence distinct from the perceiver, and therefore of the perceiving of them, where he includes in the notion of 'distinctness' both the *external* position, that is, as he soon explains (T, p. 190), their externality to, or distance from, our body, and their independence. Both independence and externality are matters of inference based upon laws (T, p. 191); impressions are therefore not only perishing but "internal" (T, p. 194), with no sign of independence. Nor do these ideas arise from (the sort of) reason that proceeds a priori from metaphysical principles (T, p. 193), since it is perfectly evident that the vulgar conceive of objects as continuing and distinct, but have not gone through metaphysical proofs of the continuing and distinct existence of body, for example, of the kind proposed by Descartes. The source of the ideas, then, must be the imagination (T, p. 193), though we must not forget that this does not condemn them as contrary to reason, since the imagination also includes the "understanding" as "the more general and established principles of the imagination" (T, p. 267) which are the best habits of causal inference (T, pp. 150, 170, 173–76).[15]

What is it, then, if it is not a continuant, which distinguishes those impressions "to which we attribute a continu'd existence"? It is, according to Hume,

> a peculiar *constancy*, which distinguishes them from the impressions, whose existence depends upon our perception. Those mountains, and houses, and trees, which lie at present under my eye, have always appear'd to me in the same order; and when I lose sight of them by shutting my eyes or turning my head, I soon after find them return upon me without the least alteration. My bed and table, my books and papers, present themselves in the same uniform manner, and change not upon account of any interruption in my seeing or perceiving them. (T, pp. 194–95)

To be sure, the constancy is not perfect, but even though objects do change position and quality, those impressions that are reckoned external have a coherence that others do not (T, p. 195). If I do notice an alteration of an object after an interruption, for example, the fire in my fireplace after leaving and returning to the room, I may still attribute externality because "I am accustomed in other instances to see a like alteration produc'd in a like time, whether I am present or absent, near or remote" (T, p. 195). If constancy is not perfect, then at least there is *coherence.*

Hume then proceeds to examine in detail how these inferences go (T, pp. 195–97).[16] It is like this. We have a series of sensible particulars a_1, b_1, c_1 with qualities F, G, H:

(a) Fa_1, Ra_1b_1, Gb_1, Rb_1c_1, Hc_1

where "R" represents that these particulars are in a continuous series. The pattern of properties is continued in other series that we observe:

(b) Fa_2, Ra_2b_2, Gb_2, Rb_2c_2, Hc_2
(c) Fa_3, Ra_3b_3, Gb_3, Rb_3c_3, Hc_3

But we now observe a 'gappy' series of two particulars a_4 and c_4, which have the F and H properties, but for which there is no intervening particular of sort G:

(d) Fa_4 . . . . Hc_4

The understanding 'fills in the gap' by forming the *idea* of a particular that is G and is R-ed by a_4 and R's c_4. Let us call this particular, of which we have no impression, only an idea, β. Then the series (d), as (re)constructed by the mind is

(e) Fa_4, $Ra_4\beta$, $G\beta$, $R\beta c_4$, Hc_4

(a), (b), and (c) are the other instances that have accustomed me to expect a G to be in a continuous series with an F and an H; this custom or habit leads me to attribute the same continuity or coherence to the gappy pattern (d); and the result is (e), which now fits the pattern (a)–(c).

Now, it would seem on the face of it that (d) falsifies the pattern that has been inferred from (a)–(c). More generally, gappy series cannot support customary inference, inference based upon mere habit, and in fact imply that those inferences very often ought to be rejected. "Any degree, therefore, of regularity in our perceptions, can never be a foundation for us to infer a greater degree of regularity in some objects, which are not perceiv'd; since this supposes a contradiction, namely, a habit acquir'd by what was never present to the mind" (T, p.

197). Nonetheless, instead of permitting (d) to falsify the inference, we to the contrary wish to maintain the inference and judge that our observations are at fault, that the series really is complete. We are, therefore, "involv'd in a kind of contradiction": "In order to free ourselves from this difficulty, we disguise, as much as possible, the interruption, or rather remove it entirely, by supposing that these interrupted perceptions are connected by a real existence, of which we are insensible" (T, p. 199).

Thus, instead of letting (d) falsify the inference based on the observational data of series (a)–(c), we to the contrary maintain the inference and judge that our observations are at fault, that the series really is complete only we do not know it, and that there is in fact a G, though we have not observed it, between the F and the H of (d). The idea β of this gap-filling particular constitutes the "idea of continu'd existence" that is essential to the idea of material objects like tables or chairs, and is a "supposition" (T, p. 199), that is, an existential hypothesis that has not been verified by observation. It is, however, a supposition or hypothesis which is believed (T, p. 199), and, indeed, is made worthy of belief by customary inferences derived from past experiences (T, p. 199). In fact, these inferences to unobserved particulars are parallel to those of the artisan explaining why the watch sometimes does not work; like the latter, the inferences to unobserved entities that fill gaps in our perceptual life arise "from the understanding, and from custom in an indirect and oblique manner" (T, p. 197). Just as the inferences of the artisan to unobserved particulars are justified by their conformity to the rules by which to judge of causes and effects, so the inferences to unobserved particulars in the series of perceptions that we experience are also rationally justified.

What is the nature of the idea that we have denominated "β"? If we take "R^2" to denote the relative product of R with itself, so that R^2xy means that y is R-ed by something that x R's, then, while we cannot say that the particular a_4 continues through the series (d) = (e) in a way such that $c_4 = a_4$, nonetheless we do have it, and quite correctly, given Russell's account of these things, that

$$(*)c_4 = (^1x)(R^2a_4x),$$

which plausibly construes c_4 is the same body as a_4.

Thus, technically speaking, we can use definite descriptions here in our inferences to fill in the gap in the series (d) to give us

$$(**)\beta = (^1x)(Rax),$$

only if R has certain structural properties, like symmetry, which together guarantee that that relation generates a continuous series; but Hume's discussion implies, though he does not know it and indeed could not have known it, that such structural properties are assumed. This being so, a statement like (*) is perfectly justified within the context of the gap-filling inferences that turn our series of impressions into bodies. This shows that Hume was essentially correct when he held that the idea of a body involves the idea of a given particular being connected with each succeeding member of the continuous series that constitutes that body.

An ordinary object like a table or a tree does in fact continue to exist. It has moreover a nature that is inseparable from it. The tradition construed such entities as simple substances with simple natures. Hume has given a very different account, one that fits with his revised concept of reason. For Hume, an ordinary thing is not a simple substance but a collection, a bundle of sensible particulars. It endures, but as a process rather than a thing. It has a nature but this nature is a matter of the parts of the process or bundle being instances of a pattern. The constancy of the nature is the persistence of a pattern. This nature is grasped not by intuition, but as all causal regularities are grasped, by (fallible) inference from experience.

Where Hume goes wrong is his notion that because the *idea* of a_4 occurs in the idea that denotes β in (**) and in the idea that denotes c_4 in (*), therefore that particular, namely a_4, continues in the objective series. This leads him to think that we attribute a "perfect identity" (T, p. 199) to the two different impressions at the beginning and the end of the series, and to think that we are "not apt to regard these interrupted perceptions as different, (which they really are)" (T, p. 199). The problem is Hume's simple inability to handle definite descriptions adequately, a problem equally evident in his famous discussion of the missing shade of blue. It is this inability that leads Hume to think that the series of perceptions that constitutes a material object contains within it a continuing particular, though one that he knows on other grounds to be "fictional," that is, something constructed by the mind.[17]

Now, for Locke, there is a distinction between some observed qualities, which are real, and the rest, which are not. Those that are real are those that directly express the real essences of things. For the rest, they are the mere appearances of things in consciousness. For Hume, in contrast, all sensible qualities are equally real in the sense that none can be distinguished from any other by reference to substances and their real essences. The distinction between those observed qualities that are somehow the 'real' properties of things and those which are

'mere appearances' is just that some cohere as parts of those patterns
that constitute material objects while others do not, and since material
objects are important to us in our lives and in our capacities to communicate with others, these objects (*not*: substances) are singled out *by convention* as defining 'reality'. We adopt a certain standpoint in assessing
the perceptible qualities we experience because this has a certain utility in communication. This is parallel, as Hume points out (T, p. 582),
to what he called the "artificial virtues," those virtues that arise only
because certain behavior is generally coordinated by convention (e.g.,
justice). In each case we have a convention. This convention is
explained by showing that it arises from self-interest in a context of constrained benevolence. In the case of justice it is an interest in establishing the property rights that are essential to peaceful living together. In
the case of perception it is an interest in communication and action: we
pick out from among all the patterns of sensible events that we experience those with respect to which we can most readily come to intersubjective agreement: "corrections are common with regard to all the
senses; and indeed 'twere impossible we cou'd ever make use of language, or communicate our sentiments to one another, did we not correct the momentary appearances of things, and overlook our present
situation" (T, p. 582).

Assessments both of the qualities of mind and character, that is,
recognition of virtues and vices, and also of the public qualities of
material objects, are extremely important in action both in society and
in the natural world. The convention therefore becomes instituted that
certain among all the qualities that we experience are to count as real.
The distinction among sensible qualities of the real and the unreal in
terms of coherence is thus artificial, but it is not therefore arbitrary.
And, of course, once the conventions of reality have become instituted,
and we talk about real colors, sizes, degrees of hardness, tastes, and the
like, then we come in turn to approve morally of conformity to these
conventions for the same reason that we approve morally of the artificial virtues, namely, because of their utility and because of our sense of
sympathy that leads us to be concerned with the needs and concerns of
others.

This, then, is the account of material objects that results when one
does away with the substances of the Aristotelian tradition. The simple
continuant disappears. Thus, on the one hand, a substance becomes an
ordered or patterned sequence of collections of qualities; predication
does not reflect the tie of inherence but rather the relation of part to
whole. The nature or form also disappears. Thus, on the other hand, to
know that a presented collection of qualities is part of that sequence

that we ran into yesterday or is part of a series that constitutes, say, a tree, is to subsume that presented collection under certain regularities that experience has taught us to apply in these circumstances; sorting things into species is a matter of coming to know laws, general matter-of-fact truths, rather than a matter of having rational intuitions of certain special properties, the 'real essences', of things. For Aristotle, change in the first place was the coming to be and the passing away of properties in substances; for Hume it is simply a matter of the transition from an earlier stage in a series to a later. But for Aristotle change was also, in the second place, the actualization in time of a real potentiality of the substance; for Hume that actualization of potentiality is simply the transition from one member of a series to the next in accordance with a general pattern or law. The order in which changes in things took place was a matter of the form or real essence of the thing for Aristotle; for Hume it is a matter of the pattern being one instance of a pattern that holds generally among all things of a similar kind. Where the substance account of body appeals to entities beyond the world of sense experience, the Humean account of body is wholly this-worldly.

SUBSTANCE AND SELF IN LOCKE

If material substance or body was handled without too much difficulty once the notion of substance and real essence was subjected to the Humean critique, the same cannot be said for mental substance.[18] But that should not surprise us. For, after all, Plotinus had added a twist to the substance tradition at this point,[19] a twist later emphasized by Descartes, that the unity of consciousness and of self-consciousness requires that one construe mind or self as an Aristotelian substance.

Rejecting the materialist claim that the world, including the soul, consists of matter in motion and that this soul is the *origin* of bodily motion, Plotinus argued that matter, as lifeless, cannot move itself; in fact it could not even stay together in a particular configuration: "body in itself could not exist in any form if soul-power did not; body passes; dissolution is in its very nature; all would disappear in a twinkling if all were body." Indeed, "Matter itself could not exist [without soul]: the totality of things in the sphere is dissolved if it be made to depend upon the coherence of a body which, though elevated to the nominal rank of 'soul', remains air, fleeting breath . . . , whose very unity is not drawn from itself" (*Enn*, IV, 7, 3). Soul, as cause, contains within itself the forms or reasons of the things the temporally ordered diversity of which it produces. This produced order reflects in time the timeless order implicit in the cause: "If the leading principle of the universe does not know the future which it is of itself to produce, it cannot produce with knowledge or to purpose; it will produce just what happens to come, that is to say by haphazard. As this cannot be, it must create by some stable principle; its creations, therefore, will be shaped in the model stored up in itself; there can be no varying" (*Enn*, IV, 4, 12). Moreover, our consciousness is in the first instance, as indeed the materialists hold, a series of events in time. However, each of these events is related to the others in the series; and they are related moreover to each other as modifications of a single consciousness, a consciousness that is a consciousness of each of them and all of them. "There can be no perception without a unitary percipient whose identity enables it to grasp an object in its entirety" (*Enn*, IV, 7, 6). The conscious self of which the events are the modifications cannot be the series as a whole, since within the series the events are successive; but at any moment the consciousness of those events does not involve a succession: "prior and past are in the things it [soul] produces; in itself nothing is past; all . . . is one simultaneous grouping of Reason-Principles" (*Enn*, IV, 4, 16). That is, while the consciousness of the series is a consciousness *of* a before and after, *within* that self-consciousness there is no before and after; within the consciousness there is no such relation between the components as there is between the events of which it is the consciousness. The consciousness that a self has of itself must lie outside the temporal sequence of events of which it is conscious. Self-consciousness must therefore be an entity outside the temporal changes of the self, an eternal entity to which the events in the temporal sequence are related as modifications.

There were already more than hints of this in the *Phaedo*: the soul that accounts for changes is *Socrates*, that is, the self that is conscious of its own self, and which is, in the light of that consciousness and in the light of its knowledge of the forms, determining the changes that take place within it. There were also more than hints of it in Aristotle. A substance is a continuant but never simply that: it is also a continuant of a certain sort, that is, it has a certain nature or form. This form has implicit within it, so far as the substance determines its own history, what has happened to it and what will happen to it: the form or nature is "the source from which the primary movement in each natural object is present in it in virtue of its own essence" (*Met*, 1014b19–20).[20] Thus, the form as the active potentiality of the substance is the whole of the substance as eternally present to its various parts, the events the sequence of which constitute its history. In particular, the soul must be a substance.

Some hold that the soul is divisible, and that one part thinks, another desires. If, then, its nature admits of its being divided, what can it be that holds the parts together? Surely not the body; on the contrary it seems rather to be the soul that holds the body together; at any rate when the soul departs the body disintegrates and decays. If, then, there is something else which makes the soul one, this unifying agency would have the best right to the name of soul, and we shall have to repeat for it the question: Is *it* one or multipartite? If it is one, why not at once admit that 'the soul' is one? If it has parts, once more the question has to be put: What holds *its* parts together, and so on *ad infinitum*. (*De An*, 411b5–14)

And so the soul, in this respect like any substance, is the atemporal source of, and eternally present to, those events that constitute its history: "the soul must be a substance in the sense of the form of a natural body having life potentially within it" (*De An*, 412a20–21). Aristotle's soul, as a simple active potentiality or form, thus contains within it in an atemporal way the series of events that constitute its history in time, at least insofar as it is self-determining; so also self-consciousness contains this history within itself. Not surprisingly, Plotinus, and the substance tradition that followed, identified the center of self-consciousness with the atemporal active substance that causes the temporal series of events unified in that self-consciousness.

On this identification, the self-consciousness that contains past and future within it is a consciousness of the active potentiality, the form of the self, which is the causal source of that past and future. But that active potentiality or form is the reason why those events occur in the sequence they do; it is that form that constitutes the necessary connection between those events. Thus, the self-consciousness is the consciousness that grasps the reasons of things. But the faculty that grasps the reasons of things is *reason*. The self-consciousness that grasps the reason for its own being and becoming is thus reason itself. Reason thus comes to be identified with the atemporal and substantial center of self-consciousness.

It is precisely this tradition that we find summarized in the Cartesian *cogito*, which is at once reason and also a center of self-consciousness *and also* a simple substance the activities of which cause the events, the doubtings, which are the events in the history of that consciousness.

Now, as Locke points out, the notion of a person is primarily a *forensic* notion, even in the theological application that the Middle Ages gave to the Plotinian tradition:

It is a forensic term, appropriating actions and their merit; and so belongs only to intelligent agents, capable of a law, and happiness, and misery. This personality extends itself beyond present existence to what is past, only by consciousness,—whereby it becomes concerned and accountable; owns and imputes to itself past actions, just upon the same ground and for the same reason as it does the present. All which is founded in a concern for happiness, the unavoidable concomitant of consciousness; that which is conscious of pleasure and pain, desiring that that self should be happy. (*Essay*, II, xxvii, 26)[21]

A person is a substance, but there is more to the identity of things than the continuity of one and the same entity throughout the sequence of events that constitute the history of the substance. To be sure, the presence of the continuant is the criterion of identity for simple substances, but in the case of substances having parts, that is, compound substances, the case is more complicated. The identity of the compound substance depends upon how the compounding occurs, that is, in effect on the relation by which the compound substance is constituted out the simple substances that are its parts. This means in particular that one cannot simply identify the continuity of a person with the continuity of a substance.

Consider some examples of compound substances. The identity of a heap of rocks through time is constituted by the identities of its parts: take away one rock and we have a different heap (II, xxvii, 4). Locke goes on to contrast the case of plants and animals. Here the parts in themselves are not essential; one particle of matter may be replaced by another, but it is the same living animal.

That being one . . . plant which has such an organization of parts in one coherent body, partaking of one common life, it continues to be the same plant as long as it partakes of the same life, though that life be communicated to new particles of matter vitally united to the living plant, in a like continued organization conformable to that sort of plants. (II, xxvii, 5)

The same pattern of continuity may be found in certain artificial machines, such as watches. Again, even if one part is replaced, the machine does not lose its identity. What is crucial is not the particular part, but *that there be* a part of that sort performing the same function as that part, that is, the same function in maintaining the entity in its characteristic activity, keeping time in the case of the watch, maintaining the process of metabolism in the cases of plants and animals. Thus, in considering whether a sequence of events forms a single identical entity one must take into account not just the inherence relation but also other relations that define the observed order in the series. We should not in fact find this surprising since, traditionally, a substance is not merely a continuant but also a form, that is, a continuant of a certain specific kind, and that kind is inseparable from the continuant. Locke continues in this tradition in that a compound substance will continue to be the same identical substance only so long as 'its' real essence remains the same. And so, in order to determine whether certain events in a sequence are parts of one and the same thing, it will be necessary to make reference to the particular sort of order that is exemplified in the sequence.

In the case of man the relevant sort of order is that of a living thing. We will have the same man if we have "one fitly organized body, taken in any one instant, and from thence continued, under one organization of life, in several successively fleeting particles of matter united to it" (II, xxvii, 7). The identity of a man is thus of a piece with the identity of an animal. But the identity of a man cannot be constituted by either his soul or his rationality. It cannot be the former, since the soul is immortal, and this would therefore allow the possibility for the transmigration of souls, discussed by the Cambridge Platonists but absurd in Locke's view, as it would entail that "men, living in distant ages, and of different tempers, may have been the same man" (ibid.). Nor can the identity of a man be constituted by his rationality, since a rational parrot, though rational, could not be counted a man (ibid.). But if the idea of man is separated from the ideas of his soul and his rationality, then man becomes something essentially corporeal, and one cannot account for the facts of personality and moral responsibility. What gives man his special position distinguishing him from other animals, is his moral status as a person, someone who can be held responsible for what he has done and rewarded or punished for that. Traditionally what this amounted to was the point that man is a substance that is not only *animal* but also *rational*. This is the point that Boethius made when he defined a person as "The individual substance of a rational nature" (*Theological Tractates, Contra Evtychen*, p. 85);[22] and it is the point that Locke makes when he asserts that a person is "a thinking intelligent being" (II, xxvii, 11).

However, following the Cartesians, and echoing the point argued by Plotinus, the consciousness of the rational being as a thinking being includes not merely thought, consciousness, but also self-consciousness; it can "consider itself as itself" (II, xxvii, 11). Locke is here accepting the Cartesian point, already argued for by Plotinus, that consciousness implies self-consciousness. We cannot, for both Locke and Descartes, think, feel, contemplate, or will anything without being conscious of, or aware of, that thinking, feeling, contemplating, or willing. As Locke says, there is a "consciousness which is inseparable from thinking, and, as it seems to me, essential to it: it being impossible for any one to perceive without *perceiving* that he does perceive. . . . Thus it is always as to our present sensations and perceptions: and by this every one is to himself that which he calls *self*." However, as Locke hastens to add, "it [is] not . . . considered, in this case, whether the same self be continued in the same or divers substances" (II, xxvii, 11). But we also remember our past actions: our consciousness here is not only conscious of itself but conscious of earlier conscious events and conscious that the earlier consciousness of *them* is the same as present consciousness.

> since consciousness always accompanies thinking, and it is that which makes every one to be what he calls self, and thereby distinguishes himself from all other thinking things, in this alone consists personal identity, i.e., the sameness of a rational being: and as far as this consciousness can be extended backwards to any past action or thought, so far reaches the identity of that person; it is the same self now it was then; and it is by the same self with this present one that now reflects on it, that that action was done. (II, xxvii, 11)

The continuity here need not be that of a substance. In fact, we do not know whether the self is a single substance or a compound of several substances. If the latter, then of course the traditional argument for immortality based on the simplicity of the substance is rendered unsound. This argument finds its origins in Plato, in the *Phaedo*, is developed by Plotinus, and made its way down through history to Descartes and More. Locke uses the argument from the separateness of certain events in experience to draw the conclusion that there is nothing in what we experience of the self to guarantee that the self is a single simple substance. The link between my present consciousness and my past is provided by memory. But memory is only a contingent tie; otherwise we would be unable to remember and then forget, we have false memories, we dream (II, xxvii, 13). There are gaps in our memory—we sleep, we are drunk—and these gaps are bridged not by some necessary tie but only by memory. We could conclude that there was a single substance only if we experience such a substance actually tying the various stages of the self together. But we do not experience substances, nor do we experience necessary connections. It follows that the self may be a compound substance (ibid.).

If the continuity is not that of a simple substance, it is also misleading to say that the link is *merely* memory. To be sure, memory is a necessary condition. That is why Locke argues as he does that when the drunkard cannot remember certain things that he has done, those things were not really done by *him*; he was not responsible for them—though, to be sure, he was responsible for getting drunk, and if he could not be punished for what he did when drunk he could be punished for becoming drunk. But as we saw, what is equally important is that the memory is one in which the self that was earlier conscious is the same self as that which is now conscious; that is, in memory we recognize the earlier self as the same as the present self. Bishop Butler argued that memory does not constitute personal identity, but rather presupposes it:

> All attempts to define personal identity would but perplex it. Yet there is no difficulty at all in ascertaining the idea. For as upon two triangles being compared together, there arises to the mind the idea of similitude; or upon twice two and four the idea of equality; so likewise upon comparing the consciousness of oneself in any two moments, there as immediately arises to the mind the idea of personal identity. . . . By reflecting on that which was myself twenty years ago, I discern that they are not two, but one and the same self. (*Dissertation of Personal Identity*, pp. 387–88)[23]

Locke agrees that in the memory you *recognize*, or, if you wish, *discern*, that the self that was conscious then is the same as the self that is conscious now. But contrary to Butler, it does not follow from this that the identity discerned is the identity of a simple substance.

Unfortunately, Locke leaves it just like this, at the discernment in memory of an identity, and does not pursue the issue further of what the nature of that judgment is. Other problems were, perhaps, more pressing.

In particular, there was the claim that memory was a necessary condition for personal identity. What, then, of the actions of the drunkard that he forgets? Or the actions of a sleepwalker? Is the drunk to be punished for what he was never really aware of doing? Is the man awake to be punished for the actions he did while asleep? Molyneux was to argue against Locke that the two cases had to be distinguished. He appealed to the *forensic* criterion that Locke himself insisted upon, that a person is *responsible for* his actions. The sleepwalker, Molyneux argued, is not responsible for what he does when he is asleep, and should therefore not be punished for anything that he might do when in that state. But drunkenness is itself a crime and so the drunkard should be punished both for it and for any other crimes that he commits while in that state (M to L, *Works of JL*, VII, p. 329).[24] Locke replied that "it is an argument against me, for if a man may be punished for any crime which he committed when drunk, whereof he is allowed not to be conscious, it overturns my hypothesis" (p. 331). But he had already argued in the *Essay* that a human judicature could not allow a drinking man to plead innocent for want of remembering something, "because the fact is proved against him, but want of consciousness cannot be proved for him" (*Essay*, II, xxvii, 22); human laws must punish both with "a justice that is suitable to their way of knowledge." But, he also went on to say, "in the Great Day, wherein the secrets of all hearts shall be laid open, it may be reasonable to think, no one shall be made to answer for what he knows nothing of; but shall receive his doom, his conscience accusing or excusing him" (II, xxvii, 22).

Molyneux was not convinced, and restated his argument for Locke: drunkenness is a voluntarily induced state, and thus the drunkard is responsible for all of the consequences thereof, while sleepwalking is involuntary, and the somnambulist ought not to be held responsible for what he does (M to L, *Works of JL*, VII, p. 334). At this point Locke resigned and gave in to the argument of his Irish friend; he admitted that "want of consciousness ought not to be presumed in favour of the drunkard" (L to M, p. 326).

But this surely is to give up his position. He has allowed that Molyneux's objection, if sound, strikes at the heart of his account of a person. And he then accepts the objection. The problem is, of course, that the criterion of consciousness and the criterion of responsibility do not coincide.

In the traditional picture deriving from Plato, Aristotle, and Plotinus, these criteria do not, of course, diverge. The self as the timeless center of consciousness sums up within itself the past that it has already, as it were, produced, and is pregnant with the future that it will, in due course, create. The self-conscious center of being is the reason why the events happen in its history, and, as that reason, that self-conscious center is also responsible for those events. It does not matter that, empirically, this self-consciousness is sometimes not conscious of itself. The position is not defended by the appeal to experience, but by transcendental arguments: the awareness of a series of events *must* lie outside the temporal series of events of which it is aware for otherwise it could not grasp them *as a whole* and *all at once*. But Locke has no recourse to this sort of argument: he is committed to the "historical plain method," and what we experience are separate and separable events contingently linked in time. We *are* self-conscious but that self being conscious of self is an event in time, and an event that we experience in time. It is part of the series, not a entity standing apart from it. It is, moreover, part of the causal order of the events in the world of ordinary experience. Given Locke's incapacity to go beyond the world of ordinary experience, there is no way that the self could play that special role that it plays in the traditional substance philosophy as the transcendental cause of the events that happen in its history. Self-consciousness no longer has that special place; it is, to repeat, an event among events, produced by events that preceded it. This is one causal process. What we must recognize is that the relations defining responsibility are also causal processes. In the traditional picture, of course, the relations of responsibility lead back to the transcendental self. But why, when one treats mind empirically, should one expect chains of responsibility always to lead back to a state of self-consciousness, and why should one expect that a center of self-consciousness should always be the starting point of a relation of responsibility? As Locke said, when we look at the concept of a person we discover pretty quickly that it is a forensic concept. To put it simply, those actions for which a person is responsible are those that define what he is as a person; and, to put it even more simply, if not crudely, we are responsible for those actions where we use the techniques of reward and punishment to control behavior. Why should we expect the area of behavior that can be controlled by reward and punishment to coincide with the area of behavior that is a product of self-conscious act? There is in fact no reason a priori to think this—other than the reason given for the traditional substance accounts of the mind and of self-consciousness, but Locke rejects these. Indeed, it is the thrust of Molyneux's appeal to the two cases of the drunkard and the sleepwalker to suggest that the two criteria of personhood may indeed diverge.

THE PROBLEM OF THE SELF IN HUME

The problem that philosophers and theologians found in Locke's account of persons was stated by Butler; Locke's "hasty observations," he says,

> have been carried to a strange length by others, whose notion, when traced . . . to the bottom, amounts, I think, to this: 'That

personality is not a permanent, but a transient thing: that it lives and dies, begins and ends continually: that no one can any more remain one and the same person two moments together, than two successive moments can be one and the same moment: that our substance is indeed continually changing; but whether this be so or not, is, it seems, nothing to the purpose; since it is not substance, but consciousness alone, which constitutes personality; which consciousness, being successive, cannot be the same in any two moments, nor consequently the personality constituted by it'. (*Dissertation of Personal Identity*, p. 392)

What Locke did when he insisted that one use the empirical method, the "historical plain method," to understand the acquisition of concepts and of knowledge, was destroy the illusion that we have any legitimate concept of substance. This in turn attacked the traditional and Christian foundations of the theory of self. When Locke argues that "*self* is *not* determined by Identity . . . of Substance . . . but only by Identity of consciousness," he is seen by his critics like Clarke and Butler as destroying the notion that there is a unitary core of personality persisting through time, replacing it by a notion of a human being as existing only from moment to moment. The important implication of Locke's position is, as Tuveson has put it, that no "unchanging soul is necessary to constitute personality." As a result, the "personality itself" becomes "a shifting thing; it exists, not throughout a lifetime as an essence, but hardly from hour to hour."[25]

Hume again takes up problems where Locke leaves off. Just as Locke for all practical purposes left the notion of body as that of a bundle of qualities, so he has left the notion of the self or person as that of a collection or bundle of events, only contingently connected together (T, p. 253). The problem was to find a basis for the stability of personality compatible with this ontological view of the self as a bundle of perceptions but yet sufficient to answer the concerns of Butler and other theologians. Or rather, Hume had to find a view of personality that sufficed for everyday purposes to meet those objections. Hume saw no need to answer the theological concerns of the Anglican divines.

Now, contrary to what some have suggested,[26] Hume does not deny that we have an idea of the self. "Ourself," he says, "is always intimately present to us" (T, pp. 320, 339, 427, 354). It is of central importance to the passions of pride and humility, according to Hume: "when self enters not into the consideration, there is no room either for pride or humility" (T, p. 277). This is not to deny that the self is a bundle of perceptions; thus, when Hume explains the exact role of the self with respect to pride, he tell us that "tho' that connected succession of perceptions, which we call *self*, be always the object of these two passions, 'tis impossible it can be their CAUSE" (T, p. 277). Indeed, the fact that the self is simply a bundle of perceptions is itself of importance in the explanation of certain mental phenomena.

> Ourself, independent of the perception of every other object, is in reality nothing: For which reason we must turn our view to external objects; and 'tis natural for us to consider with most attention such as lie contiguous to us, or resemble us. But when self is the object of a passion, 'tis not natural to quit the consideration of it, till the passion be exhausted. (T, p. 341)

What Hume does deny is that we have an idea of the self as a *simple substance*. A person is "a bundle or collection of different perceptions which succeed one another with an inconceivable rapidity and are in perpetual flux and movement" (T, p. 252). The problem is that of finding the principle that unites these into a person, and not merely into *a* person but into a person with the relatively stable character needed to carry on with the practical projects in our lives and which is presupposed by our ordinary moral principles.

The central text for Hume on personal identity is, of course, *Treatise*, Book I, Part IV, Section vi, which bears that title. In the end, however, as we shall see, we cannot limit ourselves to this text; as so often in Hume, a discussion that begins in Book I of the *Treatise* finds its completion in Books II and III. Hume signals this in Book I when he tells us that "we must distinguish betwixt personal identity, as it regards our thought or imagination, and as it regards our passions or the concern we take in ourselves. The first is our present subject (T, p. 253). But at the end of the discussion in I, IV, vi we are not given a clear account of personal identity—not as, for example, we are given clear accounts of causation and of the identity of body. One reason for this, as we shall see in the present section, is that Hume could not in his own terms address the problem that had been raised long ago by Plotinus. A second reason for it, however, as we shall see in the next section, is that the relevant relation among the parts of the self that generates the idea of our self cannot be understood apart from our passions and our system of morality, topics that are not discussed until Books II and III respectively of the *Treatise*. The issue of personal identity *cannot* be resolved without turning to our passions and the concern we take in ourselves. But this should surely not surprise us. After all, Locke had already established that the notion of a person is a forensic notion, and to say this is to say that, as the *Treatise* is written, personal identity cannot be fully understood until we complete Books II and III.

We must, however, begin where Hume begins, with the discussion of personal identity in Book I.

It is here that Hume first establishes, on the basis of the principle of acquaintance, Locke's "historical plain method," that just as we have no idea of body as a simple substance, so we have no idea of the self as a simple substance. The bundle view follows.

But as in the case of body, there is continuity in the complexity, and a relation that generates this continuity. Like Locke, Hume points out that things are often counted the same even though their parts change. A church falls down and is replaced; it is nonetheless the same church (T, p. 258). It is the same church because it serves the same end, or, as he says, stands in the same relation to the people of the parish. Similarly, the parts of plants and animals change—the small tree grows into the mighty oak, the infant into the adult—but when they are added or replaced the parts continue to function jointly to maintain the organism. What we have here is "a *sympathy* of parts to their *common end*, and [we] suppose that they bear to each other, the reciprocal relation of cause and effect in all their relations and operations" (T, p. 257). This sort of reasoning, which has worked so well in the case of plants and animals, "must be continued" (T, p. 259), Hume tells us, in the case of personal identity. Here, too, we have a succession of objects so related as to form a continuous series. The continuity we transform into an identity when we "imagine something unknown and mysterious connecting the parts besides their relation" (T, p. 254). This identity is a fictitious one, the continuing entity a fiction, creating no real bond among them (T, p. 259).

Now, Hume is here careful not to say that the relation generating the continuity is the same as that which holds for organisms or parish churches. He says only that the case appears to be *analogous* for persons. In particular there will be the sympathy of the parts serving a common end. But that need not exhaust the content of the relation generating the continuity. This relation does involve resemblance and causation, he tells us (T, p. 260), but that is not to go very far. The important point—and this distinguishes this relation from those that generate the identities of organisms and churches—is that memory has a role to play. Through memory we recall past contiguities in space and time, and this produces the association of ideas that constitutes the causal judgment. The mind then applies this to the remembered events, uniting them into a series. That is, memory is now that which locates the events that the mind unites into the series; memory discovers identity "by shewing us the relation of cause and effect among our different perceptions" (T, p. 262). Memory is also relevant in the case of resemblance. The memory recalls a past object, which resembles a present one, and this creates by association the abstract idea that links them; the mind then as it were reverses itself and applies the abstract idea to the remembered entity. In this way, then, for both resemblance and causation, memory both *produces* and *discovers* personal identity (T, p. 262). There is nothing parallel to this in the case of animals. In the case of animals, it is our thought that creates the feeling that there is a tie of necessity; and it is our thought that creates what Hume thinks of as the fictitious continuing particular. The mechanism that creates the feeling is *external to* the animal. In the case of the mind, however, the mechanism is *internal to* the entity whose parts are tied together. The memories that we have both produce and discover the identity but are at the same time part of the series to which the identity is attributed. It is this that distinguishes the case of personal identity from that of the identity of animals.

What we need, therefore, is a better grasp of what precisely is the relation that generates the continuity of mind. Recall how Hume sees these things. The relation, considered philosophically, is an association of ideas. This association is produced by some "quality" in objects; this quality is the relation considered naturally (T, pp. 13–14). Thus, in the case of causation, to judge that two things are related as cause and effect, there must be an association established between our ideas of the cause and the effect. The quality that establishes this association is a constant conjunction among things. Thus, to ask for a better account of the relation that produces the identity is to ask what "quality" of things produces the relevant association (T, p. 255). What we do know is that resemblance plays a role (T, p. 260), that causation plays a role (T, p. 261), that memory plays a role (T, pp. 261–62), and also that memory cannot be a necessary condition, since Hume contends, as Molyneux did, that causation extends our judgments of identity through gaps in our memories, even when we are not drunk—do you really remember what you were doing at precisely this time last week? (T, p. 262)—and to events prior to any memories—the infant is the same person as the adult (T, p. 257). But to say these things is not yet to give a fully developed theory.

Hume puts it this way in the "Appendix":

no connexions amongst distinct existences are ever discover-
able by the human understanding. We only *feel* a connexion or
determination of the thought to pass from one object to
another. It follows, therefore, that the thought alone finds
personal identity, when reflecting on the train of past perceptions, that compose a mind, the ideas of them are felt to be
connected together, and naturally introduce each other. However extraordinary this conclusion may seem, it need not
surpize us. Most philosophers seem inclin'd to think, that personal identity *arises* from consciousness; and consciousness in
nothing but a reflected thought or perception. The present
philosophy, therefore, has so far a promising aspect. But all
my hopes vanish, when I come to explain the principles, that
unite our successive perceptions in our thought or consciousness. I cannot discover any theory, which gives me satisfaction
on this head. (T, pp. 635–66)

Consciousness is reflected thought or perception; it is, in other
words, the perception of thought. But a perception is an impression.
So consciousness must be an impression that is of and is produced by
our thoughts. Consciousness of personal identity must therefore be an
impression of our self *qua* unified; that is, since the self is a series of
events, it must be an impression of the events of this series as a unified
whole. But the only *impressions* of which we are at a moment conscious
are the impressions that are then present to us, that is, not those in the
past (or the future), and the only impression of unity that is present is
the *feeling* of union that is present by virtue of the association among
the ideas of the events in the series that constitutes the self. This feeling is produced by a quality of the perceptions in the series that forms
the self, but is separate from the events that produced it. Hence it is
not part of the self whose unity it constitutes. Yet surely the self's
awareness of itself is part of the self. This is the problem.

Hume goes on to say how he could solve these problems if he had
either real essences, that is, objective necessary connections, or a substratum as a continuant. In either case, we would have an impression in
experience of the tie. This impression would at once be a perception of
the unity that constitutes the self and at the same time be unified into
the self by the tie of which it was an impression. But there is no such
impression (T, p. 636), and so the problem, for Hume, remains
unsolved.

In fact there are two problems for Hume. The first is this: what is
the quality of the events in the series forming the self that produces the

impression of unity? The second is this: How can the impression of unity that is produced by that quality represent the whole of which it is one part?

The second problem is, of course, the problem raised by Plotinus. On the one hand, if the felt connection is established by an association of ideas, then the complexity of the latter, including its temporal progression, cannot be a perception, which is simple. On the other hand, the simplicity of the perception would seem to imply the simplicity of what is perceived. How can a simple perception be the product of a process of association and embody within it the series of events from the past and their continuation into the future? As John Stuart Mill put it,

> If . . . we speak of the Mind as a series of feelings, we are obliged to complete the statement by calling it a series of feelings which is aware of itself as past and future; as we are reduced to the alternative of believing that the Mind, or Ego, is something different from any series of feelings, or possibilities of them, or of accepting the paradox, that something which *ex hypothesi* is but a series of feelings, can be aware of itself as a series.[27]

If we take for granted the model of psychological analysis that Hume tended to accept and which he had inherited from Locke, then this problem cannot be solved since on the model the analysis of a mental state yields just the genetic antecedents of that state. Thus, the analysis of the impression of unity of a self will, upon analysis, yield the genetic antecedents of that impression; or, in other words, analysis of the impression of the unity of the self will yield the various parts of the series that constitute the self. But, upon the Lockean model of analysis, the psychological analysis of a mental state is the same thing as a logical analysis of a concept into the parts that define it. The parts into which an idea or impression is analyzed are upon this model real parts, really and wholly present in the thing analyzed. Thus, upon the Lockean model of analysis, the impression of unity must be a whole that has within it all the various parts that constitute the self; it cannot, in other words, be simple, but must contain within itself the complexity of the series that produced it. Clearly, one cannot within this Lockean account of analysis reply to the Plotinian problem in a way that avoids that substantialist solution; and, indeed, as Hume himself saw, substantialism would provide a solution.

The solution to the problem actually consists in the rejection of the Lockean model of analysis. This is what John Stuart Mill did. As he explained it, quite correctly, psychological analysis does not locate the real parts of a mental state. Rather, what analysis does is *recover* through association elements that are normally only potentially or dispositionally present; that is, it recovers parts that are actually present only when they appear as a consequence of undertaking the analytic task.[28] These "parts" that are thus recovered are the genetic antecedents of the phenomenologically simple phenomenon that their association produced. This enables Mill to say straight out that a simple perception can "contain" a complexity of parts, to say that there is no mystery here, only a fact. Mill makes the relevant point this way:

> The real stumbling block is perhaps not in any theory of the fact, but in the fact itself. The true incomprehensibility perhaps is, that something which has ceased, or is not yet in existence, can still be, in a manner, present: that a series of feelings, the infinitely greater part of which is past or future, can be gathered up, as it were, into a single present conception, accompanied by a belief of reality. I think, by far the wisest thing we can do, is accept the inexplicable fact, without any theory of how it takes place; and when we are obliged to speak in terms which assume a theory, to use them without a reservation as to their meaning.[29]

We must take for granted, then, that a simple impression can indeed represent the complexity of the self. Why, indeed, should that be puzzling? Taken in this way, there is no further problem of the sort that Plotinus raised; the only thing left is to find an adequate account of the associational process that generates the simple perception of the unity of self, that is, to discover, as Hume put it, the "quality" of the parts of the self that yields the association of ideas that is the perception of the unity of the self.

This provides an adequate answer to the second problem that Hume faced: how can the impression of unity that is produced by that quality represent the whole of which it is one part? There remains the *first* problem: what is the quality of the events in the series forming the self that produces the impression of unity? To this issue we turn in the next section.

HUME'S POSITIVE THEORY OF THE SELF

G. Vesey has suggested that once the standard of substantial identity is abandoned, there is no remaining problem with personal identity.

Hume generates the problem, on his view, because, while he rejects the substantialist account of mind, he nonetheless insists upon substantial identity as the standard that must be met. The correct move, Vesey holds, is not only to reject substances but to reject substance as the standard criterion of identity. Once we do that, no problem remains.

> To say that there is nothing *essential* about personal identity, or that the self is not a *substance*, is to suggest that there *is* something essential about other things, or that other things *are* substances. To say that there is no just standard by which we can decide any dispute about identity is, surely, wrong. We can decide ordinary disputes—in the way in which we do.[30]

Hume would not really disagree with this. He, too, argues that once substances are abandoned many of the problems disappear.[31] Hume would also like to think along with Vesey that our ordinary concept of personal identity is more or less in order. No doubt he would recognize what Vesey ignores, that much of our ordinary discourse is infected by the Christian tradition with its view of the self as in effect a substance. But even if we agree that we can get along quite well in ordinary circumstances with our ordinary concept of a person, it does not follow that all the interesting questions about personal identity have been answered. For it remains to spell out what those ordinary procedures are, and what the criteria we ordinarily use in contexts where personal identity is an issue are. In Hume's terms, we have still to elaborate an account of the origin of the idea of personal identity that we use. And in still more specifically Humean terms, we shall need an associationist account of the origins of this idea.

To retrieve Hume's positive theory we must proceed to Books II and III of the *Treatise*. Hume does not devote a further section specifically to the topic. But he does say just enough about the idea of the self that we do have for us to suggest an adequate Humean theory of the 'quality' or relation among the parts of the self that accounts for the association of ideas of those parts into our idea of ourself.

Locke was sufficiently part of the Christian tradition that, while he gave up the notion of a substantial self, he nonetheless still had to allow for future rewards and punishments. When he came to analyze the concept of a person, he had to allow for this. The concept of a person could not, therefore, have as part of itself the concept of a man. The latter was a material object, and Locke had to allow the possibility of the separation of the person from the man. This led to his memory criterion for being a person, with the defects that Molyneux pointed out. Hume is not so bound to the Christian tradition, and so, as we shall see, he is prepared to allow that our body enters into the idea of our self. We discover through experience a distinction between our own body and those of others, and this identity of body enters into the identity of self. Since the body is relatively stable, that will in turn give a certain stability to the self. This is part of Hume's answer to critics of Locke like Butler and Clarke, who held that all stability disappeared when the substantial self was abandoned. But this is not all that Hume has to say. There is also the issue of the sufficient stability of personality for our practical purposes. Here too Hume attempts to show how the distinction between our own self and those of others arises within the world of experience, and more specifically how the stable character of the responsible person is developed through interaction with others. And of course, when Hume develops these aspects of the issue of personal identity, he is pursuing lines of thought first introduced by Locke when he insisted that the concept of a person is a forensic notion.

Hume tells us that "the idea, or rather impression, of ourselves is always intimately present with us, and our consciousness gives us so lively a conception of our own person that 'tis not possible to imagine that anything can in this particular go beyond it" (T, p. 317). The first thing to note is that this idea or impression of oneself is present in our consciousness; "ourself is always intimately present to *us*" (T, p. 320; emphasis added). There is, in other words, a *conscious state* that contains this idea or impression of oneself. Hume similarly speaks elsewhere of the "self or that individual person of whose actions and sentiments each of us is intimately conscious" (T, p. 286). The conscious state thus includes not only the idea or impression of oneself but also one's actions and sentiments. But these ideas, impressions and, among the latter, sentiments that are in one's conscious state are "intimately present" to one. This implies a distinction between those contents and the awareness of them. When I take pride in something I have done, there are on the one hand the ideas and impressions that are 'intimately present' to me, and, on the other hand, the 'me' to which they are 'intimately present'. We therefore have the following model of what it is to be a conscious state. There are, first, certain contents. Second, these contents are the contents of a conscious state by virtue of being the objects of an awareness.[32] Given Mill's point about awareness, we can treat this awareness by virtue of which various entities are among the contents of our conscious state as a simple mental act.

Consider, for example, the mental state that one *expresses* when one uses a sentence like

(+)   I feel proud that I then did so-and-so.

in the normal way. The conscious state that is expressed when (+) is used in a speech act in the normal way has among its contents the feeling of pride. This is the sort of thing that Hume would, of course, refer to as an impression. This feeling of pride has a certain object, namely, my past action. This past action becomes the object of my feeling of pride by virtue of the latter being tied to a certain idea, namely, the idea of my past action. This idea, though of course not the action itself, is also among the contents of my conscious state; it, too, is 'intimately present' to me. As a sentence, (+) *describes* the very same conscious state that is described by

(#)   David Hume [now] feels proud that he then did so-and-so.

But a speech act in which (#) is used need not *express* a conscious state of David Hume; its use may express, for example, a conscious state of James Boswell, namely, a conscious state of Boswell's that has as its content the belief that the state of affairs described by (#) actually exists. Both the first 'I' in (+) and 'David Hume' in (#) refer to, or designate, the same person; that is what it means to say that (+) and (#) both describe the same state of affairs. The difference lies in the fact that (+) is so used that it expresses the conscious state of the person to whom the subject term refers while (#) does not. This means that in the characteristic use of the word 'I' as a subject term not only does it refer to the person speaking but it also expresses the awareness that is constitutive of the conscious state of that person.[33] In this sense, although the referent is the same, the linguistic roles of the two terms differ, and, in that sense, so does their meaning.[34]

Now, the difference between an action and a mere movement is that the former is the result of a conscious intention. This means that the sentences (+) and (#) both ascribe to David Hume a certain conscious state that has preceded the one that has the feeling of pride among its contents. Call this earlier conscious state *a*. But when (+) and (#) ascribe a feeling of pride to David Hume, they ascribe a conscious state that is later than *a*. Call this later conscious state *d*. There are, let us assume, other conscious states that intervene between *a* and *d*; suppose that these states are *b* and *c*. There is a certain 'quality' or relation that connects these conscious states *a*, *b*, *c*, *d*, uniting them into the states of a single self. Call this relation *R*. (+) and (#) ascribe these two conscious states to the same person, David Hume; they *identify* them as states of the same person. The pattern here is the same as we had in the case of body: we can reasonably construe

d is the same person as a

as

$$d = (^\imath x) \, (R^3 ax)$$

Because we also have both

$$b = (^\imath x)) \, (R ax)$$

and

$$c = (^\imath x) \, (R^2 ax)$$

Hume concludes from the presence of the idea of a running throughout these that our idea of a person as an enduring entity contains the idea of a simple entity that continues throughout the series. But the principle of acquaintance excludes any such entity. It is therefore, according to Hume, "fictitious." Thus, "what we call a *mind*," Hume suggests, "is nothing but a heap or collection of different perceptions, united together by certain relations, and suppos'd, tho' falsely, to be endow'd with a perfect simplicity and identity" (T, p. 207). The pattern here is the same as in the case of body, and we may also conclude here that we can accept the main thrust of Hume's position without accepting that he needs to include in the idea of the self any "fictitious" simple particular that is supposed to endure throughout the series.

For what we are about now, the question with which we are concerned is simply this: What is the relation R?

Hume speaks of "that connected succession of perceptions which we call self" (T, p. 277). These perceptions include the perceptions of our body. Indeed, they are part of the definition of oneself, according to Hume, for he speaks of "the qualities of our mind *and body*, that is, self," and elsewhere of the "self or that individual person of whose *actions* and sentiments each of us is intimately conscious" (T, pp. 303, 286; emphasis added). In experience we distinguish a variety of bodies, including the bodies of persons. But among the bodies of persons that I can distinguish within experience there is one to which I have a unique relation; this is *my* body. As John Stuart Mill put it, "I am aware, by experience, of a group of Permanent Possibilities of Sensation which I call my body, and which my experience shows to be an universal condition of every part of my thread of consciousness. I am also aware of a great number of other groups, resembling the one that I call my body, but which have no connexion, such as that has, with the remainder of my thread of consciousness."[35]

The point Mill was getting at when he said that "experience shows" my body "to be a universal condition of every part of my thread of consciousness" is surely correct: among the contents of every conscious state there is an awareness of one's own bodily state. We often have as parts of the contents of our conscious states awarenesses of the bodies of others, but an awareness of our own body is among the contents of all our conscious states. But this awareness of our own body is unique. All other bodies we experience from the outside; our own body we experience from the inside. When I see something, I experience part of my own body—the eyebrows, the bridge of my nose, and so on. Properties like pains and pleasures are located at places *within* my body; these properties of parts of my body located within my skin are experienced by no one else but me. Conversely, there is one and only one body *B* of which it is true that I experience properties like these that are located at places inside *B*. Again, I can move my own body simply by willing it; this I can do with no other body. It is a fact of experience that we are aware of one and only one body from the inside and that among the contents of every conscious state is an awareness of this body from the inside. We can use this special sort of experience to define the symmetrical relation of 'belonging to', that is, to define what it is for a conscious state to belong to a body and what it is for a body to belong to a conscious state.[36] A conscious state belongs to a body just in case that among the contents of the conscious state is an awareness of that body from the inside; conversely, a body belongs to a conscious state just in case that among the contents of the conscious state is an awareness of that body from the inside.

Thus, if I assert that (+)

I feel proud that I then did so-and-so

then the first 'I' expresses an awareness that is constitutive of a conscious state. That conscious state has among its contents an awareness from the inside of a particular body. That body belongs to me, that is, the 'I'; that body is *mine*. But (+) also describes an earlier conscious state. This too is *mine*. Why? Because among the contents of that conscious state was an awareness from the inside of the very same body that I am now aware of from the inside when I assert (+). That earlier conscious state belonged to the very same body that is (now) *mine*. The earlier conscious state and the later conscious state are related to one another through the fact that they belong to the same unique body.

As we put it above, the earlier conscious state was a and the later one d, and the two are the same because $d = (\text{'}x)\ (R^3ax)$. We phrased the issue of personal identity as the issue of the relation R: precisely what relation is it? The Humean answer that we have given is that R is the relation that a bears to d just in case that a belongs at an earlier time to the very same body that d belongs to at a later time. If we assume that we have a nonproblematic account of the identity of bodies through time, it follows that we now have a nonproblematic account of the identity of persons through time. And once we have personal identity, the ordinary practice that we noted above of identifying mental states—believings, passions, and the like—and actions by predicating them of persons can be sustained.

This nonproblematic account of personal identity has so far been stated in non-Humean terms; it can easily be re-stated in Hume's own language. Things that stand in the relation R have a certain 'quality' in common: that of belonging to one and the same unique body. This relation creates an association among the ideas of things that stand in that relation. That is, if X's and Y's as X's and Y's stand in the relation R, then an idea of an X will introduce the idea of a Y and the impression of an X will introduce the idea of a Y, together in each case with the feeling of unity. But a and d have the quality of belonging to the same body, and therefore stand in relation R to one another. Hence, the impression of that body which is among the contents of conscious state d will introduce the idea of the conscious state a together with the feeling that a and d are a unity. As Hume would think about these things, there are three entities present. There is, first, the present impression of the body that picks out the person. Second, there is the idea of the past states of that person as picked out by that body. Third, there is the feeling that the former states, as presented by the idea, are part of a unity that includes the present conscious state that belongs to the same body. Hume makes these several connections when he speaks of "the idea, or rather impression, of ourselves [which] is always intimately present with us" (T, p. 317).

We can restate these points within the framework of Hume's associationist psychology. The conscious state d will contain an impression of the body to which it belongs. By virtue of established associations, the presence of this 'quality' in consciousness will introduce ideas of all the other states that constitute the self. But this notion that ideas of all these antecedent states are contained within the present state is clearly implausible. What one should say—as John Stuart Mill's rethinking of the notion of psychological analysis makes clear—is that d introduces the idea of the self that is an awareness of the whole as such, but does not include an awareness of the parts of that whole as really present in the conscious state. These parts are present, to be sure, but only dispositionally, not really.

As we have indicated, there is little doubt that Hume would find something along this line congenial as an account of personal identity. But this is not the central theme in Hume's reply to those, like Butler and Clarke, who held that all stability of personality would disappear if we abandon the notion that the self is a simple substance. The self, Hume holds, is also a social construct, and a stable personal identity arises in a social context. As Capaldi has emphasized, in the discussions of the passions and virtues, "the self in a public and social world is already presupposed in Hume's analysis."[37] The sort of personal identity one can have is dependent upon the social structure, the norms that Hume speaks of when he discusses the "artificial virtues," and the stability of that identity depends upon the stability of that social structure.[38]

When the statement

(+)   I feel proud that I then did so-and-so

is used in its normal way, the subject of the feeling of pride is my action of doing so-and-so. The object of pride is always oneself; the subjects are "either parts of ourselves, or something nearly related to us" (T, p. 285). The pride in an action often derives from its virtue—"the good and bad qualities of our actions and manners constitute virtue and vice, and determine our personal character, than which nothing operates more strongly on these passions [of pride and humility]" (T, p. 285); we may assume that this is so in the case of (+), but at any rate its use implies that the action is so related to *me* that *I* take pride in it. This relation is not merely that of belonging to my body. I do not take pride in the reflex acts of my arms and legs; reflex acts are not actions, they do not relate to *me*. Nor, indeed, are certain intentional acts *mine* in the relevant way. This, surely, is the point about the acts of Locke's drunk: his actions when drunk, while certainly his in the sense of being consciously intended by him, are nonetheless not his in the sense of being "out of character." The actions of the drunk are, to use Hume's terminology, the subjects of shame rather than of humility, though being a drunk may be the subject of humility. It is the element of *character* that here provides the linkage to self that is recorded in (+). (+) moreover records a knowledge of the connection of action to the self unified not only as belonging to a certain body but also as having a certain *enduring character* as its nature; and this knowledge would normally be taken as the exercise of the capacity for self-knowledge.

There are two points here. The first is that one's identity as a person is constituted by one's character. This must be added to bodily identity as part of the relation "R" that links the various parts of a person into a unity. The second is that self-consciousness is to be understood not only in terms of the awareness that constitutes my present conscious state; it is to be understood also in terms of the exercise of the capacity to survey one's actions and dispositions and to relate them to oneself *qua* having a certain character. Self-consciousness in the first sense is the immediate awareness that one always has of the contents of one's conscious states; self-consciousness in the second sense is the capacity to recognize one's various actions and dispositions as expressing and as connected to oneself as an enduring unity. The former is a simple awareness. The latter is the capacity to come to know certain *patterns in experience*. And this coming to know patterns in experience is to be understood in the Humean terms that we have already noted.

We must look at each of these points—character as providing the linkage that defines personal identity, and our own reflective knowledge of our character—in turn.

Concerning character, Hume holds, quite correctly, that our psychological dispositions, our human sentiments and passions, are dependent upon social and economic conditions, and that changes in those conditions bring about psychological transformations. He characterizes the conventions that make social life possible as "natural artifices" (T, p. 484). These have developed "gradually and acquire force by a slow progression" (T, p. 490). Such changes in the social and economic structure redirect the human sentiments and passions in various ways. There is therefore, as Hume says, a "progress of the sentiments" (T, p. 500) as the artifices that structure society develop. Traits like "selfishness and confin'd generosity" (T, p. 495) are present in presocial or natural persons. But as society forms through the institution of social conventions concerning property, contract (promising) and government, new traits such as honesty, fidelity, and loyalty, and also chastity, come into existence. And as these make possible the division of labor, so our natural abilities also develop (T, pp. 606ff.). The abilities that presocial or natural man possesses are "slender" (T, p. 484); they need to be "augmented" (T, p. 485) if life is to be at all decent. This improvement in our abilities is achieved in the social context; it is "by partition of employments, [that] our ability increases" (ibid.). Among the relevant faculties of the soul are the intellectual, such as the "faculty of placing our present ideas in such an order, as to form true propositions and opinions" (T, p. 612), as well as our manual abilities, such as "agility, good mein . . . dexterity in any manual business or manufacture" (T, p. 279). Hume also mentions "industry, assiduity, enterprize, dexterity" (T, p. 587) and later "industry, perseverance, patience, activity, vigilance, application, constancy" (T, p. 610). Besides "wit and eloquence" he includes "good humour" (T, p. 611). To "cleanliness" he adds "decorum" (T, pp. 611–12).

The various dispositions and traits that constitute one's character are, as we have seen, all to be understood as *patterns* of thought and action. The permanence of the self, then, if there be such, is the permanence of a *pattern*, not the permanence of an *entity*. The objection of Clarke and Butler to the attack on the substantial self was that it eliminated the permanent; for them the question was, as it was for Shaftesbury, "how [is] that subject continued one and the same?"[39] Too wed to the substance tradition, too wed to the Christian doctrine of the self that had appropriated the substance account of personal identity, they could not see that there could be any permanence other than the permanence of an entity. What Hume makes clear, however, is that another account of the permanence of the self is possible.

The habits, the traits and dispositions, which constitute character are themselves learned; these patterns are acquired patterns. The laws of learning are the same for all men; these patterns define a common human nature, and through them, together with different conditions of learning, we can account for the diversity, and stability, of human nature. We acquire the various traits that define our individual characters through a process of learning when we grow into the roles that are open to us in society, when we choose a role like historian or lawyer or pool hustler, or when we come to play a role to which we are led or assigned or even fated by, say, the place of our parents in society.

> The skin, pores, muscles, and nerves of a day-labourer are different from those of a man of quality: So are his sentiments, actions and manners. The different stations of life influence the whole fabric, external and internal; and these different stations arise necessarily, because, uniformly, for the necessary and uniform principles of human nature. Men cannot live without society, and cannot be associated without government. Government makes a distinction of property, and establishes the different ranks of men. This produces industry, traffic, manufactures, law-suits, war, leagues, alliances, voyages, travels, cities, fleets, ports, and all those other actions and objects, which cause such a diversity, and at the same time maintain such an uniformity in human nature. (T, p. 402)

What accounts for the stability of human character is, therefore, the fact of *causal determinism*, where by 'cause' one means, of course, "constant union" (T, p. 405).

> Whether we consider mankind according to the difference of sexes, ages, governments, conditions, or methods of education; the same uniformity and regular operation of natural principles are discernible. Like causes still produce like effects; in the same manner as in the mutual action of the elements and powers of nature. (T, p. 401)

This means, of course, that the self in the sense of that which is permanent through diversity is created by the sensible world rather than being something that transcends that world, as in the substance and Christian traditions. Hume does not neglect to point out that both common sense and the Christian tradition tend to agree with his position rather than that of the substance tradition when they recognize the efficacy of rewards and punishments in shaping human character. "'Tis indeed certain, that as all human laws are founded on rewards and punishments, 'tis suppos'd as a fundamental principle, that these motives have an influence on the mind, and both produce the good and prevent the evil actions. We may give to this influence what name we please; but as 'tis usually conjoin'd with the action, common sense requires it shou'd be esteem'd a cause, and be look'd upon as an instance of that necessity" (T, p. 410). Indeed, if we assume that causal determinism does *not* hold true, then there would be *no connection* among the actions of our lives. On the view of the libertarians who deny causal determinism, the self would turn out to be a mere bundle with nothing permanent to it, and however good or evil those actions might in themselves be, there would be no person to hold responsible for them or to praise or blame (T, p. 411).

Moreover, as Hume has explained much earlier in his discussion of cause in Book I of the *Treatise*, given that we are presented with no objective necessary connections in experience, the hypothesizing of a transcendental self as a power that produces actions will not help—however could we ascertain that the same substantial self (power) was present on two or more occasions? (T, p. 91) The *metaphysical conjecture* of a transcendental substantial self is therefore without any *practical* importance. The only notion of the permanent self that is useful is that which Hume proposes, the permanence of a pattern rather than the permanence of an entity.

We can say therefore that the unity of the self is not merely the unity of the body, though that is a crucial part of it. But the unity of the self includes also the unity constituted by the person's enduring character. As we have seen Hume say, for socialized persons, "our reputation, our character, our name are considerations of vast weight and importance" (T, p. 316). And so, in order to define the relation R that links the various stages of the self into a unity, we need to take into account not only the laws that connect the states of the body with their predecessors and successors and states of mind with states of the body but also the permanent patterns of thought and action that define our character and our name, that is, make us *who* we are, the individual person we are.

We need, however, one more thing. Since the unity of self is constituted by patterns and these can come to be known as can any patterns, it follows that the unity of the self, far from being mysterious as it appeared at the end of Book I of the *Treatise*, is in fact open and public. But the traditional self is a center of reflective self-consciousness, and this we do not yet have. It must not only be true that the self can be known but also that it be capable of *self*-knowledge; a person must have the capacity to reflect upon and monitor his own self.

Now, this itself is a character trait, and Hume's general position on the unity and permanence of the self applies in particular to the crucial trait of self-consciousness. This too is a socially acquired trait, and its enduring character can be accounted for in terms of the needs of society and of the individual in a social context.

One's character is of importance to others; they learn to discern it in order to look after their own good, as they interact, or refuse to interact, with one. One's own character is important to oneself also, for one to know how others will react to one and how one can go about achieving one's own ends in cooperation with others. Morally good character traits, recognized in a good reputation and name, are generally beneficial to both oneself and others.

In the presocial context, a person in a way has a character, in the sense of having certain natural virtues and vices, enduring traits and abilities. What one does not have is a "reputation" or even a "name." Hume links the invention of language with that of other conventions such as that of promising (T, p. 490), so one could have a "name" only in a context in which the artificial virtues were also present.[40] Similarly, one could have a reputation only in a community in which opinions are shared through language as well as sympathy. Having a reputation depends upon the existence of a common moral language (T, p. 582), and so having a reputation like having a "name" presupposes the presence of the artificial virtues. The development of society in the form of the conventions of property, contract (promising), and government also brings with it, in the form of language, the capacity to describe virtues and vices and to communicate one's judgments of character. Moreover, since an abstract idea is, for Hume, simply the association of a word with a similar class of individuals, it follows that we can have no abstract ideas, nor, therefore, any thought, apart from language, apart from linguistic conventions.[41] The capacity to *think* about ourselves, the capacity for reflective self-consciousness, is thus acquired only in the social context.

Locke recognized that the notion of a person is a forensic notion. Hume accepted this point, but went beyond it to locate the notion of a person in the broader framework of the linguistic and moral practices that define society and the social context in which we live, love, and work. Since the forensic notion of the self defines the latter with respect to responsibility, Locke discovered, in his correspondence with Molyneux, that the linkage that creates a person out of a series of events need not coincide with the casual chain that links those events. Both bodily identity and memory are crucial to personal identity, but there is more to it than that: there are also the permanent traits of character that unify one's thought and action as *one's own*. But there is yet more. As Locke also recognized, continuing the tradition coming down from Plotinus through the Christian tradition, the responsible self is one that is self-reflective. Locke was not able to free himself sufficiently from the substance tradition to recognize that this capacity had to be understood not as a simple power of a substance but as a learned capacity of a socialized being. This final step was the one that Hume took. Identity of self is not something that one can "find" in "the thought alone" (T, p. 635); reason reflecting upon its own processes cannot discover the principle that constitutes personal identity. Nor is that which constitutes the unity of the self to be found in the passions alone, the sentiments, traits and abilities that define one's character. What is required is the union of these two in a character that includes the capacity for self-conscious concern, the reflective concern of a mind for the status and being of its own self, the reflective concern of a mind "all collected within itself" (T, p. 270). This mind "all collected within itself" is the product of the social context in which each mind mirroring its fellows discovers itself: "a mind will never be able to bear its own survey which has been wanting in its part to mankind and society" (T, p. 620). The man of thought alone is a "strange, uncouth monster" (T, p. 264); once we have discovered exactly what it is that constitutes personal identity, we recognize that it is not at all surprising that he is incapable of discovering his own personal identity, that is, to put it another way, that the full solution of the problem of personal identity cannot be given in Book I of the *Treatise*, that one must wait for the completion of Books II and III. The man of character is one who can "mingle and unite in society" (ibid.) through the establishment of conventions and social artifices. Only when this is added to the man of thought do we achieve a *person*, someone capable of surveying his (or her) own being and bringing it into harmony with the deepest standards he or she has for himself or herself alone, someone responsible for his or her own identity.

This concept of person is not adopted for purely descriptive purposes. Unlike our abstract idea of, say, a natural chemical kind like gold, we do not adopt it simply because it is useful in stating the regularities that we discover to obtain in the world. That, to be sure, is part of it, since regularities, both those that define our body and those that define our character, are important in determining the utility of our concept of a person. But Locke's insight remains, that the concept of a person is also a forensic concept, in part defined as it is because it is useful in the social practices of men. Persons are, in the first instance, those entities whose enduring dispositions and traits we morally evaluate and who, on the basis of those evaluations, we reward and punish. But persons are more than entities whose behavior and traits can be shaped by the actions of others through reward and punishment. Persons are not merely responsible for what they do; they are capable of *taking responsibility* for their actions. They are capable of *self-evaluation*, and capable of acting to shape themselves, and to determine their own way of being. In Frankfurt's terms,[42] they are capable of forming second-order desires and second-order volitions. This capacity is itself useful both to the possessor and to others—it is to one's own good and that of others that one knows oneself sufficiently to anticipate the responses of others, and, where one finds it desirable, to modify one's actions and dispositions in the light of this knowledge. And since this capacity has utility, it is, upon Hume's view, a virtue. It is, however, not simply a virtue among virtues, it is a virtue that is of such special utility in social practice that we use it as a defining characteristic of those who play roles in our social system.

The reflective self-consciousness that defines what it is to be a person, a player of social roles, is achieved and maintained in a mind only in the context of social conventions, social roles, and only with the help of the mirroring minds of one's fellows. This means that those whom we recognize as persons are in the first place those with whom we interact sympathetically. And it means in the second place that there are no persons apart from the context of the conventions that define society. These conventions of course reckon as persons those with whom we often do not interact sympathetically. But then, the conventions are, as Hume argues, established not by feelings of sympathy and benevolence but by self-interest. The concept of a person and of personal identity is determined by the utility it has in defining what it is to be a role player in our system of social conventions and artificial virtues.

To understand this, we have found, we must read the whole of Hume's masterpiece. We can recognize only then Hume's point in putting on the title page of the *Treatise* the motto from Tacitus extolling the unity of thought and desire that achieves self-expression: "Rara temporum felicitas, ubi sentire, quae velis; & quae sentias, dicere licet."

NOTES

1. This view has more recently been defended by David Wiggins, *Sameness and Substance* (Cambridge, Mass.: Harvard University Press, 1980).

2. In Spinoza's terms, the 'real essence' is the *natura naturans* and the definitional essence is the *natura naturata*.

3. Cf. B. Williams' view that "an individual person has a set of desires, concerns, or as I shall often call them, projects, which help constitute a *character*." A person has a character "in the sense of having projects and categorical desires with which that person is identified" ("Persons, Character and Morality," in *The Identities of Persons*, ed. A. Rorty [Berkeley: University of California Press, 1976], pp. 197–216).

4. Page references in parentheses following a "T" are to D. Hume, *Treatise of Human Nature*, ed. L. A. Selby-Bigge (Oxford: Clarendon Press, 1888).

5. This point is of some relevance to moral philosophy, as John Stuart Mill emphasized. See the important essay by W. Donner, "John Stuart Mill's Concept of Utility," *Dialogue* 22 (1983): 479–94; and also F. Wilson, *Psychological Analysis and the Philosophy of John Stuart Mill* (Toronto: University of Toronto Press, 1990), Chapter 7.

6. M. Heidegger, *Sein und Zeit*, in his *Gesamteausgabe*, Band 2 (Vittorio Klosterman: Frankfurt am Main, 1976), Sec. 9, p. 57.

7. H. Frankfurt, "Freedom of the Will and the Concept of a Person," *Journal of Philosophy* 68 (1971): 7.

8. A. Rorty, "A Literary Postscript: Characters, Persons, Selves, Individuals," in A. Rorty, *The Identities of Persons*, p. 309.

9. Boethius, *The Theological Tractates*, trans. H. F. Steward and E. K. Rand, Loeb Classical Library (Cambridge, Mass.: Harvard University Press, 1962), p. 92.

10. Cf. F. Wilson, "The Lockean Revolution in the Theory of Science," in *Early Modern Philosophy: Metaphysics, Epistemology, and Politics–Essays in Honour of R. F. McRae*, ed. G. Moyal and S. Tweyman (Delmar, N.Y.: Caravan Books, 1985), pp. 65–97.

11. Cf. F. Wilson, "Abstract Ideas and Other Rules of Language," paper presented to the Conference on Ideas in 17th and 18th Century Philosophy, University of Iowa, Iowa City, April 1989.

12. This is awkwardly placed relative to the main argument about the nature of causation which occurs in Book I, Part iii of the *Treatise*. (The parallel discussion in the *Enquiries* is better placed.) Hume attempted to remedy this awkwardness in the "Appendix" to the *Treatise*, where he added a new paragraph to be inserted into the discussion of I, iii, 14.

13. Cf. F. Wilson, "Hume's Defence of Science," *Dialogue* 25 (1986): 611–28, and "Hume's Cognitive Stoicism," *Hume Studies* (1985 Supplement): 251–68.

14. D. Hume, *An Abstract of a Treatise of Human Nature*, ed. J. M. Keynes and P. Sraffa (London: Cambridge University Press, 1930).

15. Cf. F. Wilson, "Was Hume a Sceptic with regard to the Senses?" *Journal of the History of Philosophy* 27 (1989): 49–73.

16. Cf. F. Wilson, "Is There a Prussian Hume?" *Hume Studies* 8 (1982): 1–18.

17. For more details on this point, see F. Wilson, "Hume's Fictional Continuant," *History of Philosophy Quarterly* 6 (1989): 171–88.

18. For an excellent discussion of some aspects of this section, see Henry E. Allison, "Locke on Personal Identity: A Re-Examination," *Journal of the History of Ideas* 27 (1966): 41–58.

19. References are to Plotinus, *The Enneads*, trans. Stephen MacKenna, 4th ed., rev. B. S. Page (London: Faber and Faber, 1969). The historical connection linking Plotinus to Locke goes via Henry More and the Cambridge Platonists, though there is, of course, a good deal of the Neo-Platonic position in both Descartes and Malebranche.

20. References are to R. McKeon, ed., *The Basic Works of Aristotle* (New York: Random House, 1941).

21. John Locke, *Essay concerning Human Understanding*, ed. P. H. Nidditch (Oxford: Oxford University Press, 1975). References are given in parentheses to book, chapter, and section.

22. See note 9 above.

23. Joseph Butler, "Dissertation of Personal Identity," in Butler's *Works*, ed. W. E. Gladstone (Oxford: Clarendon Press, 1896), vol. 1.

24. John Locke, *Works of John Locke* (London: T. Longman, 1794).

25. Ernest Lee Tuveson, *The Imagination as a Means of Grace: Locke and the Aesthetics of Romanticism* (Berkeley: University of California Press, 1960), pp. 27–28.

26. Cf. T. Penelhum, "Hume on Personal Identity," *Philosophical Review* 64 (1955): 571–89; and "Self-Identity and Self Regard," in A. Rorty, *The Identities of Persons*, pp. 253–80.

27. J. S. Mill, *An Examination of Sir William Hamilton's Philosophy*, vol. 11 of *The Collected Works of John Stuart Mill*, ed. J. Robson (Toronto: University of Toronto Press, 1979), p. 194.

28. Cf. F. Wilson, *Psychological Analysis and the Philosophy of John Stuart Mill*, Chapter 3.

29. J. S. Mill, *An Examination of Sir William Hamilton's Philosophy*, p. 194.

30. G. Vesey, *Personal Identity: A Philosophical Analysis* (Ithaca, N.Y.: Cornell University Press, 1974), pp. 108–9.

31. Cf. F. Wilson, "Was Hume a Sceptic with Regard to the Senses?"

32. Compare the account of conscious states in G. Bergmann, "Acts," in his *Logic and Reality* (Madison, Wis.: University of Wisconsin Press, 1964).

33. Compare the view of Wittgenstein in *The Blue and Brown Books* (Oxford: Basil Blackwell, 1958):

To say 'I have pain' is no more a statement *about* a particular person than moaning is. 'But surely the word "I" in the mouth of a man refers to the man who says it; it points to himself; and very often a man who says it actually points to himself with his finger.' But it was quite superfluous to point to himself. He might just as well only have raised his hand. It would be wrong to say that when someone points to the sun with his hand, he is pointing both to the sun and himself because it is *he* who points; on the other hand, he may by pointing attract attention both to the sun and to himself.

The word 'I' does not means the same as 'L.W.' even if I am L.W., nor does it mean the same as the expression 'the person who is now speaking'. But that doesn't mean: that 'L.W.' and 'I' mean different things. All it means is that these words are different instruments in our language. (p. 67)

34. For this notion of 'linguistic role' and 'meaning', see W. Sellars, "Reflections on Language Games," in his *Science, Perception and Reality* (London: Routledge and Kegan Paul, 1963); and "Notes on Intentionality," in his *Philosophical Perspectives* (Springfield, Ill.: Charles C. Thomas, 1967). Also F. Wilson, "Marras on Sellars on Thought and Language," *Philosophical Studies* 28 (1975): 91–102; and "Effability, Ontology and Method," *Philosophy Research Archives* 9 (1983): 419–70.

35. J. S. Mill, *An Examination of Sir William Hamilton's Philosophy*, p. 205n.

36. Cf. F. Wilson, "Why I Do Not Experience Your Pain," in *The Ontological Turn: Essays in Honor of Gustav Bergmann*, ed. M. Gram and E. D. Klemke (Iowa City, Iowa: University of Iowa Press, 1974), pp. 276–300.

37. N. Capaldi, *David Hume* (Boston: Twayne, 1975), p. 138.

38. Concerning certain aspects of what follows, see the important essay of Annette Baier, "Hume on Heaps and Bundles," *American Philosophical Quarterly* 16 (1979): 285–95; and also her *A Progress of Sentiments* (Cambridge, Mass.: Harvard University press, 1991).

39. Anthony, Earl of Shaftesbury, *Characteristics of Men, Manners, Opinions, Times*, ed. J. M. Robertson, with an introduction by S. Grean, two volumes in one (Indianapolis: Bobbs-Merrill, 1964), 2: 275.

40. Cf. F. Wilson, "Hume and Derrida on Language and Meaning," *Hume Studies* 12 (1986): 99–121.

41. Cf. ibid.; and also F. Wilson, "Abstract Ideas and Other Rules of Language."

42. See note 7, above.

Leibniz's Principle of Individuation in His *Disputatio metaphysica de principio individui* of 1663

Laurence B. McCullough

t requires only a passing acquaintance with Leibniz's philosophical texts to appreciate that individuals occupy a central place in his philosophy. In his "Discourse on Metaphysics" (1686), for example, after seven paragraphs concerning God and God's nature, in the eighth paragraph Leibniz turns his attention to the "concept of an individual substance" and, in subsequent paragraphs, to the celebrated "complete individual concept."[1] "The Principles of Nature and of Grace, Based on Reason" (1714) begins with a consideration of substance, including simple substance, or monads.[2] Simple substances, or monads, have no parts. They cannot be broken apart, as it were, and, therefore, constitute unities. Simple substances are also distinguished from one another. In short, simple substances, or monads, are indivisible and distinct, thus displaying the two fundamental intensional components of individuality.

This chapter concerns Leibniz's principle of individuation, a philosophical topic that occupied his attention throughout his philosophical career. He first developed his views on the topic in his earliest philosophy and essentially carried those views into his mature philosophy.[3] Thus the focus of this chapter will be Leibniz's *Disputatio metaphysica de principio individui* (1663), because it is in this text that Leibniz sets out and defends his principle of individuation in a level of detail not to be found elsewhere in his work.

THREE PRELIMINARIES

Before turning to an account of Leibniz's principle of individuation, three preliminaries are in order, to set the appropriate context for that account. These include clarification of Leibniz's approach to the problem of individuation, the intension of 'individual', and the extension of 'individual'. These preliminaries provide the conceptual tools required to understanding Leibniz's principle of individuation on its own terms.

Leibniz's Approach to the Problem of individuation

Leibniz's approach to the problem of individuation is decidedly metaphysical. This is no surprise for a pre-Kantian philosopher. As a consequence, Leibniz's approach to the problem of individuation is quite different from approaches that can be found in more recent philosophy. For Strawson, for example, the problem of individuation is understood in conceptual-linguistic terms. His concern is with how we identify particulars, which involves how a "hearer" identifies the particular of which a "speaker" speaks. Strawson's account comes to this: "[a]ll that is necessary, in order for the identification to be secured, is that the hearer should come to know, on the strength of the speaker's words, what, or which, particular the speaker is in fact referring to."[4] And this the hearer can accomplish by being in possession of some "individuating fact" about the particular in question: "that such-and-such a thing is true of that particular and no other particular whatsoever."[5] These individuating facts about particulars are provided by spatiotemporal relations, because each particular occupies a unique place within the spatiotemporal matrix.[6]

Wiggins can be read as extending this conceptual-linguistic approach to its logical conclusion when he writes:

> It would appear that a theory of individuation must comprise at least three things: first, an elucidation of the primitive concept of identity or sameness; second, some however abstract account of what it is for something to be a substance that persists through change; and third . . . the beginnings of some lifelike description, however schematic, of what it is for a thinker at one time and then another to single out the same substance *as* the same substance.[7]

This last task, Wiggins goes on to say, provides the basic "framework" for this theory. As he puts the matter, "That which individuates [i.e., singles out], in the sense in which the word is used in this book, is in the first place a thinker, and derivatively a substance or predicate."[8]

Leibniz's approach to the problem of individuation is starkly different, a fact that must be appreciated if we are to understand Leibniz's principle of individuation on its own terms. Leibniz is concerned to provide an account of the metaphysical foundation of individuality in individuals themselves. Thus, Leibniz's primary concern is not to provide a conceptual-linguistic analysis of the concept of identity and of the identification and reidentification of substances in the manner of, say, a Strawson or Wiggins. Leibniz wants to understand that which in individuals, ingredient in them, *makes them individual*—quite apart from *our* attempts to identify them over time as the same individual. As Leibniz puts it in the *Disputatio metaphysica de principio individui*: "Wherefore to summarize the foregoing, we treat of something real and what is called a "physical principle," which would serve as the foundation for the formal notion in the mind of 'individual', understood as individuation or numerical difference."[9] This real or physical principle is distinct from what Leibniz terms a principle of 'knowing', which applies to the logical sense of 'individual', its use in predication.[10] The principle of knowing an individual, Leibniz would say, is the topic that concerns Strawson and Wiggins. This topic can be studied in turn on the basis of Leibniz's own topic in the *Disputatio*, a principle of 'being',[11] what it is *in re* that constitutes the individual as such.

This same approach to the problem appears in Leibniz's mature work. For example, in his *New Essays on Human Understanding* he has Theophilus—the character through whom Leibniz speaks in the dialogue—address the "relative idea of the greatest importance . . . that of identity or diversity."[12] This idea is understood in the following terms: "In addition to the difference of time and place [the whole of the story for Strawson, it would seem] there must always be an *internal principle of distinction*."[13] Shortly thereafter Theophilus goes on to add this:

> The 'principle of individuation' reduces, in the case of individuals, to the principle of distinction of which I have just been speaking. If two individuals were perfectly similar and equal, in short, *indistinguishable* in themselves, there would be no principle of individuation. I would even venture to say that there would be no individual distinctness, no separate individuals.[14]

Clearly, there must be something internal to and constitutive of individuals, 'in themselves', that accounts for their individuation.

This passage from the *New Essays* provides the context for reading the *Monadology* in the course of which the same theme emerges, namely, there is something about individuals themselves that makes them individual. Indeed, this must be the case: "It is even necessary for each monad to be different from every other. For there are never two things in nature which are perfectly alike and in which it is impossible to find a difference that is internal or founded on an intrinsic denomination."[15]

Leibniz's understanding of individuals and of their individuation is thus distinctively metaphysical in character, almost one-dimensionally so. Individuals are what exist, they occupy all of the places in Leibniz's ontology, and it is some constitutive feature of them that accounts for their individuality.

In his recent study, *Introduction to the Problem of individuation in the Early Middle Ages*, Gracia provides a thoroughgoing account of how individuals and the problem of individuation were understood in the Scholastic tradition.[16] Because, when it comes to individuals and their individuation, Leibniz inherits and works largely within the terms set by that tradition, Gracia's analysis makes available to us a powerful framework within which Leibniz's approach to the problem of individuation can be understood.

Gracia points out that there are two ways in which the term 'individuation' was understood in the Scholastic tradition: "(1) the process by which an individual acquires the feature or features which make it the individual it is, or (2) the very feature or features which render it such."[17] Leibniz's concern is with the latter. Gracia adds that 'individual' and 'individuality' have distinct meanings: "Individuality is to be distinguished from the individual. The former is the feature whereby the latter has its unique character. The individual is opposed to the universal, while individuality is opposed to universality."[18] The problem of individuation in the Scholastic tradition, according to Gracia, was concerned with a thing's "individuality, namely, with the feature of things which characterizes them as individuals."[19] In the *Disputatio* Leibniz searches for the principle of individuation that alone fulfills this role.

The Intension of 'Individual'

As a result of this feature, this internal principle of individuation, individuals, for Leibniz, have a particular intension. This intension has two main components. First, individuals are marked by indivisibility. They are something "indivisible" (1669),[20] are "finite" and have a "determinate existence" (1678),[21] are a "genuine unity" (1686-87),[22] are "indivisible" and "perfect" monads (1699-1706),[23] and are "total things."[24] Individual substance is characterized by the "perfect unity" of perception and appetition (1695-1704).[25] Individual substances are, second, marked by distinction, as the above passages from the *New Essays* and the *Monadology* make clear.

Living things or bodies, which comprise individual substances, have indivisibility and thus identity through time in virtue of the monad that is the principle of their unity, their dominant monad.

> Organization or configuration alone, without an enduring principle of life which I call 'monad', would not suffice to make something numerically the same, i.e., the same individual . . . one can rightly say that they remain perfectly 'the same individual' in virtue of this soul or spirit which makes the *I* in substances which think.[26]

Monads thus account for their own individuality and also for the individuality of the living things, bodies, that they constitute and organize into unique unities.

Gracia's analysis of the intension of individuality as a constituent element of the problem of individuation is extremely helpful here. The intension of individuality concerns "what it is to be an individual as opposed to something else."[27] The first intensional element of individuality is indivisibility—the impossibility of an individual being divided or somehow broken up into individuals of the same species as the original individual. The second intensional element of individuality is what Gracia calls distinction, "the distinction of each and every individual from all other individuals, including those belonging to the same species."[28] Each individual is unique in at least some respect, perhaps all respects. The latter view, that individuals are unique in all respects, is Leibniz's view.

Leibniz adopts this understanding of individuality. Individuals are "indivisibile,"[29] a term he uses. This accounts for their "unity"[30] and "determinate existence."[31] Individuals are also marked by their distinction, a term that Leibniz used, for example, in the *New Essays*.[32] Something intrinsic, a metaphysical principle constitutive of an individual, accounts for its difference from all other individuals.

The Extension of 'Individual'

The third and final preliminary concerns the extension of 'individual'. Leibniz was as careful to delineate rigorously the extension of 'individual' as he was to delineate its intension. Gracia notes that there are three basic views in the Scholastic tradition on the extension of individuality: (1) "Nothing that exists is individual"; (2) "Everything that exists is individual"; and (3) "Some things that exist are individual and some are not."[33] Leibniz, as we shall shortly see, in the *Disputatio* takes essentially the second view, with the important implication that—contra the common nature of the Scotists—there are no real universals. Because there can be no universals or anything common *in re*, it will also turn out that everything constitutive of individuals is itself individual, including individual accidents and properties. This basic feature of Leibniz's metaphysics is absolutely crucial for understanding his principle of individuation, as will become plain later.

LEIBNIZ'S PRINCIPLE OF INDIVIDUATION
IN THE *DISPUTATIO*

With these preliminaries in place, the basic features of Leibniz's principle of individuation in the *Disputatio* can be identified. It must be some internal, constitutive element of each individual that accounts for the individual's indivisibility and distinction. Leibniz argues in the *Disputatio* that, because everything that exists is individual, each individual is its own principle of individuation. Hence, he sometimes speaks in his mature philosophy of individuals as "total things."[34] The phrase that he uses in the *Disputatio* and that will be used here is "whole entity," *entitas tota*. The first step toward understanding what Leibniz means by 'whole entity' is to understand the principles of individuation that he rejects in the *Disputatio*.

Principles of individuation Leibniz Rejects in the Disputatio

In the *Disputatio* Leibniz considers and rejects what he identifies as the chief contenders for the principle of individuation other than whole entity. A brief review of these three contenders—negation, existence, and haecceity—will help shed further light on Leibniz's principle.

In the *Disputatio* Leibniz seeks a principle of individuation for all created, finite entities, including angels and all other creatures, that is, all material and immaterial entities other than God. Apparently, he accepts the traditional Scholastic argument that because God is infinite there cannot be many gods and so there is no problem of individuation with respect to God. But there are many finite entities: individual material substances, individual nonmaterial substances (angels), and the individual accidents and properties of individual substances. Any adequate principle of individuation must apply to all three alike. He considers, therefore, only principles of individuation that would serve to individuate all these types of entities. Thus, matter, for example, is not considered.

Negation as the Principle of individuation   Negation as the principle of individuation focuses on the intension of individuality considered as indivisibility and distinction. Indivisibility is plainly something negative, but so is distinction also because distinction means that an individual is *not* identical with any other thing. Thus, it seems quite natural to conclude that indivisibility and distinction together constitute the principle of individuation.

Leibniz begins his consideration of the view of individuation in terms of negation by doubting that it has any adherents other than "some obscure nominalist."[35] Thus, he chiefly relies on those who consider but reject this principle for his understanding of it. For example, Duns Scotus, with whose metaphysics Leibniz was acquainted, considers but rejects negation as the principle of individuation.

Scotus's account of negation as the (alleged) principle of individuation is the following: "'One' means indivision; 'indivision' means negation. Therefore, through nothing positive is an individual individuated."[36] Ramoneda, also known to Leibniz, provides a more detailed elaboration of this principle:

Since 'individual' does not express something other than what is undivided from itself and is separated through two negations, which are the negation of division from itself and the negation of identity with another, but not individual through something positive, [those who hold this view] contend that a material individual in its *esse* is not constituted through something positive.[37]

Thus, double negation—indivisibility *and* distinction *together*—can be proposed as the principle of individuation.[38]

Leibniz mounts a number of criticisms of negation as the principle of individuation.[39] His main criticism relies on Scotistic sources. Scotists had argued against negation on the grounds that being incapable of division into individuals of the same species and being incapable of being identical with other individuals are perfections. But perfections, of course, are positive determinations of being. Moreover, as Bassolius argued, individuation is an act and so cannot be something negative.[40] Finally, the Scotists argued that negation is the *same* in each individual. Hence, negation cannot account for why a particular individual is 'this' rather than 'that' individual; negation cannot, ironically, account for distinction. Distinction therefore must be a function of some positive determination of the individual. It cannot be a function of itself and still account for nonidentity with other individuals.

Existence as the Principle of individuation in the *Disputatio*
Existence is at least a positive determination of being and so Leibniz
cannot dismiss it as rapidly and readily as he does negation. Gracia
notes that for those philosophers who distinguish essence from existence, existence is understood as a "separate principle or act."[41] This
creates the prima facie plausibility of existence as the principle of individuation: "This theory has initial support in the seemingly unshareable character of existence. For who can exist for me? My existence and
yours, certainly, are distinct and unshareable, and so it seems with
everyone else's."[42] In other words, each individual's existence is intrinsic and unique to it and so accounts for each individual's distinction
and indivisibility.

In the *Disputatio*, Leibniz takes as his antagonist on this score Henry
of Ghent. Henry of Ghent's argument is, roughly, that existence is not a
separate *res* but rather a constituent element of the individual, con-
ferred on it by God, and this existence contracts the essence to which
individuality is thereby added.[43] Hence, existence is something positive
and a constitutive principle of individuation, according to this view.

Again, in the *Disputatio*, Leibniz mounts a series of objections to
existence as the principle of individuation.[44] One of most powerful
turns on Leibniz's rejection of the formal distinction of the Scotists as
a middle ground between the real distinction, between individual *res*,
and the mental distinction, either made wholly by the mind or in the
mind on the basis of some *fundamentum in re*.[45] The formal distinction
is based on *aliquia realia* that are distinct but are not separable into
individual *res*. On such a view, essence and existence could be really
distinct although metaphysically inseparable.

Leibniz's rejection of the formal distinction allows him to claim
that, to the contrary, existence and essence are not really distinct. This
is because substance is already self-individuated, Leibniz's own view. In
other words, existence as the principle of individuation simply
amounts to Leibniz's own view. Leibniz also relies on Scotistic arguments that existence, when properly understood, is always existence of
some kind. But then, existence, as the principle of individuation, in
effect presupposes the ordering of things into kinds of things, kinds
that are multiplied in many individuals. Thus, existence presupposes
individuation; existence cannot account for individuation. Existence,
after an effort on his part, is thus dismissed by Leibniz as the principle
of individuation.

Haecceity as the Principle of individuation in the *Disputatio*
Leibniz reserves most of his negative argument in the *Disputatio* for

haecceity, the Scotistic principle of individuation. Scotists were realists about universals and so held that each individual of a specific kind has a common nature, a nature that is formally the same in each of those individuals. The common nature is thus not distinct and is, clearly, divisible into the many individuals to which it is common. Common natures possess specific rather than individual unity. Hence, the common nature cannot account for individuality. Something must be added to the common nature that does so and haecceity or 'thisness' provides the requisite positive individual determination. Each individual is thus an inseparable composite of common nature + haecceity and it is haecceity within this formally distinct, but metaphysically inseparable, composite that provides for indivisibility and distinction.[46] Haecceity is thus something positive and an internal, constitutive principle of individuation, according to this view.

It is in response to the Scotists that Leibniz's nominalistic commitments are fully displayed in the *Disputatio* and, I believe, cemented unalterably in place for the rest of his life. Scotus and his followers are rejected as "extreme realists" because Leibniz rejects the scheme of common nature + haecceity altogether as a model for individuals.[47] In doing so he follows Suárez, a fact he fully acknowledges. There is, he argues in many ingenious ways, no formal distinction and no common nature. Nature in things is individuated, not common. At most, it is only mentally distinct but not because of real commonality that might serve as a *fundamentum in re*. Nature and the principle of individuation are distinct only in the realm of ideas, as creatures of the mind. The mind abstracts a common *ratio* which is only and at most an *ens rationis*. *In re* natures are distinct and only and at most similar, never common. As such they serve as the *fundamentum in re* of sameness *in conceptu, in mente*. Of course, if there is no *common* nature, there is no haecceity, because there simply is no metaphysical need for something individual to be 'added' to already self-individuated nature. Since there is no formal distinction, haecceity is not something real. If haecceity were, *mirabile dictu*, to have any status, it would only be as an *ens rationis*. But an *ens rationis* exists only in the mind and is therefore external to, not intrinsic in, individuals. Hence, obviously and finally, haecceity cannot be the principle of individuation.

The Principle of Individuation Leibniz Accepts in the Disputatio

In the *Disputatio* Leibniz is clear that he follows Suárez in adopting whole entity, *entitas tota*, as the principle of individuation.[48]

> The first opinion [of the four he considers], because it is held
> by the most distinguished men and removes all difficulties
> [that pertain to the rejected candidates], will be adopted by
> us, the confirmation of which furnishes, as it were, a general
> argument against the remaining views. Therefore, I maintain:
> every individual is individuated by its whole entity.[49]

His arguments in defense of his view rely crucially on his rejection of
the common nature + haecceity account of the Scotists. Because there
is *in re* nothing common, nature is already individuated. Nothing real,
especially nothing formally distinct, must therefore be added to the
nature to account for its individuation. The nature thus individuates
itself. Thus, for Leibniz a nature = nature + principle of indivisibility
and distinction, where '+' does not signify the joining of real, formally
distinct entities, but the addition of what is only conceptually distinct.
As *individuated*, a nature is indivisible and distinct. As *nature*, a nature
is similar to other natures of the same kind, that is, natures from which
the mind is naturally disposed to abstract a single concept, the *same*
concept, under which those self-individuated natures fall.

Whole entity, then, is the principle of individuation in the following way. Nonmaterial substances consist only of natures, that is, self-
individuated natures and so their 'whole' entity is their principle of
individuation, where 'whole' means nothing need be added, haecceity
in particular. Material substances consist of self-individuated natures
and self-individuated matters, 'this nature' or 'this form', on the one
hand, and "this matter," on the other. The two together constitute the
whole entity of a material substance.

While Leibniz, as he points out in the opening passages of the *Disputatio*, is not directly concerned with the individuation of accidents,
he indicates his interest in the topic in the course of his defense of
whole entity as the principle of individuation. There Leibniz wants to
claim that individual accidents of the same kind can differ only in number and still be in one subject at the same time.[50] This could only be the
case if the nature of an accident—accidents have natures just as substances do, after all—is self-individuated. Thus, *mutatis mutandis* the
whole entity is the principle of individuation of accidents, as well.

In summary, in the *Disputatio* Leibniz holds that the nature individuates itself, in substances and accidents alike. Thus, every constituent element of each finite substance, its nature and its accidents, is
individual and therefore unique to it. Everything that exists—substances and their accidents—is individual, through and through.
Hence, the whole entity of each individual, that is, the individual sub-

stance + its individual accidents, accounts for its individuality. Indivisibility and distinction are thus accounted for by the whole entity.

Indeed, indivisibility and distinction are closely intertwined. Individuated nature obviously cannot be divided or multiplied into many individuals, as could the common nature of the Scotists (were it, *mirabile dictu*, to exist in the first place). Individuated nature also accounts for distinction because individuated nature is at most similar *in re*. It is unique to the individual that it constitutes, whether of substance or accident.

In short, everything that exists is individual, through and through. This is because, Leibniz takes himself in the *Disputatio* to have shown, there is no commonness *in re* and hence no basis for two individual things being able to be the same *in re*, that is, common *in re*, in even one respect. To be common in this way could be possible for Leibniz only if there were real universals and, emphatically, he argues that there are not any such entities when he again and again in the *Disputatio* rejects the common nature of the Scotists.

LEIBNIZ'S PRINCIPLE OF INDIVIDUATION
IN HIS MATURE PHILOSOPHY: A SKETCH

Between his earliest and his mature philosophy, Leibniz, for a variety of reasons,[51] shifted from a static model of individuals to a dynamic model. As he says in *De transubstantiatione*, substance "subsists in itself" because it has the "principle of action in it."[52] Only minds, he continues, are subsisting substances. Hence, he concludes, all finite reality comprises nonmaterial substances that are centers of activity.

These nonmaterial substances he later names "monads," as every student of Leibniz knows well. Monads are centers of activity constituted by appetition and perception. Each perception is an act of having at a *logical* (not physical, as measured by a clock) moment the rest of the world, that is, all other monads, as an object of consciousness. Each monad, as Leibniz says in many places, is a consciousness. Each perception contains all of its predecessors and successors and so a monad's perceptions form an inseparable whole. Each perception is a nonrepeatable relational property of its monad[53] and so is self-individuated. Appetition is the principle of activity that governs the generation of the perceptions of an individual in a seamless, ordered fashion into infinity. Appetition thus ensures that *in re* the perceptions of any one monad are inseparable from each other. That is, the monad is "indivisible into parts,"[54] where 'parts' means perceptions. Appetition in any monad is a function for generation of a particular set of perceptions, namely, *that* monad's perceptions. Hence, appetition is unique to each monad. Appetition is thus self-individuated in each monad and so also accounts for that monad's distinction from all others. Thus, the two components that comprise the intension of individuality are accounted for by a monad's self-individuated appetition and the seamless, inseparable ordered set of self-individuated perceptions of that monad that are generated by the activity of appetition. In short, the whole entity of a monad is its principle of individuation.

The parallels between the earliest and the mature philosophies of individuation of Leibniz can now be drawn succinctly.

earliest principle
of individuation = whole entity = self-individuated nature of substance and self-individuated nature of its accidents

mature principle
of individuation = whole entity = self-individuated appetition and self-individuated inseparable perceptions

CONCLUSION

Leibniz's principle of individuation is whole entity. Every property of an individual is itself individual, in virtue of being self-individuated, and is thus unique to that individual. Indeed, on the basis of such a nominalistic ontology, with its deep antagonism to any commonality *in re*, the only principle of individuation that can be defended is whole entity. Thus, Leibniz's nominalistic commitments—with roots in late scholastic work, Suárez's in particular, formed at the very beginning of his philosophical career, and adapted in his mature philosophy to a dynamic model of individuals—are essential for understanding the nature of his principle of individuation and why he came to hold that principle. Leibniz's principle of individuation, it turns out, is thus not a modern one, although in his mature philosophy it is adapted to a problem that is modern: how to account for the individuation of individuals that are centers of activity.

NOTES

1. Gottfried Wilhelm Leibniz, "Discourse on Metaphysics," in Gottfried Wilhelm Leibniz, *Philosophical Papers and Letters*, trans. Leroy E. Loemker (Dordrecht, Holland: D. Reidel, 1969), pp. 307ff.

2. Gottfried Wilhelm Leibniz, "Principles of Nature and Grace, Based on Reason," in Leibniz, *Philosophical Papers and Letters*, pp. 636–42. See also Gottfried Wilhelm Leibniz, "Monadology," in Leibniz, *Philosophical Papers and Letters*, pp. 643–53.

3. Benson Mates, in his masterful study of Leibniz, *The Philosophy of Leibniz: Metaphysics and Language* (New York: Oxford University Press, 1986), has recently noted that "on the fundamental points of his philosophy, his constancy over the years is little short of astonishing" (p. 7) and continues: "For instance, from the first of his publications, at age seventeen, to the end of his life he never wavered in holding to the rather unusual and implausible doctrine that things are individuated by their 'whole being'; that is, every property of a thing is essential to its identity" (p. 7). I agree with Mates on the constancy of Leibniz's views on the principle of individuation, but I disagree with the remainder of his characterization. Leibniz's account is not unusual. Many philosophers of his era, Suárez chief among them, held similar views. Indeed, Leibniz freely acknowledges Suárez and other later Scholastic philosophers as the chief sources for the view that 'whole entity' is the principle of individuation. Nor is Leibniz's account implausible, at least by then current philosophical terms, once it is seen for what, at bottom, it is, namely, a nominalist account of individuals and their individuation.

4. P. F. Strawson, *Individuals: An Essay in Descriptive Metaphysics* (Garden City, N.J.: Anchor Books, 1963), p. 8.

5. Ibid., p. 23.

6. Ibid., *passim.*

7. David Wiggins, *Sameness and Substance* (Cambridge, Mass.: Harvard University Press, 1980), p. 1.

8. Ibid., p. 24.

9. Gottfried Wilhelm Leibniz, *Disputatio metaphysica de principio individui*, in Gottfried Wilhelm Leibniz, *Sämtliche Schriften und Briefe*, Sechste Reihe, Erste Band (Darmstadt: Otto Reich Verlag, 1930), p. 11: "Quare et haec colligam, agemus de aliquo reali, et, ut loquimur principio Physico, quod rationis individui formalis seu individuationis, seu differentiae numericae in intellectu sit fundamentum, idque in individuis praecipue creatis substantiales."

10. Gottfried Wilhelm Leibniz, *Disputatio metaphysica de principio individui*, p. 11: "Ante omnium autem statum quaestiones excutiemus. Acturi igitur

sumus de Principio Individui, ubi et Principium et Individuum varie accipitur. Et quod Individuum attinet, quemadmodum Universale, sic ipsum quoque vel Logicum est in ordine ad praedicationem; vel Metaphysicum in ordine ad rem. . . . Principii quoque vox notat tum cognoscendi principium, tam essendi."

11. See note 10.

12. G. W. Leibniz, *New Essays Concerning Human Understanding*, trans. and ed. Peter Remnant and Jonathan Bennett (Cambridge, England: Cambridge University Press, 1981), p. 229.

13. Ibid., p. 230.

14. Ibid.

15. Gottfried Wilhelm Leibniz, "Monadology," p. 643.

16. Jorge J. E. Gracia, *Introduction to the Problem of individuation in the Early Middle Ages*, 2d rev. ed. (Munich, Federal Republic of Germany: Philosophia Verlag, 1988).

17. Ibid., p. 19.

18. Ibid., p. 20.

19. Ibid., p. 21.

20. Gottfried Wilhelm Leibniz, "Letter to Jacob Thomasius," in Leibniz, *Philosophical Papers and Letters*, p. 97: "This also makes it clear why the substantial form consists in something indivisible and cannot be increased or decreased."

21. Gottfried Wilhelm Leibniz, "On the Ethics of Benedict de Spinoza," in Leibniz, *Philosophical Papers and Letters*, p. 203: "Any individual thing, or anything which is finite and has a determinate existence."

22. G. W. Leibniz, *The Leibniz-Arnauld Correspondence*, ed. and trans. H. T. Mason, with intro. by H. G. R. Parkinson (Manchester, England: Manchester University Press, 1967), p. 161. Reprinted in series, *The Philosophy of Leibniz*, ed. R. G. Sleigh (New York: Garland, 1985): "every substance has a genuine unity, in metaphysical rigor."

23. Gottfried Wilhelm Leibniz, "Correspondence with de Volder," in Leibniz, *Philosophical Papers and Letters*, p. 530: "I regard substance itself . . . as an indivisible or perfect monad."

24. Ibid., p. 534: "Substances are not mere wholes which contain parts formally but total things which contain their parts eminently."

25. Leibniz, *New Essays*, p. 318.

26. Ibid., p. 231.

27. Jorge J. E. Gracia, *Introduction to The Problem of Individuation*, p. 22.

28. Ibid., p. 26.

29. See note 20.

30. See note 22.

31. See note 21.

32. See note 14.

33. Jorge J. E. Gracia, *Introduction to The Problem of Individuation*, pp. 31–34.

34. See note 24.

35. Gottfried Wilhelm Leibniz, *Disputatio metaphysica de principio individui*, p. 144: "An vero quenquam habuerit qui defenderit, valde dubito, nisi fortasse aliquem Nominalium obscuriorem."

36. Johannes Duns Scotus, *Reportata Parisiensia* (Hildesheim: Georg Olms Verlag, 1969), II, distinction 12, question 6, Part I, p. 329b: "*Unum* dicit indivisionem, indivisio negationem, igitur per nihil positiuum individuatur."

37. Christian de Ramoneda, *Commentaria in libellum de ente et essentia Divus Thomae Aquinatis*. Perpignan: Sanson Arbus, 1596, *Disputatio de materia*, article 3, p. 380: "Cum individuum non aliud significet quam quod a se indivisum, et separatum per duas negationes, quae sunt negatio divisionis a se, et negatio identitatis cum alio, non autem per aliud positivum, individuum: materiale in esse talis individui constitutuum esse contendunt."

38. This theory of individuation anticipates to some extent the 'bare particular' theory in recent Anglo-American philosophy. This is because the bare particular theory, by emphasizing numerical difference as a basic given, adopts a single negation as the principle of individuation, namely, distinction. See Edwin B. Allaire, "Bare Particulars," in *Universals and Particulars*, ed. Michael J. Loux (Notre Dame: Notre Dame University Press, 1970), pp. 281–90.

39. For a detailed account of these criticisms see Laurence B. McCullough, *The Sources of Leibniz's Principle of Individuation* (Munich, Federal Republic of Germany: Philosophia Verlag, in press), Chapter 3.

40. Johannes de Bassolis, . . . *in Quattuor sententiarum libros*. . . . (Paris: Fullon, 1516–17), fol. 79r: "Illud non est principium individuationis aliquo genere quod non est aliquis actus quia per actum ultimatum per se ordinabilem in genere est individuatio. Sed negatio non est aliquis actus sicut nec aliquod ens, ergo etc."

41. Gracia, *Introduction to the Problem of Individuation*, p. 45.

42. Ibid.

43. See John F. Wippel, "Essence and Existence," in *The Cambridge History of Later Medieval Philosophy*, ed. Norman Kretzmann, Anthony Kenny, and Jan Pinborg (Cambridge, England: Cambridge University Press, 1982), pp. 385–410.

44. For a detailed account of these objections see McCullough, *The Sources of Leibniz's Principle of Individuation*, Chapter 3.

45. In this, as in so much in the *Disputatio* (and therefore later in his life), Leibniz follows Suárez. See Francis Suárez, *On the Various Kinds of Distinction*, trans. Cyril Vollert (Milwaukee, Wis.: Marquette University Press, 1947).

46. Johannes Duns Scotus, . . . *X11 libros Metaphysicorum Aristotelis* (Hildesheim: Georg Olms Verlag, 1968), V11 ques. 13, section vii: "Notandum, quod individuum; sive unum numero dicitur illud, quod est non divisibile in multa: et distinguitur ab omni alio secundum numerum."

47. For an account of Leibniz's argument on this score, see McCullough, *The Sources of Leibniz's Principle of Individuation*, Chapter 3. See Gottfried Wilhelm Leibniz, *Disputatio metaphysica de principio individui*, pp. 15–18.

48. For an account of Suárez's principle of individuation and Leibniz's adoption of it in the *Disputatio*, see McCullough, *The Sources of Leibniz's Principle of Individuation*, Chapter 4. Suárez's main text on individuation, the *Disputatio Metaphysicae V*, has been translated and discussed by Gracia in *Suárez on Individuation* (Milwaukee: Marquette University Press, 1982).

49. Gottfried Wilhelm Leibniz, *Disputatio metaphysica de principio individui*, p. 11: "Prima opinio, quoniam et a gravissimis viris defenditur, et difficultates omnes tollit, a nobis quoque recipietur, cujus confirmatio velut generale argumentum contra reliquas suppeditabit. Pono igitur: omne individuum sua tota Entitate individuatur."

50. Ibid., pp. 13–14: "Qui et objicit de accidentibus, quae solo numero differentia non possint esse in eodem subjecto simul, quod tamen falsum; item de partibus continui divulsis. Verum nos accidentia et entia in completa removimus a nostra tractatione."

51. For an account of Leibniz's shift from a static to a dynamic model of individuals, see McCullough, *The Sources of Leibniz's Principle of Individuation*, Chapter 5.

52. Gottfried Wilhelm Leibniz, "De transubstantiatione," in Gottfried Wilhelm Leibniz, *Sämtliche, Schriften und Briefe*, Sechste Reihe, Erster Band (Darmstadt: Otto Reich Verlag, 1930), pp. 508–9.

53. See Laurence B. McCullough, "Leibniz and Traditional Philosophy," *Studia Leibniziana* 10 (1978): 264–67.

54. See Leibniz, "Monadology," in Leibniz, *Philosophical Papers and Letters*, p. 643: "The *monad* which we are to discuss here is nothing but a simple substance which enters into compound. *Simple* means without parts."

Christian Wolff on Individuation

Jorge J. E. Gracia

*T*wo problems related to individuality are frequently confused by philosophers. One is metaphysical, the other epistemological. The first is properly speaking the "problem of individuation." The second is what I like to call the "problem of discernibility."[1]

The problem of individuation has to do with the identification of principles or causes that are responsible for the individuality of individuals. Thus, the solution to the problem involves answering the question of what makes Peter, say, or this chair on which I am sitting while writing these words, individual.

The problem of the discernibility of individuals, on the other hand, has to do with the identification of the principles or causes that are responsible for making knowers aware of individuals *qua* individuals. Thus we could ask, for example, what it is that makes it possible for me, or any other knower, to discern Peter or this chair on which I am sitting as individuals.

The distinction between these two problems would appear to be rather obvious. But, as already said, it has not been obvious to many philosophers who have concerned themselves with individuality and it took a long time for it to be explicitly stated in the history of Western thought. The first author who did so clearly was Gilbert of Poitiers (b. ca. 1076; d. 1154), but his point of view did not gain quick approval.[2] Indeed, one of the main characteristics of what I call the "Standard Theory of individuality," which dominated discussions of this topic before 1150, is precisely that it does not distinguish between these two problems. By the end of the thirteenth century, however, it had become customary for most major figures to acknowledge the distinction between them. Thomas Aquinas, for example, makes it explicit in the *Commentary on Boethius' "De Trinitate.*"[3] And, although there were occasional authors who did not follow suit, the prevailing attitude, as reflected in Francisco Suárez's *Disputatio metaphysica* V, was that the problems of individuation and discernibility are different.[4]

The importance of the stance that philosophers take with respect to the distinction between the problem of individuation and the problem of discernibility can be illustrated with respect to two points. The first is that those who make the distinction generally regard the principles or causes of individuation as different from the principles or causes of discernibility. Thus, for example, Thomas Aquinas identifies designated matter as the principle of individuation and place as the principle of discernibility, and Suárez points to entity as the principle of individuation and to location as the principle of discernibility.[5]

The second is that those who do not distinguish between the two problems usually propose theories that are most effective in accounting for discernibility but are generally ineffective in accounting for individuation. Thus we find many contemporary authors arguing that spatiotemporal relations are the principle of individuation because it is through those relations that knowers become aware of individuals *qua* individuals. And, while this makes perfectly good sense when dealing with discernibility, it does not explain the individuality of individuals apart from our awareness of it.[6]

The blurring of the distinction between the problem of individuation and the problem of discernibility returns to philosophy in the modern period with the renewed emphasis on epistemology. Not that epistemic issues had been ignored by Scholastics; indeed, the bases of the epistemic turn in modern philosophy can be traced to discussions that began in the latter part of the thirteenth century.[7] But it is true that modern philosophy gave an emphasis to epistemology that had been largely lacking prior to the seventeenth century. Moreover, this emphasis, which I call "epistemologism," had at least two important results. The first is the introduction of new problems in philosophy. The discussion of the status of the world vis-à-vis our ideas, for example, is one. The second is the recasting of well-known metaphysical problems from an epistemic perspective. One of the problems that suffered such a fate was the problem of individuation: questions about individuation became transformed into questions about the discernibility of individuals.

The investigation of how far the epistemological tendency characteristic of modern philosophy invaded metaphysics in general and the formulation and solution to the problem of individuation in particular would be an interesting task for the historian of philosophy, but one that would be beyond the scope of a chapter of this size. What I do here is more restricted. I content myself with looking at an example of a modern theory of individuation to see to what extent it was affected by the epistemologism of modern philosophy. I examine the theory of Christian Wolff (1679–1754).

The choice of Wolff's theory is justified because Wolff's philosophy displays some of the more important and fundamental traits that characterize modern philosophy. In the first place, it has important ties to premodern thought. Wolff is sympathetic with the Aristotelian perspective prevalent in the later Middle Ages and is familiar with most of the major scholastic authors in that tradition, whom he greatly admired.[8] Second, following in the footsteps of several late scholastic and early modern philosophers, he tried to present a comprehensive and systematic metaphysical system dealing in detail with fundamental metaphysical notions and issues, including individuation. And, finally, his view serves as a good illustration of the difficulties encountered by views that do not distinguish between individuation and discernibility.

Care should be taken, however, not to confuse what I characterize as "epistemologism" with another closely related, but nevertheless distinct, tendency of modern philosophy: the increasing tendency to see the object of philosophical inquiry as mental. The emphasis on mental beings, whether perceptions or ideas, rather than on the extramental reality taken for granted by scholastics, led eventually to the various versions of idealism found in the nineteenth century. This tendency also produced a particular set of problems concerned with the individuation of perceptions, appearances, and other mental phenomena as is evident from the papers by Daisie Radner and Michael Radner contained in this volume. The study of this tendency in general and in Wolff in particular has already been carried out in some detail by Campo and others, so there is no need for me to deal with it here.[9] My concern is limited to the issues of individuation and discernibility, and specifically has to do with the collapse of these two logically distinguishable issues.

A more restricted goal is to establish and characterize Wolff's theory of individuation. Moreover, I determine the place it occupies in the history of the problem of individuation.

This chapter is divided into three parts. First, I examine briefly the nature of Wolff's *Ontology*, its method, and the place that the discussion of individuality and individuation occupies in the overall structure of the text. Second, I present and characterize Wolff's view of individuation. Finally, I explore the extent to which Wolff's theory of individuation displays the influence of the epistemologism prevalent in modern philosophy. I defend two main theses. First, I claim that Wolff's theory of individuation is a bundle view with a strong accidental component. Second, I argue that the influence of the epistemologism of modern philosophy is one of the factors that led Wolff to adopt the view of individuation that he did.

THE *ONTOLOGY*

Wolff's *Ontology* is a long, systematic treatise of what had been generally called before him "metaphysics" or "first philosophy." The term 'ontology' to refer to this rather traditional discipline had antecedents before Wolff used it in the title of his book, however. In 1647 Clauvergius published a treatise with the title *Elementa philosophiae sive ontosophia* in which he explicitly argued in favor of a more precise name for what was generally called "metaphysics." The primary reason behind the shift of terminology had to do with the object of study of the discipline, which Clauvergius identified with being in general.[10] Wolff, following suit, titled his book *Philosophia prima sive ontologia* (1729), defining the subject of study as the science of being in general, that is, of being insofar as it is being.[11]

The *Ontology*, in comparison with the extensive systematic metaphysical treatises of late Scholastics, is fairly short. It is divided into three sections: a section entitled "Prolegomena" and two parts. The Prolegomena deals with the nature of ontology and of the terms and notions with which it concerns itself. In the first of the two parts into which the rest of the treatise is divided, Wolff discusses the notion of being in general and the properties that follow from it. In the second part, he is concerned with the various species of being. The first part is divided in turn into three subsections, dealing respectively with the principles of ontology, the essence and existence of being, and the general attributes of being. After Wolff discusses identity and similarity in Chapter 1, he then deals with singular and universal being in Chapter 2. Thus, the discussion of singularity, which for Wolff is equivalent to individuality, precedes the discussion of necessity, contingency, quantity, quality, relation, truth, perfections, and related notions.[12] It is also worthy of note that in the chapter devoted to individuality and universality, individuality is listed and discussed first.

The relative position that individuality occupies in relation to other fundamental metaphysical notions, including universality, indicates the importance that Wolff attached to it as well as its more fundamental and central role in the *Ontology*. Not that such importance and central role were something new. Throughout the Middle Ages there had been a progressive shift of emphasis from universality to individuality, which is clearly evident as early as the thirteenth century when Duns Scotus discussed universals in the context of individuals in the *Opus oxoniense*, contrary to what had been customary before him. This shift is most evident in Suárez's *Disputationes metaphysicae*, where individuality is given separate, prior, and more extensive treatment than all the other common properties of being.

What is most significant and different structurally speaking about Wolff's *Ontology*, vis-à-vis the later Scholastic tradition, is something else, namely, the epistemic and methodological considerations that are contained in the beginning of the work. They are found in two places. In the Preface Wolff presents some general statements about his modus operandi, indicating among other things that his aim is to make clear notions that are only confusedly found in common as well as in previous philosophical discourse, and also pointing out that he intends to follow the rigorous mathematical method popular among other modern philosophers. In Section 1, he begins the discussion with an examination of the methodological principles that guide his investigation. The principles in question are the "principle of contradiction" and the "principle of sufficient reason." The methodological concerns expressed both in the Preface and in Section 1 are certainly an indication of the epistemic bent that Wolff gave to the *Ontology* and that do not seem to have affected the work of many late Scholastics. Suárez's *Disputationes*, for example, go directly from a discussion on the nature of metaphysics to the discussion of the common properties of being and do not contain in the Preface the kind of procedural comments that characterize the *Ontology*. What distinguishes Wolff's *Ontology*, then, is that between the discussion of the nature of metaphysics and of the common properties of being he adds a section on methodological principles and that he prefaces the whole work with a series of remarks on the same topic.

Thus, although the *Ontology* aims to be a work of metaphysics, from its very beginning we are confronted with epistemic and methodological considerations. Does this mean that its contents suffered from the epistemologism that characterize most other modern metaphysical works? I argue yes at least as far as individuation is concerned.

WOLFF'S THEORY OF INDIVIDUATION

At the start, one would think that the determination of Wolff's view of individuation would be rather easy. After all, the *Ontology* contains a rather substantial chapter, covering close to forty pages in Ecole's edition, devoted to individuality and universality and of these two individuality takes up the better part. Yet the way Wolff goes about the subject matter of the *Ontology* is such that his view concerning individuality and individuation is far from clear. The difficulties involved in establishing it arise from various sources, but I mention three important ones. First, the axiomatic method used in the *Ontology* generally

excludes both the discussion of opposing views as well as the formulation of philosophical views as responses to problems. Thus, it is often
difficult to see where Wolff is going and why, as well as the differences
between his views and those of other philosophers. Second, the pervasive use of mathematical examples, even in cases in which examples
taken from experience would have been more helpful, obscures rather
than clarifies many parts of the discussion. Third, in part as a result of
the first point mentioned and in spite of the substantial extension of
the discussion of individuality, Wolff leaves entire questions about it
unanswered, such as the question dealing with the ontological status of
individuality in individuals.[13] All this makes it very difficult to establish
exactly what Wolff's theory of individuation is. Indeed, he is very far
from the deliberately clear and problem-oriented approach to philosophy characteristic of Scholastic philosophy. What follows, therefore,
can be taken only as an attempt to produce a consistent and comprehensive interpretation based on the somewhat fragmentary and often
cryptic account presented by Wolff.

To simplify matters, I divide the discussion into three parts. In the
first, I discuss Wolff's conception of individuality; in the second, I deal
with the question of the existence of individuals and universals; and, in
the third, I identify the principle of individuation.

Individuality

It is a common feature of Wolff's method to try to show that the
notions he uses adhere both to common usage and to mathematical
practice. Thus, in his discussion of individuation he tries to show that
the notion of 'individual' is present in both common and mathematical
discourses.

Since the section of the *Ontology* in which individuation is discussed deals also with universals, and since for Wolff genera and
species are universals, he discusses the three notions together. He
argues that the notion of 'individual', just like the notions of 'species'
and 'genus', are common notions that everyone uses to make distinctions among beings. However, the linguistic terms used to refer to individuals on the one hand and those used to refer to species and genera
on the other are different. Proper names are used to denote individuals. The example he gives of a proper name is 'Bucephalus', the name
of Alexander the Great's horse. In order to refer to species and genera,
on the other hand, appellative names are used. Wolff's example is
'horse'. Accordingly, and following Melanchthon, who himself relied
on a long tradition going back to the early Middle Ages, a proper name

applies only to one thing and signifies an individual, whereas an appellative name signifies the species or the genus.[14]

Strictly speaking one might quarrel with the way Wolff puts his claim, for terms such as 'species' and 'genus' are not part of common discourse. They are only part of learned or scientific discourse. The case with 'individual' is different, of course, but even here the examples that Wolff provides in order to substantiate his claim indicate that he is not thinking about these notions as explicitly acknowledged and used. Rather, it would appear that what he has in mind is that these notions are implicit in the use of certain terms such as 'Bucephalus' and 'horse'. Thus, even if the ordinary person might not talk directly about "individuals," "species," and "genera," that person is implicitly using those notions.

In the case of mathematical discourse the trouble is compounded at least for two reasons: first, as in the previous case, the use of these notions in it must be, if at all, implicit rather than explicit; second and more important in the case of individuals, proper names like 'Bucephalus' are not used in mathematical discourse. Nonetheless, Wolff tries to show that indeed all three notions are at work in mathematics. He has no great difficulty showing that some geometrical notions, such as the notion of a quadrilateral figure, encompass other notions, such as the notion of square and rhombus, and thus function toward them as genera toward species. But when it comes to the claim that mathematical discourse contains references to individuals, matters do not seem so clear, since there are no proper names in mathematics or geometry that can be used to refer to those individuals.

None of this, however, seems to disturb Wolff, a fact that suggests that he is not really concerned with the surface form of speech, or even the psychological awareness of those who use it. His concern is rather with the deeper conceptual structure that is at work in ordinary discourse, even if on the surface his claim seems to be much stronger than that. If one is to interpret his claim in a way that will not result in contradiction, one must understand it to mean not that mathematical discourse contains explicitly terms such as 'Bucephalus'. Rather, what one must accept is that the notion of 'individual' is implicit and at work in mathematical discourse in a way in which, for example, one might use general terms as part of definite descriptions to refer to individuals.

But even if that were granted, the problem remains if by 'individual' one means something like Bucephalus or even the individual color of its eyes, for mathematical entities do not seem to be of such sort, nor does mathematical discourse seem to be based on the consideration of entities such as Bucephalus or the individual color of its eyes. So one is back to square one, namely, that it is not clear how Wolff can claim that the notion of individual is involved in mathematical discourse. It would seem that either Wolff is contradicting himself or that the notion of individual that he uses is different from what one would have expected. And indeed it is the latter that holds some promise.

Wolff says that to be individual is to be "completely determinate," so to understand something as individual is precisely to understand it as completely determinate.[15] This same understanding of what it is to be an individual is repeated in the *Logic*, where he adds, moreover, that in an individual everything is determinate.[16] In contrast, a being is universal when it is not completely determinate, or has some determinations that are common to several beings.[17]

But, one can ask, what is it to be determinate? According to Wolff, for a thing to be determinate, something must be affirmed of it.[18] By contrast, for something to be indeterminate it is required that nothing be affirmed of it, even if to affirm something of it were not contradictory.[19] For a being to be completely determinate, then, it is necessary that nothing indeterminate be conceived about it.[20] Thus, in a completely determinate being there is no aspect of it about which something is not affirmed.

Now one can see how Wolff can say that the notion of individual can be present in mathematical discourse. For, indeed, as long as mathematics deals with entities that are fully determinate in the specified sense, one can hold that it deals with individuals. Thus Wolff explains that general formulas such as $(n^2 + n) \div 2$ are not individual, but when variable n is substituted by a number, say 5 in a particular case, the result is something fully determined, which in the example given turns out to be 15, since $(5^2 + 5) \div 2 = 15$.[21]

From the discussion of determinate and indeterminate being and from the mathematical examples that Wolff provides of them we can surmise two points. The first is that if number 15 represents something fully determinate and thus individual, then individuals are not noninstantiable instances. For number 15 is certainly subject to instantiation; indeed, it is subject to multiple instantiation. Second, determination and indetermination are presented by Wolff in terms of conception rather than of being. Thus the conditions of individuality and universality are epistemic rather than ontological.

The Existence of Universals and Individuals

From the definition of what is completely determinate, Wolff derives the principle that "whatever exists, or is in act, is completely determinate."[22] But since universals are not completely determinate, then, he concludes, they must not exist.[23] This leads to the further conclusion that only individuals exist.

In the *Logic*, Wolff adds that everything we perceive through sense (whether it be internal or external sense), or that we imagine, is individual. As examples he cites the horse we see, the sound we hear, the changes that our minds undergo, and the image of a lion we have in our minds.[24] By contrast, universals do not exist, although Wolff later adds that they exist through individuals.[25] Wolff reconciles his statement that universals do not exist with his statement that they exist through individuals by indicating that universals are nothing but the "similarities found among individuals," that is, "what individuals have in common."[26]

Wolff does not seem to notice that the two formulas he uses to elucidate the notion of universal, 'similarity among individuals' and 'commonality among individuals', create a problem for him. For the first formula, 'similarity among individuals', suggests that universals are nothing in individuals, whereas the second suggests that they are something shared by individuals. Indeed, the first formula is a favorite of nominalists all the way back to the Middle Ages, while the second is a favorite of realists and eclectics, going as far as back as the first one.[27] Nominalists used the notion of similarity to describe what knowers perceive to be common among individuals, rejecting that such similarity is localized anywhere but in the knower, and insisting that it has no causal basis in anything present in individuals themselves. Similarity, according to this view, arises from the failure of knowers to recognize the distinctions that characterize the objects of knowledge. Medieval realists and eclectics, on the other hand, spoke of "the common nature" that is found in individuals and is causally related to the universal concepts that knowers have in their minds. Thus we are left with three alternatives in interpreting the relation between the two *formulas* used by Wolff concerning universals: (1) they are inconsistent; (2) they are consistent but have to be interpreted nominalistically; or (3) they are consistent and must be interpreted realistically or eclectically.

Of these three alternatives, the first should be adopted only if the other two are not viable. This is in accordance with the historiographical Principle of Charity, which holds that one should impute a mistake to an author only as a last resort. So, before accusing Wolff of inconsistency we must see if alternatives (2) and (3) are viable.

Alternative (2), that the two formulas should be interpreted nominalistically, would seem to find support from three sources: Wolff's statement that only individuals exist; his view that we perceive only

individuals; and his position that everything in an individual is determinate. But none of these three can be held as clear evidence of nominalism. Take the first one, for example. Almost everyone from the thirteenth century on maintained that only individuals exist. This is, of
course, the view of such well-known nominalists as William of Ockham, but was also accepted by Thomas Aquinas and Duns Scotus,
whose views are more eclectic. For example, Aquinas held also that the
nature (what Wolff calls the "universal") can be considered absolutely
in itself and that as such it is real although neutral with respect to individual or universal existence and thus existing only as individuated in
the world or as universalized in the mind.[28] And for Scotus every thing,
including the common nature, is individualized, but nonetheless the
common nature has a being of its own that should not be confused
with existence.[29] So we cannot assume that because Wolff holds that
only individuals exist he is to be considered a nominalist of the Ock-
hamist variety. But does that mean he should then be considered a real-
ist or an eclectic? What about the second and third sources of support
for the nominalist interpretation?

As with the first, the second source where the nominalist interpretation finds support seems to have been a standard view throughout
the later Middle Ages and early modern philosophy. It was generally
accepted that the object of our perceptions is the individual; universals
were considered to be the objects of our understanding, rather than of
our perceptions. Empiricists, of course, introduced important changes
in this scheme, but among Continental rationalists the principle was
fundamentally maintained. In the Middle Ages, for example, Thomas
Aquinas would have agreed entirely with this view and have found
nothing objectionable with the examples that Wolff provides. For that
the senses perceive only individuals does not preclude the possibility
that universals have some ontological status in individuals or outside of
them. Indeed, rationalists of the Platonic variety would agree that it is
precisely because we perceive only individuals that knowledge must not
be acquired though perception, since its object has a higher ontological
status than the individuals we perceive. So again, the second source of
support of the nominalist interpretation does not seem to tip the scales
in favor of nominalism. I turn, then, to the third.

The way the third source of support for the nominalist interpretation is phrased gives a clue as to where Wolff stands when it comes to
the issue of the ontological status of universals. As stated, his formula
says that everything in an individual is *determined*, not that everything
in an individual is *individual*. The difference between being "determined" and being "individual" is significant for two reasons. In the

first place, even moderate realists and eclectics, and certainly all nominalists going back to the Middle Ages, made clear that everything in the individual is individual. Eclectics, like Thomas and Scotus, preferred to say that everything in individuals is "individuated," leaving open the door for something nonindividual in itself, like a nature, to be the subject of individuation. Those who were more nominalistically inclined, like Ockham, preferred to talk about the components of individuals as "individual," and sometimes threw in qualifying expressions such as "per se" or "essentially" in order to preclude any possibility of a nonindividual subject of individuation.

Second, the meaning of the term 'determined' as used by Wolff does not entail individuality. Individuality consists in *complete* determination, but mere determination does not imply individuality. Indeed, universals such as 'man' are determined by the genus, in this case 'animal', but by no means does that entail that 'man' is individual. In fact 'man' is universal, in the same way that other species and genera are. It is only Peter, Paul, and the like that are individual, that is, completely determinate.

In short, then, although Wolff uses what at first appear to be nominalistic formulas, a careful examination of the texts reveals that a more realistic or eclectic interpretation of his position is quite possible. The two *formulae* that Wolff uses in connection with universals, 'similarity among individuals' and 'commonality among individuals', can be interpreted consistently either nominalistically (2) or not nominalistically (3), which leaves open the question as to exactly what Wolff thought concerning the ontological status of universals. It is clear that he did not hold that universals exist *independently of* individuals, but he did not clarify what the ontological status of universals is *in* individuals. I put aside the determination of this question for the moment to turn to the issue involved in the principle of individuation, for the investigation of the latter issue leads to the answer to the question of extension.

The Principle of Individuation

Having established that for Wolff to be individual is to be completely determinate and that universals do not exist independently of individuals, I turn to the important question of what the principle of individuation is for him. Wolff tells us explicitly that it is "the intrinsic sufficient reason of the individual" and adds that such a principle is what Scholastics called "thisness" (*haecceitas*). In other words, the principle of individuation is "the reason why a being is singular,"[30] since a sufficient reason of something is the reason why something is what it is or why something exists as it exists.[31] Now, since individuality consists in complete determination and only individuals exist independently, Wolff argues that the sufficient reason of individuality must be the complete determination of beings in act, that is, of those beings that exist.[32]

But, one can ask, what are the determinations that completely determine existing beings? Determinations, according to Wolff, come in two basic varieties: they are common or proper. Common determinations are simultaneously determinations of the individual and the species, of the species and the genus, or of lower and higher genera. For example, animal is a common determination of both the individual Bucephalus and of the species horse. Proper determinations, on the other hand, do not pertain to the higher species and genera to which the being that they determine belongs. Thus, a proper determination of a lower genus is not in a higher genus, a proper determination of the species is not in the genus, and a proper determination of the individual is not in the species.[33] So, for example, rationality is a proper determination of the species human being because it is not common to the genus animal, which is above the species human being. The proper determination of a species, although not present in the genus above it, is present in the individuals that belong to that species. Thus, for example, rationality is present in both the species human being of which it is the proper determination and also in the individual Peter who belongs to that species, and of which it is a common determination. And the same applies to lower and higher genera. However, the proper determination of the individual is not present in anything but the individual, since there is nothing below the individual in the hierarchy of being. For Wolff, the proper determination of the species is the specific difference and that of the individual is the numerical difference.[34] Wolff points out that sometimes generic and specific determinations are called universal.[35]

From all this, it is clear that the individual contains both proper and common determinations. An individual man, for example, is rational (specific difference) in addition to having the singular determinations (numerical difference).[36] And this means further that individuals, insofar as they are contained under species and species are contained under genera, are determined by essential characteristics, just as species and genera are.[37] Indeed, according to Wolff, individuals are determined in the same way as species and genera.[38] But individuals cannot exist without numerical difference, for specific and generic determinations are sufficient for understanding but not for existence. That is to say, in order to know what Paul is, it is sufficient to know that he is an animal (generic determination) and that he is rational (specific determination). But actualization requires the further determination of numerical difference.[39] This goes along with the view concerning the existence of individuals and of universals only through individuals, that generic and specific characteristics are universal and it is only the individual that exists independently.

So far, then, what I have shown is that individuals are to be understood as completely determined and that their determination is in part specific and generic but also numerical. This points to a view where the principle of individuation is a bundle of the features ('determinations' in Wolff's terminology) of a thing, but I am not completely sure that is the case, for there is no text in the *Ontology* that clearly indicates a bundle view.

Fortunately, there are indications in Wolff's *Logic*, a treatise in which one does not expect to find a discussion of individuation. It is true that scholastic logics usually deal with the notion of individual and thus it is not surprising to find Wolff doing the same. But Scholastics deal with the notion of individual in books on logic because they considered part of the function of logic to provide a conceptual map of our most basic notions.[40] That is, they conceived of logic as a science or art that deals in part with the definition of basic notions, so that the analysis of both 'individual' and 'universal' is considered part of it. When it comes to the principle of individuation, on the other hand, things are different, for the search for a principle of individuation is not a matter of definition and conceptual analysis, but has to do with a fundamental *causal* analysis of reality. Thus, the principle of individuation is dealt with in metaphysical treatises or contexts.

Wolff, on the other hand, does not shy away from discussing individuation in the *Logic* and indeed it is there, rather than in the *Ontology*, where we would have expected it, that we find what appears to be a clearer statement of what he considered the principle of individuation to be. The key passage occurs in the body of one of the demonstrations of the axioms of the *Logic*. It reads: "The principle of individuation includes all differences, whether numerical, specific or generic. It is the bundle of all the differences [that constitute the individual]."[41]

Wolff confirms in the same paragraph what he had said before, in both the *Ontology* and the *Logic*, namely, that the individual differs from the universal in that the notion of individual does not contain anything that is not determined, whereas universals contain only *some* determinations, that is, they are not completely determined.

The principle of individuation, then, is a bundle of all the determinations of an individual. It involves both generic and specific determinations, although these two types of determinations are incomplete without the numerical difference which, as it were, completes the determination of an individual.[42] Specific and generic determinations are not sufficient to account for individuality because they involve what is common to many individuals and, therefore, do not make explicit that in virtue of which individuals differ from each other.[43]

In short, then, Wolff has a bundle view in which the principle of individuation is composed of three types of elements: generic, specific, and numerical determinations. He explains generic and specific determinations in the *Ontology*, but what constitutes the numerical difference without which individuation does not take place still remains to be established. What, then, is this key component of the principle of individuation?

There is nothing explicit in Wolff's *Ontology* or his *Logic* that gives a solution to this difficulty. There are, however, three ways one might interpret his view of numerical difference, which I call respectively the sui generis, the quantitative, and the accidental interpretations. The first is not based on any direct textual evidence. It is rather founded more on what Wolff does not say than in what he says, although there is some indirect textual support for it. According to it, Wolff does not give a further analysis of the notion of numerical difference because for him such difference is primitive and cannot be analyzed further into more simple notions.

The support for the *sui generis* interpretation comes from two sources. First is the fact that Wolff does not present an analysis of numerical difference anywhere in the *Ontology* or the *Logic*, or for that matter in any of his other works. Second, there is the significant fact that Wolff explicitly identifies the principle of individuation with the scholastic *haecceitas* (thisness). But, as is well known, Duns Scotus was the main proponent of the *haecceitas* theory of individuation and *haecceitas* was conceived by him as a fundamental and unanalyzable principle. All of this suggests that perhaps Wolff was taking his cue from Scotus.

The problems of the *sui generis* interpretation, however, are rather serious. Apart from the fact that Wolff never explicitly states or even hints that numerical difference is a primitive notion, there is some evidence in the *Ontology* that suggests that perhaps numerical difference can after all be further unpacked. That evidence leads to the quantitative interpretation.

According to the quantitative interpretation, numerical difference is to be identified with quantity. The support for this interpretation comes from a text in the *Ontology*, where Wolff points out that quantity is not related to what constitute genera and species but rather "pertains to numerical determinations," not to specific or generic determinations. He goes on to note that quantitative determinations are excluded from universal (i.e., specific and generic) determinations, but play a role only in singular determinations.[44] Moreover, much later he adds that quantity is what makes it possible for similar beings to differ intrinsically,[45] which is to suggest that it is quantity that constitutes numerical difference.

All of this indicates that quantity plays an important role in the determination of individuals and thus that numerical difference is not *sui generis* but can be further unpacked. Still, from the text it would be difficult to support the view that quantity is *the sole* or even *the most important* constituent of numerical difference. The most one can surmise is that quantity is *one* of the elements that can make up numerical difference. Indeed, this negative assessment is confirmed by the fact that in Wolff's philosophy there are simple substances and those substances are not subject to quantification but are nonetheless individual. Therefore, if quantity were to be construed as the sole constitutive of numerical difference, Wolff would have no way of accounting for the individuality of simple substances.

The third interpretative theory, the accidental view of numerical difference, has more promise than the other two. It is that numerical difference is for Wolff the set of accidental features that adhere to things. Wolff has three sorts of features that characterize beings: essentials, attributes, and modes.[46] The first two are tied to the essence and consist in the intrinsic determinations that make beings possible, that is, noncontradictory determinations. Thus, for example, the triple number and equality of sides are essential for an equilateral triangle.[47] The same could be said for animal and rationality for a human being, although Wolff does not give this example. The distinction between essentials and attributes is very similar to the scholastic distinction between the proximate genus and the specific difference on the one hand (e.g., animality and the capacity to reason for human beings) and properties on the other (e.g., the capacity to laugh also for human beings). In addition to essentials and attributes, there are also what Wolff calls "modes," which he explicitly identifies with the predicable accidents of the Scholastics.[48] These modes are features of things that may or may not be present in them; they are not tied to the essence of the things in which they are found, but neither are they contrary to it. Color, weight, the act of laughter, and the like are all examples of accidents commonly found in scholastic literature and therefore serve also to illustrate the Wolffian notion of mode, although he generally uses quantitative and mathematical examples to illustrate it instead.

The accidental interpretation holds, then, that numerical difference is to be analyzed in terms of modes or accidents. Thus, whereas
the specific difference of a man such as Paul, for example, will have to
do with his rationality, the numerical difference will have to do with
the color of his hair, weight, and so on, all features that he actually has
but may not have.

The accidental interpretation of numerical difference makes sense
for several reasons. In the first place, it is consistent with the bundle
thrust of the theory of individuation that Wolff explicitly defends. If
the principle of individuation has to do with a bundle of determinations (generic, specific, and numerical), and both the genus and the
species are also analyzed in terms of bundles of determinations, it
makes sense to say that numerical difference consists itself in some
kind of bundle of determinations. Moreover, since numerical determinations cannot be specific or generic (that is, essentials or attributes),
they must consist of accidental determinations, that is, modes. Second,
this interpretation of numerical difference is also consistent with
Wolff's explicit statements concerning quantity. For quantity, as a
mode, can be part of the bundle of accidents that make up numerical
difference. Third, the accidental is the only one of the three interpretations mentioned that does not have serious handicaps of the sort identified in the other two interpretations. And, finally, this view has much
in common with a traditional and well-established position concerning
the principle of individuation, by which Wolff was most likely inspired.

The major problem with the accidental interpretation is that
nowhere does Wolff explicitly identify numerical difference with a
bundle of modes. So there is no textual proof that in fact he held so,
although there is evidence to suggest that indeed that was his view or
at least the view that is implicitly contained in what he says explicitly.
The problem is not that he does not say what numerical difference is.
He does that, for example, by noting it is the "proper determinations
of the individual."[49] The problem is that he never explicitly identifies
the proper determinations of the individual with its modes. Furthermore, the examples he gives, taken as they are from mathematics and
geometry, do not clarify things for they always concern quantity. He
always gives, therefore, quantitative examples of numerical difference,
such as length and proportion.[50]

Now, if one accepts the accidental interpretation of numerical difference as the correct interpretation of Wolff's view, one ends with a
bundle view in which generic, specific, and numerical differences are
separately necessary conditions of individuality and only taken
together do they become its sufficient condition. The bundle, more-

over, contains both essential determinations as well as accidental ones, but the accidental ones provide the proper determinations of the individual *qua* individual, since both essentials and attributes are or can be common to several individuals. This feature distinguishes Wolff's theory from theories that identify essential features or elements, such as matter, form, properties (in the Aristotelian sense), or bare particulars, as principles of individuation.

Wolff's theory is fundamentally accidental in character, but he has no particular accident or accidents ("modes" in Wolff's terminology), wholly determining the individual *qua* individual. This separates the theory from those that identify, for example, spatiotemporal location or quantity as principles of individuation.

Wolff's view belongs in general to a tradition that goes back to the early Middle Ages and survives in the twentieth century in the work of Russell and others.[51] It shares with them the view that the principle of individuation is a bundle of features—whether essential or accidental—which characterize the individual or, depending on the particular ontology, make up the individual.

This interpretation of Wolff's theory also helps determine a question left open earlier, namely, the ontological status of universals. I concluded earlier that nominalistic, realistic, and eclectic interpretations of Wolff are possible, in spite of some explicit statements he makes that seem to support a nominalistic interpretation.

My determination of his view of the principle of individuation provides further support for a non-nominalistic interpretation. There are two reasons for this. The first is external and historical. Practically all authors who have adhered to versions of the bundle view have also maintained eclectic positions in which the bundles are considered individual but their components are considered universal. Consequently, it makes some sense to argue that in adopting a version of the bundle view, Wolff would follow suit and adopt also a non-nominalistic view of the components of individuals.

The second reason is internal and philosophical. If Wolff had adopted a nominalistic position in which the components of the bundles that make up individuals turned out to be individual, he would have had to account for the individuality of those components themselves. But, since he did not do so, that omission suggests that he did not see the need to do it precisely because he thought the components of individuals were not themselves individual. And this, indeed, is consistent with what he says elsewhere, and is supported by his explicit statement that generic and specific determinations are universal and exist only through individuals.

If the interpretation of Wolff's position that I present here is correct, then it turns out that his view of individuation is rather traditional, having antecedents as far back as the early Middle Ages. On the other hand, this view differs quite drastically from the positions favored by the later Scholastics that he read and admired who were almost unanimous in their view (1) that the components or features of individuals are also individual and (2) that the principle of individuation cannot be a bundle of features and least of all accidental ones.[52] Under such conditions, one might ask: What had changed between the time of the later Scholastics and Wolff that explains his return to a view of individuation that had been largely discredited and much abused since 1150? The answer to this question is to be found in the epistemologism of modern philosophy, to which I turn next.

INDIVIDUATION AS DISCERNIBILITY

Those who adopt a primarily epistemic perspective toward individuation find great appeal in bundle views, particular accidental or partially accidental ones. The reason is simple. Instead of looking for what makes or causes an individual to be individual, they search for that which makes or causes knowers to become aware of individuals *qua* individuals. And it is, of course, the features of individuals, particularly accidental ones, that make it possible for knowers to distinguish among them. Indeed, we never encounter individuals that share all their accidental characteristics, even if logically it may be possible for them to do so. Thus, it is natural to conclude that it is in fact the bundle of features of individuals, particularly accidental ones, that individuate them.

There are strong indications that Wolff suffered from epistemologism and, therefore, that this may have been the reason, or at least part of the reason, why he adopted the bundle view of individuation in which accidents play a leading role. The several pieces of evidence that point in that direction have all been mentioned in passing, but I must now gather them together to make the case more clear. Two of them are indirect and must be considered weak, but nonetheless significant if taken in conjunction with the others. The first and perhaps most obvious one is the epistemic character in which Wolff casts the *Ontology* by adding parts to it that deal with methodology. This certainly changes the overall tone of the work and underlines the importance that Wolff attached to questions of knowledge and certainty.

The second is the fact that Wolff does not distinguish between the problem of individuation and the problem of discernibility, nor does he offer a principle of discernibility that is different from the principle of individuation. Naturally, the lack of explicit distinction between these problems and principles does not entail that Wolff collapsed them. But the lack of explicit distinction between them is significant insofar as this *modus operandi* has generally characterized the discussion of individuation of those who reduce the principle of individuation to the principle of discernibility.

In addition to these rather indirect and somewhat weak pieces of evidence of Wolff's epistemologism, there are stronger indications of it. Perhaps the most significant is that the criteria for individuality used by Wolff are subject-oriented. To be individual for Wolff means to be completely determined and for something to be determined it is necessary that something be affirmed of it. And, of course, the notion of affirmation is knower-directed and dependent.[53]

A further indication of Wolff's epistemologism is his assertion that the principle of individuation is the sufficient reason of an individual's individuality. At first this might appear to be a fundamentally ontological analysis involving no epistemic dimension. But the epistemic import of the analysis becomes clear when we compare it with other more ontological analyses, for the latter are concerned not with the sufficient *reasons* of why things are individual, but rather with the *causes* or *principles* that *make* them individual. That is the language, for example, used by most Scholastics. The expression 'sufficient reason,' used by Wolff, carries with it a knower connotation that is lacking in words such as 'cause' or 'principle'.

A further piece of evidence is the fact that Wolff discusses individuation in the *Logic*. Prior to Wolff, it was customary to discuss the notion of 'individual' in logical treatises, because such procedure involved conceptual analysis. But investigations concerning the principle of individuation were generally restricted to metaphysical contexts. Logical treatises dealt with the analysis of concepts and sometimes, as in the case of Aristotle and Aristotelians, with epistemic questions; they did not generally include metaphysical discussions of issues such as individuation.

Next, consider the very language that Wolff uses when discussing the principle of individuation. He always speaks of the principle of individuation as a type of "difference" and composed of "differences." The principle of individuation is composed of generic, specific, and numerical differences, and of course, the notion of difference is a relational one. The use of this notion does not by itself entail an epistemic perspective, but it is often the case that those who view individuality as difference rather than as, for example, indivisibility or noninstantiability, cast the principle of individuation in epistemic terms, for it is easy to see how differences might lead to a subject that differentiates.

Finally, the understanding of numerical differences in terms of modes or accidents also confirms Wolff's epistemic leanings. Accidents are the most obvious features of things whereby we distinguish among them, and it is certainly in virtue of them, as Wolff recognizes explicitly, that we distinguish among members of the same species.[54]

There are, then, strong pieces of evidence in Wolff's doctrine of individuation that suggest that the epistemologism of modern philosophy affected him and in fact may have been part of the reason why he adopted a view of individuation contrary to the more recent Scholastic tradition and closer to early medieval theories. The search for a principle of individuation that would function epistemically as principle of discernibility may have been one of the reasons that led Wolff to defend a bundle view with a strong accidental component. In doing that, however, he was not only stepping backwards in time but also anticipating the views of later philosophers who, having also been affected by modern epistemologism, followed along the same road, collapsing the problem of individuation and the problem of discernibility into one problem and adopting a principle of individuation that could function as principle of discernibility. The study of Wolff's view of individuation, then, has value insofar as it illustrates how the epistemic emphasis of modern philosophy affected metaphysics.[55]

NOTES

1. I have explained the distinction between these problems in some detail in the Prolegomena to *Individuality: An Essay on the Foundations of Metaphysics* (Albany: State University of New York Press, 1988), pp. 16-24.

2. Gilbert makes the distinction in *De Trinitate*, in N. Häring, *The Commentaries on Boethius by Gilbert of Poitiers*, ed. N. Häring (Toronto: Pontifical Institute of Mediaeval Studies, 1966), pp. 77-78. I discuss the significance of this text and of Gilbert's position in general in my *Introduction to the Problem of Individuation in the Early Middle Ages*, 2d rev. ed. (Munich and Vienna: Philosophia Verlag, 1988), pp. 155-78.

3. Thomas Aquinas, *Expositio super librum Boethii "De Trinitate"*, ed. B. Decker (Leiden: Brill, 1959), q.4, a.2, p. 155.

4. For Suárez, see sec. 3, pars. 28-34 in particular. In *Opera omnia*, ed. Carolo Berton, vol. 25 (Paris: Vivès, 1861), pp. 172-75.

5. For Suárez, see the reference in the previous note. For Thomas, see *De ente et essentia*, ed. M. D. Roland-Gosselin (Paris: J. Vrin, 1948), Chapter 2, p. 11, and the *Expositio super librum Boethii "De Trinitate"*, q.4, a.2, pp. 142–43.

6. For discussions of spatiotemporal location as principle of individuation, see J. W. Meiland, "Do Relations Individuate?" *Philosophical Studies* 17 (1966): 65–69, and V. C. Chappell, "Particulars Re-Clothed," *Philosophical Studies* 15 (1964): 60–64. For my discussion of this view, see *Individuality*, pp. 150–55.

7. A key text in this turn is Henry of Ghent's *Summae questionum ordinariarum*, ed. E. M. Buytaert (St. Bonaventure, N.Y.: The Franciscan Institute, 1953), I, a.1, q.1, where he begins the investigation with questions concerning the possibility of knowledge.

8. See Christian Wolff, *Philosophia prima sive ontologia*, ed. Jean Ecole (Hildesheim: Georg Olms, 1962), par. 169 *et statim*, p. 138 and elsewhere.

9. See Mariano Campo, *Cristiano Wolff e il razionalismo precritico*, 2 vols. (Milan: Società Editrice Vita e Pensiero, 1939). In vol. 1, Chapter 6, Campo has a section entitled "Mentalizzazione," in which he discusses the progressive mentalization of modern philosophy and particularly of Wolff's metaphysics. Pages 179–83 deal explicitly with individuation. See also my "Suárez's Conception of Metaphysics: A Step in the Direction of Mentalism?" *American Catholic Philosophical Quarterly* 65 (1991): 287–310.

10. Etienne Gilson has discussed at length the implications that Clauvergius's definition of metaphysics and change of terminology had for the discipline in *Being and Some Philosophers* (Toronto: Pontifical Institute of Mediaeval Studies, 1952), pp. 112ff.

11. *Ontologia*, par. 1, p. 1: "*Ontologia* seu *Philosophia prima* est scientia entis in genere, seu quatenus ens est." The emphasis in all Latin texts is that of Wolff.

12. Not all authors use the terms 'singularity' and 'individuality' interchangeably. As far back as the early Middle Ages, Gilbert of Poitiers and others introduced distinctions in their meaning. See my *Introduction to the Problem of Individuation*, Chapter 3.

13. For a recent discussion of Wolff's method and its impact on his ontology, see Marco Paolinelli, "Metodo matematico e ontologia in Christian Wolff," *Rivista di Filosofia Neo-scolastica* 66, 1 (1974): 3–39.

14. *Ontologia*, par. 245, pp. 196–97: "nomina propria individua denotant; appellativa vero nunc species, nunc genera."

15. Ibid., pars. 227 and 229, pp. 188–89: "*Ens singulare*, sive *Individuum* esse illud, quod omnimode determinatum est." The same text is repeated in par. 229. The use of the notion of 'determination' in connection with individuals is present in Scholastics. The individual was regarded as "determinate,"

while the universal as "undetermined." See, for example, Thomas Aquinas, *De ente et essentia*, Chapter 2, p. 11.

16. *Philosophia rationalis sive logica*, ed. Jean Ecole (Hildesheim, Zurich, New York: Georg Olms, 1983), part 1, sec. 1, Chapter 2, par. 74, Band 1.2, p. 152: "Apparet hinc, *Individuum* esse ens omnimode determinatum, seu in quo determinata sunt omnia, quae eidem insunt."

17. *Ontologia*, par. 230, p. 190: "*Ens universale* est, quod omnimode determinatum non est, seu quod tantummodo continet determinationes intrinsecas communes pluribus singularibus, exclusis iis, quae in individuis diversae sunt." *Logica*, part 1, sec. 1, Chapter 2, pp. 153–54, repeats the same point. The terminology of "determination" in connection with individuality is used by other modern philosophers in addition to Wolff. Most Scholastics prefer other terms such as 'indivisibility' and 'incommunicability'. Wolff uses both terms in connection with God, but he does not say that God is individual. See *Theologia naturalis*, part 2, pars. 41 and 51. In J. Ecole's ed. (Hildesheim and New York: Georg Olms Verlag, 1981), pp. 25, and 30.

18. *Ontologia*, par. 112, p. 92: "Est adeo *determinatum*, de quo aliquid affirmari debet."

19. Ibid., par. 105, p. 88: "*Indeterminatum* adeo est, de quo nihil adhuc affirmari potest, etsi de eo quid affirmari posse non repugnet."

20. Ibid., par. 225, p. 187: "*Ens omnimode determinatum* dicitur, in quo nihil concipitur indeterminatum, quo nondum determinato cetera, quae insunt, actu esse nequeunt."

21. *Logica*, part 1, sec. 1, Chapter 2, par. 74, pp. 152–53.

22. *Ontologia*, par. 226, p. 187: "*Quicquid existit vel actu est, id omnimode determinatum est.*"

23. Ibid., par. 235, p. 193: "*Ens universale existere nequit.*"

24. *Logica*, part 1, sec. 1, Chapter 1, par. 43, p. 132: "Quidquid sensu percipimus, sive externo, sive interno, aut imaginamur, id singulare quid est, soletque *Individuum* appellari."

25. Ibid., par. 56, p. 138: "*Genera et species non existunt, nisi in individuis.*" Species and genera are universal, as Wolff points out in par. 57, p. 139: "Cum adeo genera et species sint notiones universales . . ."

26. Ibid., par. 44, pp. 132–33: "Quoniam species non designat nisi similitudinem individuorum; ideo notionem speciei non ingreditur, nisi quod individua inter se commune habent."

27. In this chapter I understand by 'realists' those who hold that nothing that exists is individual, by 'nominalists' those who hold that everything that

exists is individual, and by 'eclectics' those who hold that some things that exist are individual and others are not. See my *Individuality*, pp. 60ff., where I discuss these views at length.

28. Thomas Aquinas, *De ente et essentia*, Chapter 3, pp. 23–29.

29. John Duns Scotus, *Opus oxoniense*, in *Opera omnia*, ed. Carolo Balić (Vatican City: Typis Polyglottis Vaticanis, 1973), II, d.3, p.1, q.6, pp. 474–84.

30. *Ontologia*, par. 228, p. 189: "Per *Principium individuationis* intelligitur ratio sufficiens intrinseca individui. . . . Quamobrem *per principium individuationis* intelligitur, cur ens aliquod sit singulare."

31. Ibid., par. 56, p. 39: "Per *Rationem sufficientem* intelligimus id, unde intelligitur, cur aliquid sit." A literal translation of this text would be "by sufficient reason we understand that whence it is understood why anything is." The formula as it stands is ambiguous, for it could refer to that whereby it is what it is or that whereby anything exists. Most likely Wolff had both meanings in mind since he, following many Scholastics, viewed that whereby anything is what it is as that whereby it exists. For a discussion of the principle of sufficient reason, see John E. Gurr, *The Principle of Sufficient Reason in Some Scholastic Systems 1750–1900* (Milwaukee: Marquette University Press, 1959), pp. 31–49.

32. *Ontologia*, par. 229, p. 189: "*Principium individuationis est omnimoda determinatio eorum, quae enti actu insunt.*"

33. Ibid., par. 238, p. 194: "*Determinationes communes* sunt, quae individuis et speciebus, vel speciebus et generi, vel generibus inferioribus et generi superiori simul insunt, seu quae simul insunt inferioribus et superiori, sub quo continentur; *determinationes* autem *propriae*, quae inferioribus tantum insunt, non autem superiori, sub quo eadem continentur, veluti quae insunt tantum singularibus, non autem speciebus, vel insunt tantum speciebus, non autem generi, vel denique generibus inferioribus tantum insunt, non autem superiori."

34. Ibid., par. 239, p. 194: "Determinationes individuis propriae sunt id, quod *differentia numerica* appellatur: determinationes autem speciebus propriae sunt id, quod *differentia specifica* vocatur." Wolff also refers to the numerical difference as "singular difference."

35. Ibid., par. 236, p. 193: "Nonnumquam *determinationes* genericae et specificae simul vocantur *universales*." Elsewhere he states that genera and species are universal, as already noted above. See, for example, *Logic*, part 1, sec. 1, Chapter 1, pars. 54 and 57, pp. 137 and 139.

36. *Ontology*, par. 240, p. 194: "*Notio individui componitur ex notione speciei, sub qua continetur, et differentia numerica.* Notio enim individui continet determinationes singulares, adeoque praeter proprias etiam specificas. . . ."

37. Ibid., par. 254, p. 209: "Quia genera et species per essentialia determinantur, *singularia eadem essentialia habent, quatenus sub eadem specie continentur.*

et species atque genera inferiora eadem essentialia habent, quatenus istae sub eodem genere, haec sub eodem genere superiori continentur."

38. Ibid., par. 253, p. 208.

39. Ibid., par. 261, p. 213: "*Sunt* nimirum *ea determinationes numericae, sine quibus genesis actu dari nequit;* ex adverso autem *specificae sunt, per quas rei genesis sufficienter intelligi, non tamen actu dari potest.*"

40. This is the case of John of St. Thomas, for example. See his *Logica*, in *Cursus philosophicus thomisticus*, ed. Beato Reiser (Turin: Marietti, 1930), part 2, q. 9, pp. 425–35.

41. *Logica*, part 1, sec. 1, Chapter 2, par. 75, p. 154: "Principium autem individuationis complectitur differentias omnes, sive numericae fuerit, sive specificae, sive genericae. Est adeo omnium differentiarum complexus."

42. Ibid., par. 76, p. 154: "Differentia specifica consistit in determinationibus, quibus datis adhuc indeterminata sunt, quae differentiam numericam absolvunt."

43. Ibid., par. 73, p. 151: "Species ea continet, quae individuis communia sunt: cetera igitur, quibus individua a se differunt, in notione speciei non determinantur." The epistemic tone reflected in this statement is even more evident in a statement of Wolff found in an article he published in the *Acta Eruditorum* in 1707: "Iam cum omnimoda determinatio eorum, quae *in perceptione* totali distinguntur, principium individuationis constituat. . . ." See *Meletemata mathematico-philosophica* (Halle, 1755), 1:11–7. Cited by Campo, 1:9.

44. *Ontology*, par. 267, p. 220: "Quoniam quantitatis non habetur ratio in generibus et speciebus constituendis, propterea quod non intelligi, sed tantummode dari potest, atque adeo quantitatis determinatio ad numericas pertinet, non ad specificas, multo minus genericas. . . ."

45. Ibid., par. 348, p. 273: "Quoniam similia differre nequeunt, nisi quantitate; *Quantitas* in genere definiri potest, quod sit discrimen internum similium, hoc est, illud, quo similia salva similitudine intrinse [*sic*] differre possunt."

46. I give here only a summary discussion of these features. For a more detailed exposition, see John V. Burns, *Dynamism in the Cosmology of Christian Wolff: A Study in Pre-Critical Rationalism* (New York: Exposition Press, 1966), pp. 21–50.

47. *Ontology*, par. 143, p. 120.

48. Ibid., par. 148, p. 123.

49. Ibid., par. 239, p. 194, in the text cited earlier, n. 34.

50. Ibid., par. 236 and 239, pp. 193 and 194.

51. See Bertrand Russell, *An Inquiry into Meaning and Truth* (London: Allen and Unwin, 1940), p. 93, and *Human Knowledge: Its Scope and Limits* (New York: Simon and Schuster, 1948), pp. 77ff., 292ff.; and A. J. Ayer, "The Identity of Indiscernibles," in *Philosophical Essays* (London: Macmillan, 1954), pp. 26ff.

52. See the various articles on late scholastic and Counter Reformation figures in my *Individuation in Scholasticism: The Later Middle Ages and the Counter Reformation* (Albany: SUNY Press, 1994).

53. In an early text, where Wolff discusses Leibniz's view, he writes: "*principium individuationis* omnimodam determinationem eorum, quae in perceptione totali distinguuntur." In "De propositionibus identicis, principio individuationis," *Meletemata mathematico-philosophica* (Halae Magdeburgicae: Bibliopoleo Rengeriano, 1755; rep. Hildesheim and New York: Georg Olms Verlag, 1974), p. 20. As stated in note 15 above, Scholastics used the notion of determination in connection with individuals, but their understanding of it was generally not epistemic.

54. Indeed, it is not surprising to find other modern philosophers, such as Régis and Desgabets, who understand individuals in terms of modes and who think of modes in accidental and epistemic terms. See the article by Lennon in this volume.

55. I would like to express my gratitude to Ky Herreid for the many useful suggestions he made after reading a draft of this chapter. I also wish to thank Nicholas Rescher for permission to reprint here an expanded version of the article "Christian Wolff on Individuation," *History of Philosophy Quarterly* 10, 2 (1993), 147–64.

Substance and Phenomenal Substance: Kant's Individuation of Things in Themselves and Appearances

Michael Radner

In the current climate of Kant studies, substance perhaps seems off-center, for two reasons. First, many commentators stress the contemporary relevance of Kant, and substance appears to be a dated concept. Second, present-day readers of the *Critique of Pure Reason* see a severely circumscribed dual role for substance: (1) In the Dialectic, Kant attacks the use of substance by metaphysicians (for instance, in the Paralogisms and in the Second Antinomy). (2) In the Analytic, Kant tames metaphysical substance. It becomes a category that is meaningful only for sense experience. Interpreters do not usually pursue the substance concept beyond these two roles.

Admittedly, substance is an awkward concept vis-à-vis modern mathematical physics and, further, was under attack by empiricists such as Hume on epistemological grounds. Why, then, did Kant retain it as a category? The substance philosophy was the framework both of the Cartesian tradition and of the German Scholastics. Kant was heir to these traditions. It makes sense to assume that he retained substance because he subscribed to that common framework.

Two methodological devices serve to transmit traditional concepts into Kant's system. One is the 'metaphysical deduction' of the categories, whereby fundamental philosophical concepts are coordinated to the logical forms of judgment. This device was not Kant's invention. It was already found in some works in his time, as Giorgio Tonelli has revealed.[1] The metaphysical deduction relies on general logic and does not depend on the synthetic a priori judgments of Kant's transcendental logic. The other device is analytic judgments, the instrument of conceptual analysis. This is a methodology common to Kant and his predecessors, including metaphysicians such as Wolff.[2]

Substance and other categories (and their subsidiary concepts) enter Kant's system via these devices. The categories are pure concepts of the understanding. They are not abstracted from sense experience; they are a priori. The 'objective reality' of the categories depends on their applicability to sense experience. But the categories were already located, in their conceptual structure within human understanding, by the metaphysical deduction and conceptual analysis. Insofar as Kant and his predecessors agreed on the results of conceptual analysis, including the concept of substance, they had a common philosophical basis. Kant calls the results of analytic judgments a "scaffolding" for metaphysics, rather than metaphysics proper.[3] Metaphysics itself goes astray by purporting to advance our knowledge, without having any tools beyond the merely explicative device of analytic judgments. So Kant can take over the scaffolding without acceding to the metaphysical architectural products of his predecessors. Kant is so confident of the heritage that he shares with Wolff and others, that he refers readers of the *Critique* to the "ontological manuals" for the task of adding the "derivative and supplementary" pure concepts of the understanding. (B108).[4]

Kant's exposition of the substance concept does involve synthetic a priori judgments, and hence is tied to possible experience. But one should not lose sight of the fact that conceptual structure can be understood by analytic judgments. In the usage of the *Critique*, the analytic teasing out of concepts does not count as 'knowledge', for knowledge requires an intuitional grasp of an object to which a predicate can be applied. And since human intuition is sensible, knowledge cannot exceed the bounds of possible experience. For philosophers, though, conceptual structure should count as knowledge: it is information about the layout of human understanding. This layout is not conventional, nor does it differ among individual minds. In our study of substance, then, there is no need for us to limit ourselves, at the outset, to possible experience.

I am focusing on the substance concept because its consideration enables me to shed light on some fundamental problems of Kant interpretation. In particular, the distinction between appearances and things in themselves is intimately bound up with the notion of substance. Questions of individuation hinge on this basic Kantian distinction.

SUBSTANCE

The *Critique of Pure Reason* contains the components of a fully fledged substance concept. Substances are logical subjects; their states change over time, but the substance persists; they act to cause changes in other things; they have distinctive inner properties (traditionally called "essence"). The discussions of these characteristics are dispersed throughout the *Critique*. The passages on substance are dispersed, owing to the fact that the *Critique* is not a book about substance, that is, a textbook of metaphysics, but a treatise on methodology and epistemology. To say that is not to deny that the *Critique* has 'metaphysical' consequences. Substance philosophy enters into it as an overall categorial scheme.

Substance officially enters the *Critique* in the table of categories, within the substance-attribute relationship. That relationship is coordinated to the logical relation of subject-predicate in the table of judgments, from which the table of categories was derived. At this stage, the categories are unschematized. They are not interpreted into sense contents and spatiotemporal forms.

Elsewhere in the *Critique*, Kant identifies the basic notion of substance: "[that of] something which can exist as subject and never as mere predicate" (B149; cf. A246, B300, B288). This notion is the one Aristotle introduced at the beginning of the fifth chapter of his *Categories*. Substance is not *defined* as logical subject for, according to Kant's theory of definitions, one cannot define but only give expositions of philosophical concepts. The 'logical subject' mark is one of the constituents of the substance concept. Other marks must be extracted from the concept, as the concept is thought. Analytic judgments can only reveal what is contained in the concept.

Not everything that was previously thought to be contained analytically in the substance concept is really so contained, according to Kant. Substance is necessarily permanent, but this claim is synthetic a priori, not analytic.[5] Kant distinguishes what is contained in a concept from what belongs to it necessarily without being contained in it. For particular concepts, such as substance, though, Kant does not always explicitly classify the marks according to this distinction. The issue is important, because a metaphysician practicing conceptual analysis can legitimately infer only the marks contained in the concept. Marks inferred by synthetic a priori judgments are tied to the spatiotemporal framework of possible experience.

I have given 'Substance is permanent' as an example of a synthetic a priori connection. The Third Analogy supplies another: "Each substance (inasmuch as only in respect of its determinations can it be an effect) must therefore contain in itself the causality of certain determinations in the other substance, and at the same time the effects of the causality of that other" (B259).

Clearly, 'Substance is logical subject' is analytic (B300). So is the relation of essence to substance: "As object of the pure understanding, every substance must have inner determinations and powers which pertain to its inner reality" (B321). Another interesting case is unspecified: "Causality leads to the concept of action, this in turn to the concept of force, and thereby to the concept of substance" (B249).

Whether the links be analytic or synthetic a priori, the main point is that Kant adheres to a fully developed substance concept. One can then use this information to explicate the concepts of appearance and thing in itself. That distinction rests on perhaps the most characteristic feature of Kant's philosophy, the ideality of space. In turn, the substance framework serves to explain the ideality of space. I will begin there and work back to appearances and things in themselves.

Substance philosophy supplies a set of pigeon-holes (substance, attribute, mode, etc.) by which to classify entities. One could say space is 'real' if it were a substance, or an attribute of substance, or relations among substances. Space is ideal or mental, however, because it fits nowhere in the 'real' pigeon-holes of the substance scheme. All the 'real' options are closed, by arguments Kant himself advanced or which were available to him.[6] His decisive move was the introduction of the argument from incongruent counterparts.

Space as mental or ideal gets around the problem of finding things (*relata*) on which to found spatial relations. For instance, one might conjecture that points are the requisite things. Then space would be constituted of points, and spatial relations would be parasitic on the points. But paradoxes concerning point-sets, known in Kant's time, block this option.[7] As relations that are mental, spatial relations can do without absolute (nonrelational) relata. One portion of space, say, is *outside* another. The terms of the relation are themselves made up of relations and in turn can be decomposed, without any assumption that eventually one will reach the absolute terms. This is admissible for ideal space, not for space as real.

Of course, the arguments about points are just one stage of a complete demonstration that space cannot be real. But they suggest that the status of relations in the substance philosophy plays a crucial role in Kant's philosophy.

It is important to note that the arguments do not just prove that space is ideal, but prove that it is ideal because it is not real. That result settles a notorious interpretive question raised in the nineteenth century. Adolf Trendelenburg defended the view that Kant's space could be ideal *and also real*. Kuno Fischer opposed him: space could only be real or ideal—an exclusive disjunction.[8] Since the arguments for ideal-

ity proceed by exclusion of all 'real' options, Fischer is right and Trendelenburg is proved wrong.

The ideality of space profoundly affects the role of substance in
the system. The substances that are employed (hypothetically) in the
ideality arguments end up nonspatial as a result of the arguments.
Now the question arises: If there are any substances, what is their relation to space and extension? Kant explores part of this problem in the
Second Antinomy, where he rejects the view that extended objects are
composed of simple substances, or that simple substances can verifi-
ably occur in sense experience.

The problem about the relation of substance to space (as
expressed in traditional substance philosophy terms) is closely related
to the problem (in Kantian terms) of the relation of things in themselves to appearances. So I will begin by translating the Kantian problem into more traditional form. Kant states clearly that appearances
are relational. Appearances, of course, were originally characterized in
terms of intuition (B34). "Everything in our knowledge which belongs
to intuition . . . contains nothing but mere relations; namely, of locations in an intuition (extension), of change of location (motion), and of
laws according to which this change is determined (moving forces)"
(B66–67). From this starting point, Kant advances an argument that he
says confirms "the ideality of both outer and inner sense, and therefore
of all objects of the senses, as mere appearances" (B66). "What it is
that is present in this or that location, or what it is that is operative in
the things themselves apart from change in location, is not given
through intuition. Now a thing in itself cannot be known through mere
relations; and we may therefore conclude that since outer sense gives
us nothing but mere relations, this sense can contain in its representation only the relation of an object to the subject, and not the inner
properties of the object in itself" (B67).

Now let us read the argument from the point of view of substance
philosophy. The context is human perceivers looking at ordinary physical objects in their environment. One would presume that tables and
books are substances. They are appearances, technically speaking.
Appearances, being relational only, have no inner properties and thus
no essences. Therefore they are not true substances. The genuine substances that act are the *things themselves*, or things in themselves,
emphasizing their essence aspect. Appearances can represent no more
than the relation of those things to the perceiver.

The argument does not purport to demonstrate the 'existence' of
things in themselves (genuine substances). It is, rather, aimed at confirming the ideality of appearances (what we perceive in space and

time). It is a confirmation, not a complete proof, since appearances could be real in other ways than being substances themselves (e.g., relations between substances).

That appearances cannot be genuine substances is an important result for Kant, one that requires more detailed treatment here. First, I must clear away a terminological hurdle. Readers of the *Critique* can easily jump to the conclusion that the things we perceive in our everyday world are substances. The Second Analogy, for example, seems to back up this surmise. The category of substance applies to physical objects in space and their causal relations. These things, however, as far as they occur in experience, are *phenomenal substances*, not true substances. Kant is well aware of the difference. It suits his purposes to use the honorific title 'substance' for phenomenal things, because the *Critique* stresses knowledge as verifiable by sense experience. The empirical meanings of substance and causality are, thus, important in the *Critique*. But when Kant seeks to compare his position with traditional philosophy (for instance, Wolff), in the Concepts of Reflection section, he must bring out the difference in substance concepts. "In an object of the pure understanding that only is inward which has no relation whatsoever (as far as its existence is concerned) to anything different from itself. It is quite otherwise with a *substantia phaenomenon* in space; its inner determinations are nothing but relations, and it itself is entirely made up of mere relations" (B321). Here Kant is in accord with the standard metaphysical doctrine, as expressed in Baumgarten's textbook: "Accidents, if considered as subsisting by themselves, are *phaenomena substantiata*."[9]

Present-day philosophical readers are accustomed to the postulation of relational structures to reconstruct things and processes. Bertrand Russell was, of course, a pioneer in this approach. In Kant's time, when substance dominated philosophy, the situation was quite different. "It is certainly startling to hear that a thing is to be taken as consisting wholly of relations. Such a thing is, however, mere appearance, and cannot be thought through pure [unschematized] categories; what it itself consists in is the mere relation of something in general to the senses" (B341). Relations cannot be left hanging about, else one would fall into the scholastic error of substantial forms—properties that are not present in or predicated of a substance.

Granted that a substance must have an essence, why could not the essence be relational? The answer is that there is a notion of 'independence' of substances, correlated with a notion of dependence of their attributes and relations. Indeed, in the *Principles of Philosophy*, Descartes introduced his substance concept via the theme of independence: "By *substance* we can understand nothing other than a thing which exists in such a way as to depend on no other thing for its existence."[10] Kant is wary of this approach, because he believed that it led to Spinoza's philosophy. So Kant preferred the formulation in terms of logical subject.[11] The logical subject (never a predicate) is itself a model of independence-dependence. If a substance had a wholly relational essence, it would be 'essentially' dependent on other things.

The problem of the relation of substance to space has evolved into the problem of the relation of things in themselves to appearances. Of course, appearances are not just space and time, although space and time constitute the forms of appearances. The original substance concept is now distributed over both sides of the appearance/thing-in-itself distinction. Logical subject (in the strictest sense) and essence belong to things in themselves. Since temporal predicates fall on the appearance side, phenomenal substance has permanence and temporal causality. The logical model of causality (noumenal causality) can still apply to things in themselves.

The issue of things in themselves is a complex one; I am sketching one approach to it via substance. A complete treatment would also involve the related concepts (and inconsistently used terminology) of 'noumenon' and 'transcendental object'. The substance approach explains the need for things in themselves, at least at the conceptual level. It also helps to explain Kant's allusions to the unknowability of things as they are in themselves (e.g., Bxx). The essence of things is unknowable in two ways. First, one cannot know that appearances *have* absolutely inner natures. Second, even if one assumes that there are such natures, one cannot pin down a uniquely specified essence.

Things in themselves are not completely mysterious entities, either as intellectual objects or as the inner nature of things. Kant is able to specify some conditions that such an essence must satisfy, according to the structure of our understanding. Thus, essences must be "simple," in agreement with Baumgarten and Wolff (B322). However, Kant has so disconnected genuine substances from appearances, that hypotheses about essences must remain speculative.

The unknowability of things in themselves must be distinguished from the unknowability of a featureless substratum for properties. Moltke Gram has suggested that some critics, such as Hegel and Fichte, were misled by an analogy between the appearance-thing-in-itself relation and the property-substratum relation.[12] The analogy is faulty in at least two respects. First, it would imply that spatial predicates apply to things in themselves, which is false. Second, Kant's substance concept, like that of Descartes and others following him, does not countenance such a substratum. The 'ultimate subject' is not the prime matter of the Scholastic tradition, but is itself an essence. In fact, Christian Wolff attacks the notion of substratum as metaphorical.[13]

INDIVIDUATION OF APPEARANCES

At this point is is necessary to take a closer look at the nature of appearances. In turn this requires that the notion of a form of sensibility be explicated. Previously we could assume in a preliminary fashion that concepts are different from intuitions, and concentrate on concepts, which are more familiar to philosophers. I will discuss only appearances of outer sense, that is, things in space. We suppose that material substances are the items of interest, and ask how they are individuated. Kant holds that the only substances that we can know to exist are material. In the Paralogisms, he argues that mental substances are not verifiable.

An appearance is the undetermined object of an empirical intuition. "That in the appearance which corresponds to sensation I term its *matter*; but that which so determines the manifold of appearance that it allows of being ordered in certain relations, I term the *form* of appearance" (B34).

Suppose one sees a red ball. One can abstract from the representation of the ball what is thought about it, for example, its being subject to mechanical forces. Also one can 'remove' the sensation qualities, such as the red color, and its impenetrability. The ball is still being represented as filling space and having a spherical shape. These latter characters, Kant says, belong to pure intuition, which has spatial and temporal structure (B35). One can identify three kinds of representations that are involved in appearances: pure (nonsensational) concepts of the understanding, empirical (sensation-based) qualities, and forms of sensibility (space and time). These are the building blocks that are available for the individuation of appearances. The pivotal factor is space. One must comprehend how it fits together with the other constituents of appearances in order to find out how individuation operates.

So far in this section I have been laying out some of Kant's apparatus for appearances. But now the rationale for those claims will be presented.

The analysis of the ontological 'location' of space reveals that it is not a substance, not an attribute either of matter or of God, and not relations between bodies, and since it is obviously not nothing at all, it must be something ideal or mental.[14] To say that space is ideal (not ideal in the sense of the Ideal of Pure Reason) is not to remove it from the substance ontology; it remains a mode or modification of 'mental substance'. Of course, the notion of mind or mental substance is strictly circumscribed by the Paralogisms.

To develop more exactly the role of space in Kant's philosophy, beyond its being mental, demands a discussion of the doctrine of 'ideas' (Locke) or 'perceptions' (Descartes). Kant prefers 'representation' as the most general classificatory term (B376). These mental entities represent or make known material objects and their behavior. Ideas or representations have a dual aspect. Ontologically, they are modes or modifications of mental substance. Epistemologically, they have a representing function: they make known something besides themselves.

The representative function of ideas allows the epistemology to sidestep some problems that crop up in a substance ontology, when confronted with the problem of knowledge. An idea can be *present in* a mind without being *predicated of* it. Thus a person seeing blue does not have a blue mind. And one can get around an objection to space being mental: space is infinite but minds are not. Presumably, the infinity of space can be assigned to the representative function of the idea.

The ontological analysis of space, together with mathematical arguments, establishes that space is a network of relations without relata, such that the whole is prior to the parts. The priority of whole to parts is an outcome of the arguments, not an unsupported assumption of Kant. The advantage of treating space as a representation is that it can be that network of relations and still be a respectable member of the substance ontology.

In a section of the Transcendental Dialectic entitled "The Ideas in General," Kant presents a classification of the various kinds of representations. Perceptions that relate "solely to the subject as the modification of its state" are called "sensations." Those that relate to objects are termed "cognitions." The latter are divided into intuitions and concepts. An intuition "relates immediately to the object and is singular," whereas a concept "refers to it mediately by means of a feature which several things may have in common" (B377). The concern in our discussion is with concepts versus intuitions, specifically as they relate to space. Is space a concept or an intuition? In order to answer this question, the difference between these two kinds of representations must be examined in more detail.

A concept is a representation that relates to several objects. For example, the concept of metal represents all those properties that are common to gold, silver, copper, and so on. Concepts are lower or higher according to whether they are under other concepts or have subordinate concepts under them. The higher concept is the genus, the lower is the species. Thus gold is a species under the genus metal. 'Higher' and 'lower' are, of course, relative terms; a concept that is a species under one concept may in turn be a genus over others. The more specific the concept, the smaller the extension. All this is a familiar scheme of classification. There is, however, no bottom concept or lowest species that refers to one and only one individual. Kant writes in the Appendix to the Transcendental Dialectic: "For since the species is always a concept, containing only what is common to different things, it is not completely determined" (B683). "Completely determined" means that it is so specific that for every possible predicate P, either P or not-P belongs to it (B601). Only if the concept is completely determined can it properly represent one and only one individual.[15] But it would take an indefinitely long sequence to run through all the possible predicates of a thing. How, then, could one ever conclude that a determination is complete? Either the whole sequence must be traversed step by step, or else the set of predicates must be comprehended all at once. Neither alternative corresponds to the facts of human knowledge. One would never know if the sequence, taken step by step, was completely traversed. Nor do humans have insight into the entire conceptual structure of a real thing. Some other kind of representation is needed to explain human knowledge, namely, sensible intuition. The situation for concepts alone will be taken up again in the section on the individuation of things in themselves.

An intuition, Kant maintains, is a representation that relates immediately to the object and is singular. Commentators have remarked that Kant gives little indication of how immediacy and singularity are to be explicated and how they relate to each other. But Kant never favors his readers with initial definitions of his key terms, in a strict sense of definition. Indeed, his doctrine of definition as expressed in the Transcendental Method part of the *Critique* cautions us to expect only gradual and partial clarification of philosophical terms. This is especially true of 'intuition'. Immediacy and singularity are not defining characters, but ways to get at a notion which can only be well understood after one has gone through much of the *Critique*, including the sections on the philosophy of mathematics. Not all the aspects of intuition are needed for the discussion of individuation.

Kant argues in the Transcendental Aesthetic that space is a form of intuition. There are two main stages to his argument. The first is that space has to be classified with intuitions rather than with concepts.

The second is that space must be classified as a form rather than as matter of intuition.

To get space classified with intuitions rather than with concepts, Kant first establishes that space is not empirical but a priori. One perceives objects as being outside oneself and alongside one another. One could not do this, says Kant, unless the representation of space is presupposed. Why could not our representation of space be derived from our experience of things in space? The reason is that space is not reducible to properties or relations of bodies. This reason follows from the ontological analysis of space and does not appear in Kant's epistemological arguments in the *Critique*. The basis for this claim is the argument from incongruent counterparts, which Kant presented in his 1768 essay on "Regions in Space" (and elsewhere, later on, drawing various conclusions from it). According to this argument, the property of orientability is ascribable only to the whole space and not to objects or their relations.[16] The argument assumes nothing about the ontological status of the objects, and in particular, it does not assume that they are substances as opposed to representations. To get the argument going, all that is needed is a depiction of the objects as being in space and as spatially related to one another. The argument from incongruent counterparts shows that the representation of space is not derived from representations of objects in space. And since space is not "an empirical concept which has been derived from outer experiences," it must be a priori and necessary with respect to outer experiences (B38). Next Kant establishes that space is not a concept at all, whether empirical or a priori, but a pure or a priori *intuition*. He cites two properties of space that prevent it from being classified as a concept. The first is that space is singular: there is one unique space, of which diverse spaces are parts. The parts of space are not constituents out of which the whole space is composed; nor can they be thought of as being under the whole space as species under a genus. On the contrary, they can only be thought of as *in* space.

One can divide space into parts, but one cannot build up space out of parts. In Kant's time, the paradoxes of the relationship of points to lines were familiar. For instance, a longer line segment would have to contain more points than a shorter one if lines were made up of points, but the diagonal of a square and one of the sides demonstrably have the same number of points. Points have no length, so how could an aggregate of such points have a length? Starting with standard units of extension, which have a finite length, one runs into the problem of the incommensurability of the diagonal of the square with respect to its side.[17] So the parts cannot be prior to the whole space; it must be the other way around. The parts are produced by limiting the whole space in various ways. Given a line, one can limit it at two points by intersecting it with two parallel lines. The result is a line segment. Given a plane, one can limit it by four lines intersecting at right angles. The result is a rectangle, a portion of space differentiated from the surrounding space by its boundaries. The many spaces, produced by introducing limits into the whole space, are particulars. The space that is limited to produce them cannot stand to them as genus to species, for when space is limited, it has spaces *in* it, and species are not *in* a genus but *under* it. Space is not simply that which is common to a circle *et cetera*. The circle and the square *are* space itself which has been divided according to certain mathematical rules.

The second property is that space is an infinity, that is to say, it contains an infinite number of representations within it. The sense of 'infinite' that is relevant here is not only that of endless extent. Although Kant believes that space stretches out to infinity, with parts beyond every part, that is not all he means when he says that "the parts of space coexist *ad infinitum*" (B40). He is referring as much to the parts in any one region as to the entire extent of space. Since the parts of a line must be given with the line, any given line segment actually contains an infinite number of parts. This is not to say, however, that the *division* of the line into an infinity of points is given. The process of subdividing the line into two, four, eight, sixteen, and so on, segments, with their associated boundary points, is only potentially infinite, for it never ends (cf. B551–52).

"Now every concept," declares Kant, "must be thought as a representation which is contained in an infinite number of different possible representations (as their common character), and which therefore contains these *under* itself" (B40). The concept of metal, for instance, is contained in the concepts of a gold ring, a silver spoon, a copper bowl, and so on. The concept of a gold ring is *under* the concept of metal; the concept of metal is *within* that of a gold ring. In general, representations *under* a concept are species of which the concept is the genus, whereas representations *within* a concept are parts of its intension. Kant goes on: "but no concept, as such, can be thought as containing an infinite number of representations *within* itself." Conceptual analysis is the process for concepts analogous to the division of a line, where component concepts correspond to subsegments of the line. Suppose that conceptual analysis were an infinite process. Then, at each stage of analysis, one or more properties uncovered would in turn be capable of further analysis. But conceptual analysis is unlike the division of a line in this important respect: at every stage of the division one knows how to proceed (for example, bisect the segment) and that the method has a definite result, whereas in conceptual analysis there is no method except to look for constituent concepts with no guarantee of finding them. The difference can be summed up in Kantian terms by saying that the infinity (if such there be) of representations is not *given* in the original concept as the parts of a line are given in the line.

So far it has been established that space is to be classified with intuitions. That space is a *form* of intuition remains to be seen. What does Kant mean by 'form' and 'matter'? He explains the distinction in the Amphiboly of Concepts of Reflection, an appendix to the Transcendental Analytic.

The Kantian distinction between form and matter is an adaptation of traditional meanings of the terms. Form and matter are correlative terms. Kant writes: "The one [matter] signifies the determinable in general, the other [form] its determination. . . . Logicians formerly gave the name 'matter' to the universal, and the name 'form' to the specific difference" (B322). The universal *animal* is indeterminate as to species; it is made determinate by adding the specific difference *rational*. So long as the form-matter distinction is confined to concepts, as it is in definitions, it will not do the work that Kant demands of it. Kant needs to reformulate the distinction, which he does by using the notion of relations: the items ordered by the relations are the matter, and the relations are the form. He gives two examples of form and matter in this sense. The first has to do with judgments: "In any judgment we can call the given concepts logical matter (i.e. matter for the judgment), and their relation (by means of the copula) the form of the judgment." The second has to do with objects: "In every being the constituent elements of it (*essentialia*) are the matter, the mode in which they are combined in one thing the essential form." In both cases the core of the traditional meaning remains; the form is still a determination of a determinable matter. The advantage is that now the form-matter distinction can be applied to sensible intuition.

One perceives a red expanse of a certain shape. Which factor is the determinable and which is the determination? Kant's answer is that sensory qualities such as color and hardness provide the matter for determination by space (and time, which Kant treats analogously). Why not the other way around? Could not space be the determinable and could not color determine a particular shape? A painter makes us see figures on a canvas by applying pigments to a bare surface. Could it not likewise be that the expanse of space that we see when we look out toward a wood is determined to represent here an oak and there a maple only by the diverse sensations of color associated with different portions of it? This is precisely the doctrine advocated by Malebranche. Space or extension in general, which he called "intelligible extension," is "rendered particular" by acts of sensation.[18] Simply put, we see circles and squares by seeing red and green. In Kant's system, however, this cannot be. Space cannot be made particular by color, since it already *is* particular.

Although Kant does not bring in his old standby, incongruent counterparts, to show that space is a form of intuition, he might well have done so. For the orientability of space is a particular characteristic of space that cannot be brought into being by acts of sensation. One can construct triangles by coloring them in, but no amount of seeing red will prove that space is orientable—that figures cannot change into their mirror images by moving through some path in space. For Kant the situation is the reverse of that for Malebranche. Rather than space becoming determinate by being perceived redly, a color becomes determinate by being perceived in an act that confers spatial location, extent, and shape on it.

Kant says in the Transcendental Aesthetic that space is "the form of all appearances of outer sense" (B42). By this he means that when we locate the matter of sensation—the colors, hardness, impenetrability, and so on—by fitting them together in a network of spatial relations, we perceive things as outside us. He adds that space is "the subjective condition of sensibility, under which alone outer intuition is possible for us." When he says that space is the condition of the possibility of outer sensible intuition, he is not offering a definition of "form of outer sense" but stating a corollary of the principle that space is the form of outer sense. If to see a thing outside us is to see it ordered spatially, then without the network of spatial relations there would be no world of outer sense.

Appearances, then, become particular as a consequence of their being located in specific spatial extents and shapes. The spatial extent by itself is not the object; it is what particularizes the sensations. Material things have geometrical form, but they are not constructed wholly by geometry. The geometer can superimpose figures on each other, construct figures within one another, imbed solids inside solids, and so on. Matter does not behave that way.

Matter, that is, material substance, requires some additional factor to distinguish it from purely geometrical entities. That factor, for Kant, is impenetrability. Material bodies are compressible in varying degrees—but not penetrable. Impenetrability is a sensation-property which is in turn explained by the concept of force.[19] Impenetrability is, of course, rendered particular by spatial form; the principle of individuation is still space. The claims about force emerge from Kant's physics. From his earliest publications, Kant concerned himself with the controversies over the nature of forces, in which Leibniz, Wolff, Euler, J. Bernoulli, and others participated. *Metaphysical Foundations of Natural Science* (1786) represents the physics of Kant's 'critical period'.

P. M. Harman, writing on Kant and Euler, remarks that for Kant, force is ontologically prior to matter.[20] Harman is interested in the ramifications of that claim for natural philosophy. In the context of substance philosophy, however, it has special significance. Kant states in the Second Analogy: "Wherever there is action—and therefore activity and force—there is also substance. . . . Action signifies the relation of the subject of causality to its effect" (B250). The activity of matter in filling space, then, signifies the presence of substance. Naturally, the substance is phenomenal, not genuine substance.

Kant characterizes material substance, in dynamics, as "that in space which of itself, i.e., separated from all else existing outside it in space, is movable."[21] The movability is not purely geometrical. To change the state of motion of something requires a force. Kant then links the concept of material substance to the traditional notion of substance as "the ultimate subject of existence, i.e., that which does not itself in turn belong merely as predicate to the existence of another." This "ultimate subject" still remains in the realm of appearance.

In space, any part may be marked off so as to constitute a geometrical individual. Space is infinitely divisible, so this may be accomplished in innumerable ways. A similar result holds for material substance. "All parts of matter will likewise be substances insofar as one can say of them that they are themselves subjects and not merely predicates of other matters. . . . They are themselves subjects if they are of themselves movable."[22]

Thus Kant has set up a correspondence whereby he identifies an individual characterized by being a part of matter with the individual as substance. We would expect that, according to substance philosophy, individual material things are substances. Kant does not disappoint us.

INDIVIDUATION OF THINGS IN THEMSELVES

The question of the individuation of things in themselves is not the same as the question of their existence. This is so for Kant, and for Wolff and Baumgarten, too. Fortunately, I can discuss the problem of individuation without entering into the vexed question of its tie-in with existence.[23]

The things in themselves that we want to individuate are not the internal natures of phenomenal things. For if they were such, the appropriate principle of individuation would be that for appearances, contrary to Kant's assertions. The notion of things in themselves that is relevant here is that of intelligible object. There are two applications of the concept. The first is to objects (for example, disembodied minds) which might exist in addition to our world of sense experience. The second is just our everyday world but interpreted as a purely intellectual structure. The latter is the Leibnizian approach of intellectualizing appearances, which is discussed in the Amphiboly of Concepts of Reflection. That section provides access to the individuation question.

The concepts of reflection include *identity* and *difference*, *inner* and *outer*. Philosophers have arrived at diverse interpretations of these terms, owing to their failure properly to grasp the sensibility-understanding distinction. "In a word, Leibniz *intellectualised* appearances, just as Locke ... *sensualised* all concepts of the understanding, i.e., interpreted them as nothing more than empirical or abstracted concepts of reflection" (B327). Kant does not explore the Lockean alternative further, but pursues the Leibnizian direction. For Kant himself, of course, sense experience was neither entirely sensible nor wholly intellectual. But philosophical extrapolations beyond experience are purely intellectual.

Since the individuation principle comes out the same for either application of thing in itself mentioned above, we can conveniently utilize the discussion of Leibnizian thought to yield the desired principle. Kant introduces his answer in an epistemological setting. Suppose "an object is presented to us on several occasions." On what grounds can one conclude that it is the same object or is numerically different? If one take it as an object of pure understanding, it is the same if it has the same "inner determinations (*qualitas et quantitas*)" in the two instances (B319).

For appearances, inner determinations do not suffice. We have already seen that there are no absolutely inner determinations in appearances. Spatiotemporal structure enters into the question essentially. Here, however, we are asked to consider things as if completely characterized by concepts. For this situation, Leibniz's principle of the identity of indiscernibles is valid.

The epistemological criterion of identity and difference restricts the relevant properties to inner determinations. Something more is needed to transform the criterion into a proper principle of individuation. *Complete determination* is the requisite condition for Kant, as one learns in the Ideal of Pure Reason. The *ens realissimum*, or most real being, is the case that Kant treats there. It represents the complete store of possible (positive) predicates. Such a concept, he says, is "the concept of an individual being" (B604). Further, "only in this one case is a concept of a thing—a concept which is in itself universal—completely determined in and through itself, and known as the representation of an individual."

The *ens realissimum* differs from the case of an existing object, say a piece of quartz, in important respects. Admittedly, everything that exists is completely determined. But for the quartz, some possible predicates apply to it and, for others, their denial holds. To know the piece of quartz completely (by concepts), "we must know every possible [predicate], and must determine it thereby, either affirmatively or negatively. The complete detemination is thus a concept, which, in its totality, can never be exhibited *in concreto*" (B601). Nor can one run through the complete list for the *ens realissimum*. Rather, one can think of the conditions that specify it uniquely: all possible positive predicates, excluding derivative predicates. The *ens realissimum* can be thought, but only on this metaconceptual level. The conditions ensure that the concept being described is an individual concept such that a decision rule is specified for the list of possible predicates: affirm every positive predicate. One could not specify the results a priori for the quartz. Humans get around the problem for the quartz by perceiving it, thus verifying its existence and, secondarily, its complete determination (cf. B272). But in doing so, they use sensible intuition, not pure concepts alone.

What justification can one present for Kant's individuation principle for things in themselves? Given that things in themselves can only be determined conceptually, it does look like a natural answer to the question of individuation. But it is also the same solution given by Wolff and Baumgarten.[24] According to Baumgarten, if all mutually possible determinations are present in a thing, it is completely determined. Such an entity is singular or individual. If the entity is less than completely determined, it is universal. Has Kant merely appropriated a readily available answer? Not from his point of view. Wolff and Baumgarten are representatives of traditional philosophy based on conceptual analysis. I have remarked earlier that the *method* of analysis was shared by Wolff and Kant. More important, some of the *content* of Wolff's (and Baumgarten's) philosophy reappears in Kant's system. The principle of individuation for things in themselves is an example of Wolffian content transferred to Kant.

The Concepts of Reflection section again supplies some answers. Kant there derives 'Leibnizian' metaphysics, more properly the

Wolff–Baumgarten philosophy. We have already seen that Kant views it as an intellectualizing of appearances. Let us look more closely at what that phrase signifies. The forms of sensibility allow one to represent features of sense experience in a way concepts cannot duplicate. The way in which the understanding attempts to mimic the structure of sense experience is, however, canonical. That is, there is a *standard* way in which the understanding imitates intuition. "If I attempt, by the mere understanding, to represent to myself outer relations of things, *this can only be done* by means of a concept of their reciprocal action; and if I seek to connect two states of one and the same thing, *this can only be* in the order of grounds and consequences" (B331, emphasis added).

Now the following difficulty arises. From the point of view of history of philosophy, the Leibniz–Wolff metaphysics is just one of a number of a priori schemes that claim to describe correctly the structure of human understanding. Conceptual analysis by itself is impotent to decide which philosophy is correct. A philosopher may assert that he has given the right concept of force, say, in contrast to his opponents. But human minds are not capable of the requisite kind of *insight* into concepts and their interrelations. In many cases, analytic judgments can only be verified quite indirectly, by inferring a remote contradiction from the denial of the judgment. The subject concept of the judgment is itself not reliably grasped directly. This uncertainty is characteristic of philosophy; it does not, of course, apply to mathematics.

Kant's solution to this problem lies in the notion of system articulated in the preface to the second edition of *Critique*. "For pure speculative reason has a structure wherein everything is an *organ*, the whole being for the sake of every part, and every part for the sake of all the others, so that even the smallest imperfection, be it a fault (error) or a deficiency, must inevitably betray itself in use" (Bxxxvii–xxxviii). Any mistake generates a contradiction which a meticulous philosopher can uncover. Each part of the system does not necessarily have an independent justification. "A philosophical work cannot be armed at all points, like a mathematical treatise, and may therefore be open to objection in this or that respect, while yet the structure of the system, taken in its unity, is not in the least endangered" (Bxliv).

The Leibniz–Wolff metaphysics is derivable from the Kantian system by taking the concept of a thing in general and developing it purely conceptually, without introducing the spatiotemporal framework of intuition (B339). The concept of a thing in general is, however, only justified in the whole system. It must be considered as dependent on the full notion of object of sense experience, which includes synthetic principles such as the law of causality. The concepts on which the Leibniz–Wolff philosophy is based are found in human understanding and were discovered before Kant formulated his system. And Kant does introduce the notion of an object in general through the correspondence between the table of judgments and the table of categories, before it receives its proper interpretation (via schematization). Kant maintains, nevertheless, that only the complete system, with its synthetic a priori judgments, is capable of ending the wrangling over which basic philosophical concepts are correct.

The principle of individuation for things in themselves thus results from a nonarbitrary conceptual extrapolation from the Kantian system. It coincides with Wolff's principle, Kant would maintain, not because he took it over from Wolff uncritically, but because it is, like other Wolffian claims, a natural consequence of the system.

As we have seen, Kant's system yields not just one but two principles of individuation. The role of substance explains why there are two such principles. For the substance framework leads to the ideality of space and thence to a sharp distinction between appearance and thing in itself. Many critics of Kant believed that Kant's sytem would be improved at little cost by dropping the notion of 'thing in itself'. That move would leave only the spatiotemporal framework as the mechanism for individuation. Yet Kant could only drop things in themselves by doing violence to the 'substance' concept, certainly a major alteration to the system. To discard the 'substance' concept would be to abandon the goal of reconciling the old metaphysics with modern mathematical science.

NOTES

1. "Die Voraussetzungen zur kantischen Urteilstafel in der Logik des 18.Jahrhunderts," in *Kritik und Metaphysik*, ed. F. Kaulbach and J. Ritter (Berlin: Walter de Gruyter, 1966), pp. 134–58.

2. Michael Radner, "How Are Analytic a priori Judgments Possible for Kant?" *Southern Journal of Philosophy* 14 (1976):189–96.

3. Immanuel Kant, *Prolegomena to any Future Metaphysics*, ed. Lewis White Beck (Indianapolis: Bobbs-Merrill, 1950), p. 20; *Ak* 4:271. *Ak* 4 refers to the fourth volume of *Kants gesammelte Schriften*, ed. Königlich Preussischen Akademie der Wissenschaften (Berlin: Walter de Gruyter, 1902–).

4. B-numbers denote the pages of the 1787 edition of the *Kritik der reinen Vernunft*; A-numbers refer to the 1781 edition. When a passage occurs in both

editions, I list only the B-number. Translations are taken from *Immanuel Kant's Critique of Pure Reason*, trans. Norman Kemp Smith (London: Macmillan, 1958).

5. Wolff presumably thought it was analytic. See Christian Wolff, *Gesammelte Werke*, ed. Jean Ecole and H. W. Arndt (Hildesheim: George Olms, 1962–), 2d ser. Lateinische Schriften, vol. 3, *Philosophia prima sive ontologia*, ed. Jean Ecole (1962), p. 574. At B227 Kant says, "the proposition, that substance is permanent, is tautological." He cannot mean that literally, as one sees from the argument supporting the proposition. In his essay against Eberhard of 1790, Kant correctly labels the proposition as synthetic. See *Ak* 8:229–30; *The Kant-Eberhard Controversy*, ed. and trans. Henry E. Allison (Baltimore: Johns Hopkins University Press, 1973), p. 142.

6. For the whole set of arguments, see Michael Radner and Daisie Radner, "Kantian Space and the Ontological Alternatives," *Kant-Studien* 78 (1987):385– 402.

7. Kant's familiarity with the point problems is indicated in the Second Antinomy, B468.

8. A survey of the controversy is found in Hans Vaihinger, *Commentar zu Kants Kritik der reinen Vernunft*, (Stuttgart: Union Deutsche Verlagsgesellschaft, 1892), 2:290–326.

9. Alexander Gottlieb Baumgarten, *Metaphysica* (1779; rep. Hildesheim: George Olms, 1963), p. 58.

10. *The Philosophical Writings of Descartes*, trans. John Cottingham, Robert Stoothoff, and Dugald Murdoch (Cambridge: Cambridge University Press, 1985), 1:210.

11. Henry E. Allison, "Kant's Critique of Spinoza," in *The Philosophy of Baruch Spinoza*, ed. Richard Kennington (Washington, D.C.: The Catholic University of America Press, 1980), pp. 205–7.

12. "Things in Themselves: The Historical Lessons," *Journal of the History of Philosophy* 18 (1980):420–21.

13. *Philosophia prima sive ontologia*, pp. 575–78.

14. "Kantian Space and the Ontological Alternatives," p. 386.

15. See also Immanuel Kant, *Logic*, trans. Robert S. Hartman and Wolfgang Schwarz (Indianapolis: Bobbs-Merrill, 1974), pp. 103, 105; *Ak* 9:97, 99. Further discussions are found in Rainer Stuhlmann-Laeisz, *Kants Logik* (Berlin: Walter de Gruyter, 1976), pp. 77–80; and Jules Vuillemin, "Reflexionen über Kants Logik," *Kant-Studien* 52 (1960–61):314–18.

16. For further details, see "Kantian Space and the Ontological Alternatives."

17. Nowadays, mathematicians formulate measure-theoretic axioms to tell a consistent though not unparadoxical story of how points make up a line. This development occurred long after Kant's time.

18. See the article on Malebranche by Daisie Radner in this volume.

19. Immanuel Kant, *Metaphysical Foundations of Natural Science*, trans. James Ellington (Indianapolis: Bobbs-Merrill, 1970), pp. 41, 46; *Ak* 4:497, 501.

20. "Force and Inertia: Euler and Kant's *Metaphysical Foundations of Natural Science*," in *Nature Mathematized*, ed. William R. Shea (Dordrecht, Holland: D. Reidel, 1983), p. 230.

21. *Metaphysical Foundations*, p. 48; *Ak* 4:502.

22. Ibid., p. 49; *Ak* 4:503.

23. On this topic, see Anneliese Maier, *Kants Qualitätskategorien*, Kant-Studien Ergänzungsheft (Berlin: Pan-Verlag Kurt Metzner, 1930) no. 65, pp. 18-19; Mariano Campo, *Cristiano Wolff e il razionalismo precritico*, 2 vols. (Milan: Vita e Pensiero, 1939), 1:170-76; Mario Casula, *La metafisica di A. G. Baumgarten* (Milan: U. Mursia, 1973), pp. 102-4.

24. Wolff, *Philosophia prima sive ontologia*, pp. 187-89; Baumgarten, *Metaphysica*, pp. 42-43.

Notes on Contributors

Martha Brandt Bolton. Ph.D., University of Michigan. Associate Professor, Rutgers University. Publications: "The Real Molyneux Question and the Basis of Locke's Answer", in G. A. J. Rogers, ed. *Locke's Philosophy: Content and Context* (Oxford: Oxford University Press, expected 1994); "The Epistemological Status of Ideas: Locke Compared to Arnauld", *History of Philosophy Quarterly* 9 (1992); "Leibniz and Locke on the Knowledge of Necessary Truths", in J. Cover and M. Kulstad, eds. *Central Themes in Early Modern Philosophy* (Indianapolis, IN: Hackett, 1990); other articles on topics in early modern philosophy.

Daniel E. Flage. Ph.D., University of Iowa, 1977. Associate Professor of Philosophy, James Madison University. Publications: *Berkeley's Doctrine of Notions: A Reconstruction based on his Theory of Meaning* (London: Croom Helm, 1987); *David Hume's Theory of Mind* (London: Routledge, 1990); numerous articles on the history of modern philosophy.

Don Garrett. Ph.D., Yale University. Associate Professor, University of Utah; co-editor of *Hume Studies*. Publications: (ed.) *The Cambridge Companion to Spinoza* (Cambridge: Cambridge University Press, forthcoming); "The Representation of Causation and Hume's Two Definitions of 'Cause,'" *Noûs*, 27, no. 2 (1993); "Spinoza's Necessitarianism," in Yirmiyahu Yovel, ed. *God and Nature: Spinoza's Metaphysics* (Leiden: Brill, 1991); "*Ethics* Ip5: Shared Attributes and the Basis of Spinoza's Monism," in Jan Cover and Mark Kulstad, eds. *Central Themes in Early Modern Philosophy: Essays Presented to Jonathan Bennett* (Indianapolis, IN: Hackett, 1990); and various other articles on early modern philosophy.

Jorge J. E. Gracia. M.A., University of Chicago, 1966; M.S.L., Pontifical Institute of Mediaeval Studies, 1970; Ph.D., University of Toronto, 1971. Professor, State University of New York at Buffalo. Publications: *Suárez on Individuation* (Milwaukee: Marquette University Press, 1982); *Introduction to the Problem of Individuation in the Early Middle Ages* (Munich, Vienna, and Washington, D.C: Philosophia Verlag and The Catholic University of America Press, 1986, 2nd ed. 1988); *The Meta-*

physics of Good and Evil According to Suárez: Disputations X and XI, with Douglas Davis (Munich and Vienna: Philosophia Verlag, 1990); *Individuality: An Essay on the Foundations of Metaphysics* (Albany, NY: State University of New York Press, 1988); *Philosophy and Its History: Issues in Philosophical Historiography* (Albany, NY: State University of New York Press, 1992); (ed.) *The Transcendentals in the Middle Ages,* issue of *Topoi* 11, no. 2 (1992); (ed.) *Individuation in Scholasticism: The Later Middle Ages and the Counter-Reformation* (Albany, NY: State University of New York Press, 1994).

Emily R. Grosholz. Ph.D., Yale University, 1978. Professor, The Pennsylvania State University. Publications: *Cartesian Method and the Problem of Reduction* (Oxford: Oxford University Press, 1991). Numerous articles on history and philosophy of science, and Rationalism.

Thomas M. Lennon. Ph.D., Ohio State University, 1968. Publications: (Trans. with P. J. Olscamp), N. Malebranche's, *The Search After Truth*; (trans.) *Elucidations of the Search After Truth, A Philosophical Commentary* (Columbus: The Ohio State University Press, 1980); (ed. with J. M. Nicholas, J. W. Davis) *Problems of Cartesianism* (Kingston and Montreal: Queens-McGill University Press, 1982); with Patricia Easton, *Bibliographia Malebranchiana: A Critical Guide to the Malebranche Literature into 1989* (Carbondale: Southern Illinois University Press, for the *Journal of the History of Philosophy* Monograph Series, 1992); with Patricia Easton *The Cartesian Empiricism of François Bayle* (New York: Garland Publishing, 1992); *The Battle of the Gods and Giants: The Legacies of Descartes and Gassendi, 1655-1715* (Princeton: Princeton University Press, 1993); articles and reviews dealing primarily with early modern philosophy.

Laurence B. McCullough. Ph.D., University of Texas at Austin, 1975; Post-Doctoral Fellowship, Hastings Center, Hastings-on-Hudson, NY 1975-76. Professor of Medicine, Community Medicine, and Medical Ethics, Center for Ethics, Medicine, and Public Issues, Baylor College of Medicine, Houston, Texas. Publications: with Tom L. Beauchamp, *Medical Ethics: The Moral Responsibilities of Physicians* (New York: Prentice-Hall, 1984), translated into Spanish, 1987 and into Japanese in 1992); with Frank A. Chervenak, *Ethics in Obstetrics and Gynecology* (Oxford: Oxford University Press 1994); *The Sources of Leibniz's Principle of Individuation* (Munich and Vienna: Philosophia Verlag, in press). Currently working on a book on John Gregory and Thomas Percival, the two leading figures of the British Enlightenment in medical ethics.

Daisie Radner. Ph.D., University of Minnesota, Associate Professor, SUNY at Buffalo. Publications: *Malebranche* (Assen: Van Gorcum,

1978); with Michael Radner, *Science and Unreason* (Belmont, CA: Wadsworth, 1982); with Michael Radner, *Animal Consciousness*, (Buffalo: Prometheus Books, 1989); several articles on early modern philosophy in various journals.

Michael Radner. Ph.D., University of Minnesota, 1968. Associate Professor, McMaster University. With Daise Radner, *Science and Unreason* (Belmont, CA: Wadsworth, 1982; *Animal Consciousness* (Buffalo: Prometheus Books, 1989); (co-editor with Stephen W. Vinokur) *Minnesota Studies in the Philosophy of Science, Vol. 4: Analyses of Theories and Methods of Physics and Psychology* (Minneapolis: University of Minnesota Press, 1970); "How are Analytic A Priori Judgments Possible for Kant?" *Southern Journal of Philosophy* 14 (1976): 189-196; "Possible Theories," *Synthese* 41 (1979): 397-415; with Daisie Radner, "Kantian Space and the Ontological Alternatives," *Kant-Studien* 78 (1987): 385-402.

Fred Wilson. Ph.D., University of Iowa, 1965. Professor, University of Toronto. Publications: with A. Hausman, *Carnap and Goodman: Two Formalists*, Iowa Studies in Philosophy, Vol. III (Martinus Nijhoff: The Hague, 1967); ed. with L. W. Sumner and J. G. Slater, *Pragmatism and Purpose: Essays in Honour of T. A. Goudge* (Toronto: University of Toronto Press, 1980); *Explanation, Causation and Deduction* (Dordrecht, Holland: D. Reidel, 1985); *Laws and Other Worlds* (Dordrecht, Holland: Kluwer, 1986); *Psychological Analysis and the Philosophy of John Stuart Mill* (Toronto: University of Toronto Press, 1990); *Empiricism and Darwin's Science* (Dordrecht, Holland: Kluwer, 1991).

Index of Proper Names

DATE DUE